Professional services agreements

Leslie Edwards and Rachel Barnes

Published by Thomas Telford Publishing, Thomas Telford Ltd,
1 Heron Quay, London E14 4JD.
URL: http://www.thomastelford.com

Distributors for Thomas Telford books are
USA: ASCE Press, 1801 Alexander Bell Drive, Reston, VA 20191-4400, USA
Japan: Maruzen Co. Ltd, Book Department, 3–10 Nihonbashi 2-chome,
Chuo-ku, Tokyo 103
Australia: DA Books and Journals, 648 Whitehorse Road, Mitcham 3132,
Victoria

First published 2000

Also available from Thomas Telford Books
Civil engineering construction contracts. Michael O Reilly. ISBN: 0 7277 2785 0
Construction law handbook. J. Baster, A. Minogue, M. O Reilly and V. Ramsey.
ISBN: 0 7277 2883 0
The NEC engineering and construction contract: A user's guide. Jon Broome.
ISBN: 0 7277 2750 8
A catalogue record for this book is available from the British Library

ISBN: 0 7277 2884 9

© Leslie Edwards and Rachel Barnes and Thomas Telford Limited 2000

Typeset by Academic & Technical Typesetting, Bristol
Printed and bound in Great Britain by MPG Books, Bodmin, Cornwall

Contents

Contents

Foreword

The RIBA first published a professional services agreement for its members in 1872. The conditions ran to some 16 pages – and the pages were little bigger than those of a pocket diary. More remarkable still, it was only 100 years later that a substantial revision was printed. In the last 30 years, a series of standard forms of agreement have been published by both the RIBA and ACE – each edition having a shorter shelf life, and tending to be longer than the last.

Moreover, nowadays, the construction professional who wins a new job, or is hoping to win one, is often presented with a bespoke form of contract. The contract documentation may (sometimes) be short and to the point, or it may be delivered in lever arch files. Beware any professional who does not read through this documentation from beginning to end. Unusual, indeed unconscionable, liabilities may be lurking within the small print.

This book should be on the desk of all those reviewing professional services agreements before they are signed, and those who refer to them once they are signed. There has been a need for a book of this kind for some time, and Leslie Edwards and Rachel Barnes have taken on a daunting task. As is evident from the wealth of helpful detail and examples, they have enormous experience of their subject.

Bidding for a job is not only about assessing the fee to undertake the services. It is also important to assess the risk of everything not going to plan. Only in that way can the construction professional in the twenty-first century remain competitive. This book will be an invaluable tool in making that assessment.

Frances A Paterson
Former Director of Legal Affairs at the
Association of Consulting Engineers
May 2000

Preface

The idea for this book arose when it was realised that there was no readily available material for professionals on how to identify and manage risks in professional services agreements. It was also realised that such information that was available often did not permeate to the levels in a professional organisation that should be concerned with such issues.

This book therefore attempts to describe comprehensively, and relatively simply, the more usual risks inherent in professional services agreements and how such risks might be managed. Also included are collateral warranties, assignments and novations, each of which could incorporate risks similar to those arising from professional services agreements. Of necessity the book also describes the cover provided by typical professional indemnity insurances.

It is hoped that the book will provide a practical, easily understood source of reference for those at any level in a professional organisation who need to understand and deal with such matters.

The book's basic aims are therefore to:

- make all appropriate levels of a professional organisation aware of the potential risks inherent in professional services agreements, possible methods of managing those risks and the scope and limitations of professional indemnity insurance;
- provide sufficient background information to enable a professional to realise when it needs advice from insurers, brokers or lawyers, and to understand that advice.

As a result, the book will assist the professional to make the correct commercial decisions on whether or not to accept the risks inherent in those agreements.

It is also hoped that this book will demonstrate the need to establish, review regularly and, if necessary, amend management procedures to achieve the foregoing aims.

Leslie Edwards and Rachel Barnes
September 2000

Biographies of authors

Leslie Edwards is a Senior Disputes Manager with Mouchel Consulting Limited.

Leslie has spent more than fifteen years providing Expert technical and risk advice on a wide variety of construction issues for private, insurance market, solicitor and contractor clients. The scope has included contractual and contractor's all risks insurance claims, structural defects, professional negligence, workmanship and personal injury investigations. In 1995, he became, by examination, the first practising engineer to be elected a Fellow of the Institute of Risk Management.

He has been a member of several institutional committees connected with risk and insurance matters, including an Advanced Study Group of the Insurance Institute of London, where he was responsible for the construction risk factor chapters for *Construction Insurance*, the leading insurance industry publication on the subject. He is also the author of *Practical risk management in the construction industry* and joint author of *Civil engineering insurance and bonding*, both in the Thomas Telford Management Series.

Rachel Barnes is a partner in Beale and Company and joined the firm in 1973.

For the first ten years or so as a practising solicitor Rachel was mainly concerned with construction litigation. This involved defending consulting engineers in high court cases and in arbitrations in the UK and overseas. From 1985 Rachel has worked on the non-contentious side of the firm's practice, giving advice to construction professionals and others on conditions of engagement and collateral warranties for all types of projects. She has also advised on building contracts, novation agreements, bonds and tenders, architectural competitions and joint ventures.

Rachel also lectures and topics have included the CDM Regulations, the Construction Act payment provisions and the Contracts (Rights of Third Parties) Act. She assisted the Association of Consulting Engineers in drafting the *ACE conditions of engagement 1995* and later editions.

She is a regular contributor to *Building* magazine, and with Tim Foley, formerly of WS Atkins, is currently contributing the section on Engineer's Appointments in the forthcoming *Construction law handbook*.

Acknowledgements

The authors would like to thank Kris Hannah for typing every word of this book (and many of them more than once) and for her help in presentation and achieving consistency. They would also like to thank the directors of Mouchel Consulting Limited and the partners of Beale and Company for their enthusiastic support for this project and in particular Derek Tadiello for undertaking to read the whole and for checking for errors in law. Thank too are due to Charles Abbott, who undertook much of the legal research.

Abbreviations

ACA	Association of Consultant Architects
ACE	Association of Consulting Engineers
ACOP	Approved Code of Practice
ADR	Alternative Dispute Resolution
APM	Association for Project Management
BPF	British Property Federation
CIC	Construction Industry Council
CDM	Construction (Design and Management)
CDR	Centre for Dispute Resolution
FIDIC	Fédération Internationale des Ingénieurs-Conseils
HSE	Health and Safety Executive
ICE	Institute of Civil Engineers
JCT	Joint Contracts Tribunal
LLP	Limited liability partnership
RIBA	Royal Institute of British Architects
RICS	Royal Institution of Chartered Surveyors

List of cases

ADT Limited *v* BDO Binder Hamlyn (1995) LTL 7/12/95 — unreported elsewhere

Alfred McAlpine Co *v* Panatown (2000) LTL 27/7/2000

American Cyanamid Co *v* Ethicon (1975) 1 All ER 504

Bosky *v* Shearwater Property Holdings (1992) 61 BLR 64

British Fermentation Products Limited *v* Compare Reavell Limited (1999) 2 All ER (Comm) 389

British Sugar plc *v* NEI Power Projects Limited and Another (1997) 87 BLR 42

Caparo Industries plc *v* Dickman (1990) 2 AC 605

Chesham Properties Limited *v* Bucknall Austin Project Management CILL (1996) 53 Con LR 1

Coco *v* A N Clark (Engineers) Limited (1969) RPC 41

Croshaw *v* Pritchard (1899) 16 TLR 45

Deepak Fertilizers & Petrochemical Corporation *v* Davy Kee (1) ICI Chemicals (2) (1998) 2 Lloyd's Rep 139

George Mitchell *v* Finney Lock Seeds (1983) 3 WLR 163

Hedley Byrne *v* Heller (1963) 2 All ER 575

Henderson *v* Merrett (1995) 2 AC 145

IBM UK Ltd *v* Rockware Glass Ltd (1980) FSR 335

Jobson *v* Johnson (1989) 1 WLR 1026

John Mowlem & Company *v* Eagle Star and Others (1995) 44 Con LR 134

Lancashire Churches *v* Howard & Seddon (1993) 3 AER 467

McKenzie *v* Potts and Dobson Chapman (1995) CA 50 Con LR 40

Midland Land Reclamation Limited and Leicestershire County Council *v* Warren Energy Limited (1997) LTL 8/9/97 — unreported elsewhere

Mitsui Babcock *v* John Brown Engineering (1996) 51 Con LR 129

Moores *v* Yakeley Associates (T&CC October 1998) 1999 52 Con LR 76

Murphy *v* Brentwood District Council (1991) AC 398

Omega Trust Company Limited and Banque Finindus *v* Wright Son & Pepper and Barker & Co (unreported) (1997) 73 P & CR D39/1997 PNLR 425

Chapter 1

Introduction

1.1 General

Effective internal risk management is crucial to the continuing existence of all construction organisations offering professional services. These include consulting engineers, architects, quantity surveyors and project managers.

Like all commercial concerns, it is to be hoped that professionals already have procedures (and review them periodically) to ensure the following are undertaken in an effective manner as follows.

(1) The receipt of invitations to bid for work.
(2) The satisfactory negotiation of rates that achieve a reasonable proportion of successful assignments and which also provide an opportunity for making an acceptable profit.
(3) The undertaking of the assignments won and achieving those profits.
(4) Obtaining payment for work done and within a reasonable time.

Professional organisations currently in business are clearly getting much of the foregoing right. For those that feel they need advice there are a reasonable number of reference books and similar documents available. Such matters are therefore not considered in detail in the text.

However, those professionals who provide construction litigation and litigation support services will realise that a significant part of their income derives from the fact that other professionals accept overly onerous terms in their agreement with clients to provide professional services.

The text of this book is therefore focused on the risks inherent in professional services agreements and associated issues and the liabilities these could give rise to which would adversely affect a professional's opportunity for maximising profit.

1.2 Liability

Liability for professional organisations can arise in a number of ways and these are explained in the text. Liability to the client will generally arise as a result of a breach of a term of the contract with the client. A professional will also owe a concurrent duty in tort to the client to use reasonable skill and care in carrying out services. Other liabilities to clients and third parties can also arise in tort. Statutes can impose duties on individuals and organisations with civil or criminal liability if there is a breach. The occasions on which this can happen are explained in the text, as is a general description of the sort of damages that could be payable.

Sometimes liabilities are recognised and accepted as commercial risks. Sometimes liabilities are not recognised. It is essential that the exposure to possible liability is understood and that proper management procedures are in place for handling it.

Professionals will often be obliged by a client to maintain professional indemnity insurance so that the client is reassured that claims should be covered by insurance. This is sound commercial practice anyway. However, it is essential for both professionals and clients to realise that it will be the insurance policy that is in place when any claim comes in that will be the relevant policy and that it is possible that at that time there could be different restrictions on cover or possibly no cover at all for certain claims. This topic too is dealt with in the text.

Even if the professional has professional indemnity insurance, claims could be made which are outside professional indemnity insurance cover, or within the cover but below an excess or above the ceiling of the indemnity provided. This will result in direct uninsured costs. Even if a claim is inside insurance cover, increases in premiums and/or the excess and/or other onerous conditions or exclusions could be imposed on future insurance cover if high-value or frequent claims have been made.

1.3 Conditions of engagement

Standard professional services conditions of engagement are written in terms discussed with, and which are generally acceptable to, the professionals and professional indemnity insurers for the professional sector concerned. The division of risks between clients and professionals within the standard conditions have therefore been considered and the risks carried by the professional will generally be covered by professional indemnity insurance.

In the main text, extracts from the following standard conditions are included for comparison and ease of reference.

(1) The ACE *Conditions of Engagement 1995, 2nd Edition 1998, Agreement A(1)* published February 1999 (ACE (Second Edition 1998)).

(2)   The RIBA *Conditions of Engagement for the Appointment of an Archi-tect (CE/99) for use with a Letter of Appointment. Updated April 2000*, published 1999 (RIBA (CE/99)).

(3)   The RICS *Appointing a Quantity Surveyor: A Guide for Clients and Surveyors with form of Enquiry, Schedule of Services, Fee Offer, Form of Agreement and Terms of Appointment*, published January 1999 (RICS (1999)).

(4)   The APM *Standard Terms for the Appointment of a Project Manager 1998*, published 1998 (APM (1998)).

While standard conditions are not always entirely suitable for a parti-cular appointment, and some might be stronger than others in some areas, particular problems arise in relation to non-standard professional services agreements and collateral warranties. Provisions may not be comprehensive or can be omitted altogether. The wording may be onerous and can impose severe or unacceptable risks on professionals. If the risk is uninsured, any successful claim would have to be met by the professional from other sources, for example cash flow, loans, sale of capital assets, etc. The same applies to excesses for each insured claim. This could have a catastrophic impact on profitability or even the continued existence of an organisation.

The following chapters describe the matters that should be included in most professional services agreements, the consequences of their non-inclusion, or of the incorporation of more onerous wording. Ways are also suggested as to how those risks might be managed.

1.4 The commercial nature of the management of agreements

A decision on how to tackle incomplete or onerous wordings in profes-sional services agreements should always be a commercial one. It can depend on many factors. For example, a professional might consider that a relatively low-priced job in an urban area could cause a large potential liability if it goes wrong, whereas a high-priced but technically simple job in a rural area might be straightforward with minimum risk. Some clients may be one-off, others may have a continuing workload for which the professional would like to be considered. Past experience may indicate that some clients are amenable to discussion and may have agreed changes to their agreements in the past; other clients may be inflexible. The professional might consider that the work is an absolute necessity to maintain minimum staff workload. The professional might have several other risky contracts in hand and not want to increase exposure. The professional may have a particular expertise not readily available elsewhere and hence be in a stronger negotiating position.

It is therefore most important to recognise that a decision to accept any particular risk is for the professional, as only the professional will have all the technical and commercial information necessary and have had a lawyer's and/or insurer's advice (where appropriate) to make such a decision.

Chapter 2

The client

2.1 Identification of the client

It is essential to identify the client so that the professional knows to whom contractual obligations are owed. The extent of the obligations undertaken and the level of risk can also be affected because of the nature of a particular client. For example, the professional may not wish to be engaged directly by a known '*difficult*' client, or a client of doubtful or unknown liquidity or of dubious '*pedigree*'. On other occasions, the professional may be prepared to be engaged by a particular client as long as some other, reputable, organisation is responsible for fees. Elementary problems concerning the client can arise. Some of these problems will be considered in this chapter.

2.2 Agent acting for the client

A professional can believe it is appointed by one person as a client, whereas in fact that person is acting as an agent for another person or organisation but does not clearly state that fact, perhaps because the agent genuinely considers that it is '*trade and custom*' knowledge in the sector concerned. Although the professional is entitled to enforce obligations such as payment against an agent, difficulties can arise if, for example, the client refuses to pay and the agent is impecunious, or if the client argues that things done by its agent are outside its authority and therefore do not bind the client. It is prudent, therefore — if it is thought that a person is acting as an agent for a client (perhaps because invoices are to be sent to a third party) — to clarify the position and the extent of the agency as soon as possible. Where an agent is formally appointed on behalf of a number of parties, the appointment itself will usually set this out and confirm the extent of the agent's authority, for example to act in all matters on behalf of its principals in relation to that project. The position can be less clear where there is no formal appointment document and, in these circumstances, the ultimate client, not the agent, should be asked to clarify the position. Always address invoices to the ultimate client unless specifically authorised by the client to address them to the agent. Where a professional is employed for expert work in relation to arbitration or litigation, the instructing solicitor will usually make clear the identity of the client and who is responsible for the professional's fees. If the solicitor does not do so, the solicitor must reimburse the professional's fees, whether or not money is received by that solicitor from the ultimate client. More rarely, a solicitor may act for a client in engaging professionals and letting the main construction contract. In those cases, the usual agency principles apply.

The situation in which a professional might be an agent for a client, and a further discussion of the principles of agency, are set out in chapter 10.

2.3 Client acting on behalf of, or for the benefit of, third parties/Panatown/Contracts (Rights of Third Parties) Act 1999

A client can often commission a project on behalf of other parties, such as another company in the same group, or for a particular purchaser or tenant, and can also enter into complicated trust arrangements with funders or others. None of these will be formal agency arrangements of the type described in section 2.2.

Professionals and contractors have been alerted by recent cases (such as *St Martins Corporation Limited* v *Sir Robert McAlpine & Sons Limited* (1994) and *Alfred McAlpine Co* v *Panatown* (2000)) that substantial damages could be recovered from them either by clients (who have suffered no loss) for and on behalf of certain owners/occupiers or direct by an owner/occupier who was not the client and who had no contractual relationship with the professional or contractor. Such damages will normally only be recoverable where there is a close relationship between the client and owner/occupier and the professional or contractor knows that the development was being built for the benefit of that owner/ occupier.

The right of the client to recover on behalf of an owner/occupier, which is an exception to the rule of privity, will not exist where the professional or contractor (as the case may be) has given a direct collateral warranty to the owner/occupier. It does not matter that the damages recoverable under that collateral warranty are different or less generous.

The right to recovery could arise in circumstances where the client could be acting, or could decide subsequently to act, on behalf of, or for the benefit of, others. This should be considered for each appointment and, if it appears to be the case, legal advice should be sought as to whether or not any limitation should be put on the client's right to recover damages on behalf of those third parties.

One way to limit the client's recovery of damages to those the client alone has suffered would be to add the following clause to the appointment document.

> *The Client confirms that it is entering into this agreement wholly on its own behalf and not on behalf of, or for the benefit of, any other party and agrees that in the event of any claim arising out of, or in connection with, this agreement it shall be entitled to recover from the [professional] only the losses, if any, it has itself suffered.*

The Contracts (Rights of Third Parties) Act 1999 confers rights on a third party to enforce any term of a contract if the contract expressly provides that it may, or if the term purports to confer a benefit on the third party unless it appears on a proper construction of the contract that the parties did not intend the term to be enforceable by the third party. The Act applies to most sorts of contracts and therefore applies to appointments, collateral warranties, building contracts and sub-contracts.

The third party has to be expressly identified but can be referred to as a member of a class or answering a particular description. Thus, the Act is wide enough to catch not only named parties but also all parties referred to generically, such as *'contractors, consultants, tenants, purchasers'*, etc.

Some terms which come within the Act will be fairly easy to identify and the professional will then be able to assess the risks involved, for example *'The [professional] will provide [the named contractor] with [certain specified drawings] at a certain time and [the named contractor] shall be entitled to enforce this term.'* The professional will know that if late, the contractor (as well as the client) will be able to sue direct for damages.

Other terms which may come within the Act may not be so clear and/or the consequences of any breach may be difficult to assess, for example a term such as *'The contractor and all members of the professional team may in their own right enforce any term of this contract which is for their benefit or is necessary for the proper performance by them of their obligations.'* This will give rights to the contractor and other members of the professional team to sue the professional direct, but it may not be clear which terms in the appointment are for their benefit and what the consequences of any breach of those terms may be. It will become more difficult still if the third parties who are given the right to enforce a term are referred to as *'tenants'*, *'purchasers'*, etc., because any tenant or purchaser will then be able to sue.

The third party has the rights to the same remedies as the client, for example damages, injunctions and specific performance.

Various limitations on the third parties' rights are permissible, for example it would be possible to limit a tenant's right to the cost of repairs. All the defences and rights of set-off which would have been available if the client had brought the claim would also be available to a claim brought by a third party.

Once a third party has been given a right, it cannot be altered or extinguished unless that third party consents. It is, however, possible to provide that this part of the Act will not apply. Clients may exclude in their contracts the necessity of obtaining third party consents because they will not want the practical difficulty of obtaining a tenant's or sub-contractor's consent, for example.

One of the objectives of the Act was to remove the need for collateral warranties (see chapter 17). At the time of writing, it is considered likely that they will continue to be used for establishing express obligations between professionals and funders, purchasers and tenants until the effectiveness of the Act has been tested by the courts.

Excluding the provisions of the Act would remove any uncertainties as to whether obligations in the appointment, such as an obligation to give information to the contractor for passing to a sub-contractor, gave that sub-contractor a right to enforce the term directly. Wording to achieve this could be incorporated in a professional appointment as follows.

Nothing in this Agreement confers or purports to confer on any third party any benefit or any right to enforce any term of this Agreement pursuant to the Contracts (Rights of Third Parties) Act 1999.

2.4 Receivers as clients

Construction contracts often contain provisions relating to the receivership or liquidation of a party. Such provisions may, for example, result in automatic termination of the employment of an insolvent contractor or give an employer the right to terminate the insolvent contractor's employment. Certain sub-contracts may cater for such events, but this is rarely the case in professional appointments, for example professionals engaged by a design and build contractor. Banks who fund developments often take security over the development property and require the right to appoint receivers to complete the project in the event of the insolvency of the developer or contractor.

A receiver must be an individual and a qualified insolvency practitioner.

The appointment of a receiver will often have no immediate effect on professional appointments. It will be a matter for the receiver to decide whether the company should continue with existing contracts, including any appointments.

Care must be taken by professionals when contracting with administrative receivers or liquidators. Appointments may arise either as entirely new appointments to complete a project that was under way at the time of insolvency or out of an existing appointment or collateral warranty.

Any attempt by an insolvency practitioner to avoid personal liability should be resisted. If a professional is appointed by a receiver, or has an appointment taken over by a receiver in circumstances where personal liability has not been excluded, the professional should invoice on a regular basis and have the ability to terminate or refuse to continue to work if invoices remain unpaid.

Usually a receiver has a right, but not an obligation, to take over a professional appointment, or to enter into a fresh contract on identical or similar terms. Under the latter arrangement, the receiver may well have no obligation to discharge any fees due and arising under the original appointment. The professional should ensure that, on insolvency of its employer, the professional does not lose copyright or give a licence to an insolvency practitioner without either outstanding fees being paid or a fresh contract being entered into.

2.5 Joint clients

Occasionally a professional may be asked to act for joint clients, that is two or more clients. It is important to establish, preferably in the appointment itself, the responsibilities of each of the clients. In relation to payment of fees, the joint clients should be made jointly and severally liable for all fees and additional payments, so that if one does not pay, the other(s) are wholly responsible. If, as sometimes occurs, the joint clients wish to pay only a proportionate part of all monies due, provision should be included for the professional to terminate if one of the clients does not pay its share. A similar right to terminate should be included if one of the joint clients is wholly responsible for the payment of fees and is in default of those obligations.

Each of the client's obligations should be considered carefully. Who is responsible for providing information or making decisions? Does the decision of one bind the other? What happens if there is a conflict of instructions or a delay in instructions being given or decisions being made? These matters should be addressed in the professional's appointment and a mechanism included for resolving them or for termination if this is not possible. One solution might be for the joint clients to appoint a project manager who has complete authority to act on their behalf, leaving any dispute to be resolved between the clients. This would not, however, resolve any problems concerning the payment of fees.

Where a professional is engaged by a joint venture made up of two or more parties or partners, the potential problems for a professional are the same as where there are joint clients. If, however, a special joint venture company has been formed, that company will usually be the client and the same assessment of the risks of accepting an appointment from such a client needs to be made as for any other company client. It is perhaps more likely that such a company will be a 'shell company' (see section 2.8). In that case, particular consideration will need to be given to the joint venture company's ability to pay, remembering that a shell company may cease to have any significant assets or even cease to exist when its purpose, the construction of a project, is completed, but there may remain outstanding fees still to be paid. Guarantees should be sought from one or more of the joint venturers.

2.6 Design and build contractor clients

Professionals are often engaged by a contractor employed in a design and build capacity. The main difficulties in such appointments can relate to: (i) the design obligation taken on by the contractor which the contractor will seek to pass on to professionals, and (ii) the question of inspection or supervision during construction. Unless expressly stated otherwise in the contractor's contract, a contractor will have undertaken an obligation to ensure that the construction will be fit for its intended purpose. This is a different and more onerous obligation from that imposed on designers under the common law, which is to use reasonable skill and care in carrying out their design (including specifications and drawings) (see sections 4.1 and 4.2). However, commonly used standard conditions for such contracts, such as JCT and ICE, state that a contractor's design liability shall be the same as a professional's. Others, such as ACA and ACA/BPF, stipulate a fitness for purpose obligation.

While a professional will normally undertake periodic inspection for a client, no inspection or supervision will normally be undertaken for a design and build contractor. Construction and supervision of the works are the contractor's responsibility and there are dangers inherent in the professional undertaking an obligation of this nature (see section 5.6).

2.7 The Crown Government, local authorities, and other statutory body clients

The Crown can enter into contracts with non-government bodies and individuals. The Attorney-General will enforce obligations under those contracts on the Crown's behalf and may be sued under the same rules of court as other individuals. The Crown does, however, retain certain privileges, for example no injunction or order for specific discovery may be granted, although the court can make declarations concerning the parties' rights. The Crown may be required to provide documents under the rules of discovery or disclosure, but it may claim public interest immunity to justify withholding some or all of those documents.

The *ultra vires* doctrine does not apply to contracts entered into by the Crown as the Crown has the power to enter into contracts without any statutory authority. The professional therefore does not have to check whether the Crown has power to enter into any form of contract. The powers of government ministers to enter into contracts may, however, be limited by statute or statutory instrument and this would need to be checked.

The main concern for a professional contracting with a public authority will be whether the relevant authority is permitted to enter into the proposed contract, as the powers of all authorities are defined by statute. In particular, the powers of local authorities derive from the Local Government Act 1972. Normal professional appointments should not create difficulties, but if the appointment covers more than the usual professional services these powers should be checked.

2.8 'Shell company' clients

For some projects a new company will be set up. However, even though the parent or holding company may be substantial, it cannot be assumed that the parent company will ensure the new company fulfils its obligations. Indeed, the new company may well have been set up to take on the project so as to shield the parent from liability. Problems can also arise when it comes to payment of fees. The new company may be formed with only, say, £100 share capital and have no other assets at all — the funding for the project coming from third parties. Further, the professional should not assume that the company entering into the appointment necessarily owns the site. Even if it does, it is likely that the site will be charged to funders. In these circumstances, there would be no automatic recourse to the assets of any parent or holding company to meet claims, including unpaid professional fees, against the new company. It is always worth while making enquiries as to the financial standing of the new company, such as one might with any new client. Certain public information may be easily obtainable from credit references searches, company searches or land registry searches to ascertain the ownership of the land or site. These can be done at little cost, although the information gathered may not always be up to date.

Where the shell company is located overseas, particularly where it is in an offshore tax haven, it may not be possible to obtain any financial information in this way.

If there is concern about any shell company client's ability to pay, the schedule for the payment of professional fees should reflect this so as to reduce the credit risk, for example time for payment should be kept as short as possible, time for payment should be stated to be of the essence and a specific right to terminate for non-payment included. A better alternative would be to obtain a third party guarantee, perhaps from the substantial parent company so as to underwrite the new company's obligations. Unless this is done, a claim for recovery of fees against the parent needs to rely on technical arguments based on the principles of agency, that is that the shell company was merely the agent of the parent. If the shell company goes into insolvent liquidation, there might then be a route to the directors of the company on the basis of *'wrongful trading'*. Such cases are rarely straightforward and, in any event, any recovery from the directors would simply be part of the liquidation and be divided amongst all the company's creditors. It is better to avoid these difficulties. No client putting forward an insubstantial company as a contracting party should object to giving a parent company guarantee.

2.9 Another professional as a client

Sometimes one professional will employ a sub-consultant to perform some of the professional's services. It is important to remember that, even though the sub-consultant's appointment may be *'back to back'* with the professional's, the professional will have obligations to the sub-consultant, particularly in relation to payment, the provision of information and taking decisions. The appointment document between the professional and sub-consultant should therefore deal with these specifically (see also chapter 9). Sub-consultancy appointments have often provided that any payment to the sub-consultant would depend on payment by the ultimate client (*'pay when paid'*). Such clauses are prohibited by the Housing Grants, Construction and Regeneration Act 1996 (*'the Construction Act 1996'*) where the professional services agreement is a *'construction contract'* as defined in the Construction Act 1996, except where insolvency is concerned (see section 21.4 for more comments on *'construction contracts'*). Professional services agreements will usually be 'construction contracts'.

2.10 Use of correct name

Once a client is identified, the correct name should be used in any professional services agreement, including the correct form of *'Limited'*, *'Ltd'*, *'plc'*, *'& Partners'*, etc. Otherwise the appointment might refer to a non-existent organisation, a different one within a group, or even a different organisation entirely from the one intended.

Chapter 3

Forming the appointment

3.1 General

In order for there to be a contract (or appointment) between a professional and a client, there has in law to be an offer to do something by one party (for example, to carry out certain services) and an acceptance of that offer by the other party. This turns the offer to carry out the services, for example, into a contractual promise. There also has to be consideration for the promise — generally an obligation to pay for the services. Other formalities may be required but a detailed consideration of what constitutes a contract is outside the scope of this book.

This very simple form of contract — where a professional offers to carry out certain services for an agreed fee, which is accepted by the client — rarely exists now. Contracts often contain lengthy provisions detailing the rights and obligations of the parties and extend to matters well beyond the services to be performed and the fee to be paid.

A professional services agreement should define in writing all the terms and conditions under which work is to be carried out, the services to be undertaken and the obligations of each party to the other. The appointment will often be on the basis of standard conditions such as those published by the ACE, RIBA, RICS and APM, or the client may wish to use its own non-standard professional services agreements. Such an appointment will then constitute the contract between the professional and the client.

It is clearly advisable to have an agreed written appointment before work commences. In practice this is not always possible, no matter what a quality assurance or management system might require, particularly if an early start is necessary. Where this happens and commercial risks have been assessed and accepted, the best procedure is that a letter should be sent to the client as soon as possible stating the professional's terms and conditions and other matters agreed, requesting the client's confirmation and, if appropriate, stating that work has commenced.

3.2 An appointment comprising several documents/ incomplete drafts

Where initial proposals have been made concerning an appointment and agreement reached in correspondence, perhaps by reference to other documents, the correspondence and the documents (if any) will comprise *'the appointment'*. If a formal document is then produced which is to comprise *'the appointment'*, it is important that either all the matters previously agreed are incorporated or that the correspondence and documents are specifically referred to and agreed as forming part of the appointment. Frequently an appointment document will contain a provision which states that the document contains all the agreed terms and/or supersedes all previous agreements and arrangements between the parties. Such a provision should not be accepted if, in fact, the appointment document does not include, or incorporate by reference, everything that has been agreed.

It is a common feature of many proposed appointments that reference is made by the client to other documents (such as the brief, the proposed contract between the contractor and the client, or forms of collateral warranties) but these documents are not provided with the draft appointment. Such documents must be provided before the appointment is agreed and signed as they might contain unacceptably onerous conditions and obligations. For example, the appointment might say that the professional must *'comply with all the obligations relating to the Services as stated in the Brief'* but the brief has not been provided or has not been finalised. It is essential to see it (and in its final form) so that the obligations can be assessed. Are they, for instance, practicable? Are they within the professional's discipline? Do they have an effect on the fee or on how the professional is proposing to carry out the work? If the brief has not been finalised, how does the appointment deal with changes to the required services and/or the fee?

Another example is that the professional must *'carry out the Services having due regard to the obligations of the Client contained in ...* [various other contracts]'. What is *'due regard'*? At the very least it would require the professional to look at the client's obligations in those documents to see whether the things the client has to do affect what the professional has to do and how to do it. If there could be a significant effect, the client should be warned and the matter discussed and any changes agreed before signature. The very task of looking at such things as development agreements and draft leases could be a time-consuming and expensive one for the professional.

Many draft appointments initially omit fundamental details, such as the basic services to be provided, possible additional services and the basis of the fee calculation and reimbursement. Even if the professional is content with all the other conditions, it must be made clear to the client that any agreement to the appointment depends on agreeing those details. If the services details are absent, the professional should supply a draft. This has two advantages:

(1) The professional will be able to set out in detail the services to be provided (which are not always what the client understands will be provided).
(2) The professional's own wording can be used or the services adopted from a form of standard conditions.

Draft appointments should also be checked to see that they contain the provisions that are essential to the professional, for example time limits for payment of fees, revisions of fees in appropriate circumstances, copyright clauses, information needed from the client, termination provisions, etc. These should be put forward by the professional at an early stage of the negotiations and, if not accepted, will alert the professional to potential problems.

3.3 Tenders

Professionals can be invited to tender for certain work and often the tender documents will include the form of appointment or the conditions that will apply if the tender is accepted by the client.

An invitation to tender does not normally constitute an offer of an appointment which can be accepted by the successful tenderer, but constitutes *'an offer to treat'*. It is therefore not necessary for such an invitation to state that the client does not undertake to accept the lowest or any tender. It is the professional's tender that is *'the offer'* as far as contract law is concerned and acceptance of that tender by the client then completes the contract.

In some circumstances an invitation to tender can constitute an offer, for example where a client agrees to accept the lowest tender.

EC and UK legislation has laid down specific procurement rules and requirements concerning the tenders for particular sorts of work (such as works contracts over a certain value let by a public body or utility) but these are beyond the scope of this book.

3.4 Letters of intent

It can often take a considerable period of time for contracts to be negotiated and executed, particularly where the details of the contractual obligations are extremely important or complex. Alternatively, a building contractor may need to sub-contract elements of its contractual obligations, such as groundworks, and the tender price will depend on the cost of the sub-contractor's work. The contractor will not want to enter into contracts with the sub-contractors until its own tender has been accepted. Sometimes a client will not want to enter into any long-term contracts until funding has been obtained. Similar issues can occur in relation to appointments between a client and a professional.

In an attempt to resolve these problems, the use of a letter of intent has become widespread, particularly with contractors, but it can also be used for professionals. By the letter of intent the parties indicate their intention to enter into a formal contract and may agree that in the interim the work can begin.

The contractual status of these letters depends on their precise terms. They may simply state an intention to enter into a contract at a later date without a specific request to undertake work or to enter into a sub-contract. On the other hand, they often create an obligation to pay for any work performed in reliance on them. Thus letters of intent have often been regarded as short-term contracts, existing only until the main contracts are entered into. The letter is regarded as an offer, which is accepted by the contractor or professional either expressly or through its conduct in performing the work or services.

Although a party issuing a letter of intent will often draft it in a way that tries to avoid creating rights and obligations on either party, the courts will strive to reject this argument where the parties have spent considerable time and effort in reliance on the letter. If no basis of payment is stated in the letter, the contracting parties will be entitled to claim payment for work done on a *quantum meruit* basis (see section 3.9). If there is a basis of payment proposed in the letter but it is unacceptable, it must be resolved to the satisfaction of both parties and a new letter of intent agreed before any work commences.

It will be apparent that letters of intent can have the same effect as contracts, although the courts have described their status in different ways. The letters can, however, only act as contracts where it is clear that the parties intended to be bound by their terms and that they intended them to have legal status.

Thus, where a professional is asked to start work under a letter of intent, the basis of payment must be acceptable and the work to be undertaken sufficiently particularised. Sometimes whole appointments can be carried out under letters of intent and this may be acceptable. If it is not, it would be prudent to have a time limit within the letter for agreeing the formal contract and provisions for what should happen, for example in relation to payment and the scope of the services to be undertaken, if no formal agreement is reached within that time limit.

Letters of intent can be very complex and contain almost as many obligations as the final appointment documents — including, for example, the obligation to give licences, collateral warranties, etc. In this event, each obligation should be considered as if it were contained in the final appointment document.

Generally, letters of intent are designed to be short-term arrangements until the final contract or appointment has been entered into or, less often, a project or commission aborted. It is important to ensure that when the final contract or appointment is entered into, it supersedes the letter of intent and that the letter of intent is of no further effect. Normally, the final contract or appointment will be retrospective, governing the rights and obligations of the parties from inception of the services. The professional should ensure that any payment not received under the letter of intent is payable under the final appointment.

3.5 Incomplete contracts

Sometimes much of an appointment can be agreed but some items are unresolved and/or the parties have recorded that some matters are '*to be agreed*'.

The courts have often recognised that in commercial contracts it is often difficult to finalise the details of a contract before work is due to begin. It is also likely that, in contracts which are to last for a significant period of time, the parties will want to allow for revision of some of the contract terms at a later date. It may therefore accept that a contract is binding on the parties, despite the fact that there are significant terms which are not included in the contract. In the event that the parties never reach agreement on the outstanding matters, the court will try to imply the missing terms into the contract, either by using a standard of reasonableness, or through statutory provisions, or as a result of the conduct of the parties. The courts will attempt to uphold the remainder of the appointment wherever possible, and the courts will only refuse to recognise the entire contract where it is unworkable or too uncertain without the missing items.

As with letters of intent, the courts look for the parties' intention to be bound by the contract to determine the validity of the contract. It will usually be easier to infer this intention where the parties have acted on the basis that the contract is valid for a significant period of time.

In some cases the parties may start work while they are negotiating the terms of a proposed contract. In those circumstances, it can be difficult to establish whether a concluded appointment has been reached and, if so, the terms of the appointment. If all the essential terms have been agreed, the court will strive to imply any other terms necessary to give the appointment business efficacy. If not, the court will have to hold that there is no contract and the parties will be entitled to payment for work done on a *quantum meruit* basis.

The courts [*Mitsui Babcock* v *John Brown Engineering* (1996)] confirmed the principles to be used in deciding whether a binding contract was in place as follows:

(1) The items outstanding are so peripheral to the main purpose of the contract as to be irrelevant to a decision on whether a contract exists or not.

(2) The language and surrounding circumstances (in this case there was an acknowledged letter of intent) inferred that the parties intended to be bound by the incomplete document.

(3) The parties operate as if a contract is in place (in this case payment was being made in accordance with '*the contract*').

3.6 Implied terms

The courts are prepared to imply terms into a written contract where a contract is otherwise incomplete. The justification for incorporating the terms into the contract is that the parties intended that the terms should have been included from the outset.

In assessing the intention of the parties, the courts will be looking at two indicators of intention against the background of the negotiation of the contract. The first indicator is the '*business efficacy*' test. This test involves looking at the contract objectively and considering whether the contract would be workable without the term sought to be incorporated. If the missing term is essential to the contract, it is likely that the parties would have intended to include it from the outset, and the term will be incorporated. The second indicator is the '*officious bystander*' test. If it would be obvious to a third party watching the negotiations taking place that a term ought to be included, and the parties appear merely to have overlooked it, perhaps because it was obvious, the term will be included.

The courts will, however, never incorporate an implied term where it contradicts a term which has been expressly included in the contract. It will also be hard for a party to argue for the inclusion of an implied term where the contract appears to have been carefully and comprehensively drafted.

Terms may also be implied into contracts based on custom or trade practice, where both parties are familiar with the relevant trade. In order for such terms to be incorporated, the trade practice must be widely known and both certain and reasonable, and it must be a well-established custom in the particular trade.

Terms may also be implied into a contract based on a previous course of dealings between the parties, particularly where the parties have contracted with each other on several occasions before on the basis of those terms.

3.7 'Entire' contract

Some non-standard professional services agreements contain *'entire'* agreement or contract clauses, such as:

> *Each party acknowledges that this contract together with all documents referred to in this contract represents the entire understanding and constitutes the whole agreement between the parties relating to the subject matter of this contract and without prejudice to the generality of the foregoing excludes any warranty, condition or other undertaking implied at law or by custom.*

The effect of such a clause is that the parties are limited to their rights under the express terms of the appointment and neither party can argue that there are implied terms. This could be dangerous because, as set out in section 3.6, such terms could be necessary to give business efficacy to an appointment. For example, if there was no obligation in the appointment on the client to give any necessary information to the professional, this would usually be implied. If an *'entire contract'* clause had been included in the contract, the professional would not be able to bring a claim should the client not provide information and this resulted in delays and extra cost to the professional.

A professional would also not be able to rely on any written or oral misrepresentation made prior to it entering into the contract, unless the statement was fraudulent (see section 3.8). Clients need expressly to exclude fraudulent misrepresentations from *'entire'* agreement clauses or the clause itself may be struck down because it fails the *'reasonableness'* test under the Unfair Contract Terms Act 1977 (see chapter 13).

3.8 Misrepresentation

During the negotiation of an appointment, many statements about the appointment may be made. Some of the negotiated terms and statements will be expressly included in the final appointment, so that if they turn out to be untrue the injured party can sue for breach of warranty or condition. If, however, any of the preliminary statements not included in the final appointment turn out to be untrue, the injured party can only sue the party making the statements for misrepresentation. Some oral statements can be terms of the contract, depending on the intentions of the parties, but it is assumed for the purposes of this section that oral statements are only representations.

A representation is a statement of fact, as opposed to a statement of opinion or intention; a misrepresentation is simply an untrue representation. The motives of the maker of the statement are irrelevant in classifying misrepresentations, but they will be relevant in assessing the level of compensation payable to the injured party.

In order to sue on the misrepresentation, the injured party must show that the statement induced it to enter a contract, and that it would not have entered the contract but for the misrepresentation. The injured party has no cause of action if it knew that the statement was untrue or if it only learned about the statement after making the contract.

Once a misrepresentation is established, it must be considered whether it was made fraudulently, negligently or innocently. A fraudulent misrepresentation is made when the person making it knows or believes it to be untrue. A negligent misstatement is made when the person making it is careless as to whether it is true or false. An innocent misrepresentation is made when the person making it honestly believes it to be true.

The effect of a misrepresentation is to make the contract voidable by the injured party, that is, it can choose whether to set it aside and treat it as if it had never been made or to continue with the contract. The contract is not automatically void. The choice will not be open for ever, though, and the right to reject the contract can be lost in certain circumstances.

The right to reject the contract is lost:

(1) By affirmation — where the person to whom the representation has been made chooses to proceed with the contract with full knowledge of the facts.
(2) By lapse of time — this may be treated as evidence of affirmation.
(3) Where it has become impossible to restore the parties to their pre-contract positions, for example where the subject matter of the contract has altered in some substantial manner.
(4) Where a third party would suffer if rescission was permitted.

The usual remedy for misrepresentation is damages, and the level of damages will depend on the nature of the misrepresentation. An injured party can claim compensation for all losses resulting from a fraudulent misrepresentation, whereas losses resulting from a negligent misrepresentation will usually be restricted by the courts to foreseeable losses under the 'Hedley Byrne v Heller' principles. In that case, the House of Lords established that the duty to take care when making statements extended to circumstances where there was a 'special relationship' between the parties, and that the existence of such a relationship created a duty of care in tort. The assessment of damages under such a claim would therefore include considerations of causation and foreseeability.

The Misrepresentation Act 1967 introduced a claim for damages for negligent misrepresentation, and case law has indicated that damages under the Act will be assessed as if the statement had been made fraudulently. The burden of proof then falls on the party in default to show that the misrepresentation was not made fraudulently. At common law the remedy for innocent misrepresentation is rescission of the contract (that is, where the contract is treated as being at an end) with no damages being awarded. However, under Section 2(2) of the Act the court has power to award damages in lieu of rescission.

Misrepresentation is also discussed in chapter 11, which deals with statements, certificates and reports.

3.9 *Quantum meruit*

As stated earlier, it may often be necessary for work to start on a contract before the details of how a party is to be paid for its services under the contract have been finally determined. Alternatively, work may be done by a party in the belief that there is a contract, but in fact there is no concluded contract for various reasons. In these circumstances, the party providing the services is, unless the work was speculative, entitled to claim reasonable remuneration for work done, on what is called a *'quantum meruit'* basis. *Quantum meruit* is applicable to several situations, but the basis of the claim is that a party has provided a benefit which cannot be returned, in circumstances where neither party expected the services to be provided free of charge. The claim can also be regarded as one which compensates a party for its *'reliance'* losses, that is, the losses suffered because of the party's belief that the contract existed.

The general principle is that a successful party in a *quantum meruit* claim can recover the reasonable value of any services provided at the date on which they were provided. *'Reasonable value'* may include an element to represent the profits of the provider of services, although this is not always available. It is possible that a *quantum meruit* award will be greater than an award in damages for the service provider's loss because the *'reasonable value'* represents the true market value of the services, whereas the contract price is only a bargain between the parties and is therefore only evidence of the value of the services. This approach has been confirmed by the courts [*Sanjay Lachhami & Another v Destination Canada (UK) Limited* (1997)], which held that a fair value ought to provide for a reasonable or normal profit margin over and above the costs incurred in carrying out contract works. The court also held that only costs which were reasonably and necessarily incurred should be reimbursed, which indicates that not all costs can be claimed, particularly where the supplier has not acted efficiently. The court did, however, hold that any pricing level put forward by a building contractor should be considered in assessing what the fair value for the work should be, even if applying this level would mean that the contractor would suffer a financial loss. This principle would appear to be relevant, for example where a professional charges on an hourly rate basis. The court would consider these rates when assessing a *quantum meruit* claim, and it would be open to the court to find that there should be no profit margin as a result.

There has been some discussion of whether the party receiving the services needs to receive any benefit therefrom so as to entitle the party providing the services to a *quantum meruit* claim. The widely held view is that the receiving party must obtain at least a tangible benefit, so that a *quantum meruit* claim fails if the party undertaking services has only carried out preparatory work of no value to the receiving party.

3.10 Speculative work

A client may request a professional to undertake work on the basis of the professional being paid only if the project concerned proceeds. A letter of appointment is still necessary, not least to record what was actually required to be undertaken initially and to set out the arrangements agreed should the project proceed. It should include a provision whereby if the project does proceed the client will pay the professional's fees to date, the basis of fees being recorded in advance in the appointment. It may be appropriate for fee rates to be higher than normal to reflect the risks inherent in the speculative nature of the initial work. It is important to note, however, that the professional will be liable if found negligent in performing that work or in giving advice, even though there has been no payment.

3.11 Trading conditions and similar

Sometimes clients will seek to order or accept offers of professional services by means of pro forma purchase order forms which are not designed for the provision of professional services; for example, they may be intended principally for the engagement of contractors or the suppliers of materials. Forms may incorporate trading conditions, usually on the reverse side. Those trading conditions should not be accepted.

If a professional has submitted an initial proposal including terms of engagement and the client confirms acceptance with a purchase order (which incorporates these trading conditions), the purchase order (and trading conditions) will constitute a counter-offer. A contract is only formed when the acceptance of an offer is unqualified. Any attempt to accept the offer on different terms will constitute a revised offer. The question will then be whether the professional by commencing work has accepted the counter-offer. Generally the answer will be that it has and thus has accepted the trading conditions. To avoid this the client should be told that the trading conditions cannot be accepted and the professional should not start work until an appropriate form of appointment has been agreed.

3.12 Checking revised drafts

Non-standard professional services agreements will often go through several revisions. All amendments should be checked to ensure that they correctly incorporate what has been agreed.

It is also necessary to check the rest of the document. It is dangerous to assume that because amendments are highlighted or indicated in different type that these are the only parts that need to be checked. Amendments may have been made to other parts and no indication made that this has happened. A final recheck should also be carried out before signature.

3.13 Appointments signed towards the end of an assignment

A check is particularly important where an appointment is not being signed until near, or even after, the completion of the services. Leaving aside the question of whether the professional might be better off without the appointment (if the appointment contains terms that are particularly onerous to the professional, it may be better if it is never agreed and signed), it is essential that the appointment accurately records what has been done. Things may have happened during the project to alter what was originally agreed.

It is also arguable that if an appointment is signed, either under hand or as a deed, the applicable limitation periods start from the date of signing and not the date otherwise prescribed by law, which could be earlier (see section 3.15). This could be dealt with by adding a term to the effect that the limitation periods will be those that would have applied if the appointment had been signed when the services commenced.

Ancillary documents such as collateral warranties should be checked to ensure they are in favour of the people to whom the professional has agreed to give them and are in the form of any agreed draft. If they are being signed after the duties have been completed, any references to continuing duties, such as *'the professional will continue to exercise reasonable skill and care'*, should be deleted or the courts may interpret this as meaning there were further duties, such as an obligation to revisit a design in the light of later technical developments (see also chapter 17 on collateral warranties).

3.14 Signing under hand or as a deed

Whether the appointment is to be signed under hand or as a deed must be checked early on. The main difference relates to limitation periods, it being 6 years for the former and 12 years for the latter (see section 3.15). If it is the professional's policy not to sign appointments and warranties as a deed, this should be resolved during negotiations.

In general, contracts can be made informally, either orally or in writing (that is, *'under hand'*), although some statutes prescribe that certain contractual documents must be made in writing, and furthermore they must be made by deed. (This is the same as signing a document *'under seal'*.) There are no such statutory requirements applying to professional appointments, although many appointments are required by clients to be signed as a deed or under seal to take advantage of the longer limitation period.

There are no specific formalities for executing a contract in writing. There may be either a single document which both parties sign, or alternatively there may be two copies of the document, with each party signing its copy, and the copies are subsequently exchanged. A duly authorised signatory can sign on behalf of a company or a partnership, and it is usual to state that he or she is signing in this capacity. The signature of an authorised signatory does not have to be witnessed.

The formalities for executing a deed depend on whether an individual or a company is executing the deed.

A document executed by an individual as a deed must state clearly that it is intended to be a deed and it must be signed by the individual in the presence of a witness attesting to the individual's signature. Alternatively, the individual can direct that the deed be signed by another person, but two witnesses are required in this situation. Finally, the document must be delivered as a deed, which means that the individual must state in writing his intention to be bound by it as a deed. There is no longer a requirement that an individual must affix his seal.

If a company is executing a deed, the document must be signed by a director and by the company secretary, or by two directors, and the document must state that it is executed by the company. Only if the company has not been incorporated under the relevant Companies Acts is it still necessary to affix the company's seal to the document. The document must also be delivered as a deed.

If the contract is executed as a deed, the general contractual requirement for some form of consideration actually to be exchanged between the parties does not apply. A gratuitous promise made in a deed can be enforced. Thus, where no consideration or payment is to be made to a professional signing a collateral warranty (see chapter 17), it will be asked to sign it as a deed, or the warranty will be unenforceable by the other party. However, if some consideration is given, even if this is as little as £1, this would be sufficient consideration. If receipt of that sum is acknowledged, even if it is not paid, that too would be sufficient consideration.

3.15 Effect of signing appointment under hand or as a deed

The time during which a professional can be sued for breach of contract is 6 years after the breach if the appointment has been signed under hand or 12 years if the appointment has been executed '*as a deed*' (or '*under seal*'). Signing as a deed or under seal should, therefore, be resisted if possible. If an appointment or a collateral warranty is being signed as a deed well after the services have been started, or even after their completion, consideration should be given to reducing the number of years for bringing any claims (see section 13.6).

It is important that all the appointments relating to a particular project are signed in the same manner. For example, where the professional is a lead consultant, all sub-consultants' appointments should be signed as deeds if the professional's appointment is so signed. If that is not so, the professional could find that it can be sued by the client but is unable to sue the sub-consultants under their appointments because the claim is time-barred.

Chapter 4

General clauses

In this chapter some matters which commonly occur in appointments are considered. It will be realised that in professional appointments (as well as in documents produced by the professional such as specifications) loose or careless wording, or wording that might have more than one meaning, or mean one thing to a technical person and another to a layman, can carry inherent risks, and the legal interpretation of certain words can carry different implications to everyday or even technical usage.

4.1 Duty of care

The standard of care imposed on a professional at common law is to carry out its services with *'reasonable skill and care'*. The test is that of the ordinary skilled and competent practitioner in the relevant profession. This is imposed regardless of whether it is specifically referred to in the appointment. It is also imposed on the provider of services by the Supply of Goods and Services Act 1982, Section 1.

All the standard conditions of engagement incorporate this obligation, often with the additional duty to proceed with *'diligence'*, that is, within a reasonable time.

ACE (Second Edition 1998) provides:

B2.3   *The Consulting Engineer shall exercise reasonable skill, care and diligence in the performance of the Services.*

RIBA (CE/99) provides:

2.1   *The Architect shall in performing the Services and discharging all the obligations under this Part 2 of these Conditions, exercise reasonable skill and care in conformity with the normal standards of the Architect's profession.*

RICS (1999) provides:

1.1   *The Quantity Surveyor shall provide the services with reasonable skill, care and diligence.*

APM (1998) provides:

2.1   *The Project Manager shall, in the performance of the Services, exercise the skill, care and diligence reasonably to be expected of a project manager holding himself out as being competent to perform such services in connection with the Project. Nothing in this Agreement shall impose a higher duty of care on the Project Manager.*

Appointments can impose a higher and more onerous duty of care. In such cases, the professional is more likely to be in breach of this duty which could lead to more successful claims, higher damages and ultimately increased insurance premiums.

Alternative wordings to *'reasonable skill and care'* are often proposed in non-standard professional services agreements, such as:

(1)   *'all skill and care'*
(2)   *'all proper skill'*
(3)   *'due professional skill'*
(4)   *'due skill and care'*.

These are clearly different from *'reasonable skill and care'* and could impose a higher duty. *'Proper'* skill, for example, could be a higher degree of skill than *'reasonable'* skill.

Often appointments contain a duty of care expressed in the following or similar terms:

The professional shall exercise the skill, care and diligence to be expected of a properly qualified [relevant discipline] experienced in carrying out work of a similar size, scope and complexity to the Project.

This is a higher duty than that imposed by common law. Whether or not it is acceptable will depend on many factors, including the nature of the project, the experience of the particular firm, any professional indemnity insurance restrictions and whether all other professionals, sub-consultants, sub-contractors, or others with design or other responsibilities that may affect the services, have undertaken an equivalent duty of care.

Any provision implying a continuing obligation to exercise reasonable skill and care once the services have been completed should not be accepted without a full appreciation of what this might require — for example, an obligation to keep the design under review or warn of problems revealed by later knowledge.

Be careful too of using statements that *'the professional is a specialist in'*. The professional will then be judged as such and therefore against higher standards and not against the criteria for using reasonable skill and care.

Wherever possible, more onerous clauses than *'reasonable skill and care'* should not be agreed to unless the risk in practice is minimal or other commercial considerations apply and the risk can be accepted.

4.2 Warranties for fitness for purpose

'*Fitness for purpose*' requirements often arise in non-standard professional services agreements, including collateral warranties. They are important enough for detailed consideration.

Building contracts are governed by the Supply of Goods and Services Act 1982 (as amended), and there are also warranties which are implied into building contracts by common law. The warranties to be implied are:

(1)   The materials used in the works and the completed works them-selves will be reasonably fit for the purpose for which they are required.
(2)   The materials used will be of '*satisfactory quality*' (the Sale and Supply of Goods Act 1994).
(3)   The work will be carried out in a good and workmanlike manner.

A contractor under a design and build contract may take on a '*fitness for purpose*' obligation in relation to design and seek to pass this on to professionals engaged directly to assist it, or attempt to impose a site supervisory role on the professionals that could involve the professional in the construction '*fitness for purpose*' aspects.

It should be noted that the ICE and JCT standard form of design and build contracts do not impose fitness for purpose in relation to design. The ACA and ACA/BPF forms do contain fitness for purpose obligations.

In the ICE form the design obligation is as follows.

8(2)(a) *In carrying out all his design obligations under the Contract including those arising under sub-clause (2)(b) of this Clause (and including the selection of materials and plant to the extent that these are not specified in the Employer's Requirements) the Contractor shall exercise all reasonable skill care and diligence.*

In the JCT form:

2.5.1   *In so far as the design of the Works is comprised in the Contractor's Proposals and in what the Contractor is to complete under clause 2 and in accordance with the Employer's Requirements and the Conditions (including any further design which the Contractor is to carry out as a result of a Change in the Employer's Requirements), the Contractor shall have in respect of any defect or insufficiency in such design the like liability to the Employer, whether under statute or otherwise, as would an architect or, as the case may be, other appropriate professional designer holding himself out as competent to take on work for such design who, acting independently under a separate contract with the Employer, had supplied such design for or in connection with works to be carried out and completed by a building contractor not being the supplier of the design.*

If this obligation is undertaken by the contractor, there will be no problem for a professional in accepting a similar obligation provided *'the separate contract with the Employer'* would be deemed to have included a duty of care obligation only. A warranty for fitness for purpose as to design should, however, be resisted.

In some cases these implied terms can be displaced. The Court of Appeal [*Rotherham MBC* v *Frank Haslam* (1996)] has stated that, where a client has produced its own design, specification and arrangements for inspection and approval, a client cannot claim to be relying on a contractor's judgement. Of particular interest to designers is the statement that:

> ... *where the efficacy of a building or other object depends upon a designer it is the designer who may be expected to bear the responsibility for ensuring the suitability of the components incorporated into it ... the designers of the building indisputably were ... [the] architect and engineer'*

and that:

> *the specification ... coupled with the architect's entitlement to test, inspect and approve materials, denied the likelihood that the contractor had been relied upon.*

In other words, the contract documents took away the contractor's fitness for purpose obligations in those circumstances.

The Court of Appeal considered *'fitness for purpose'* and *'merchantability'* (now *'satisfactory quality'*) separately. It considered that the material − in this case specified slag − was perfectly adequate (merchantable) for many applications but not for the application in question, that is, it was not fit for its intended purpose.

Express terms as to *'fitness for purpose'* agreed by a contractor in a contract create inescapable obligations. Where terms have to be implied, much depends on how detailed the client's requirements are in terms of design, specification and drawings. For a contractor's design and build contract the client's requirements are likely to be more in outline and the contractor's obligations correspondingly more onerous.

The Supply of Goods and Services Act does not require professionals (that is, those who provide services) to give such warranties. They are required to use reasonable skill and care.

If a professional gives a warranty that completed works will be fit for their purpose and they are not, liability will arise even if reasonable skill and care were used and therefore the professional has not been negligent. The damages flowing from a breach of warranty (which are the cost of making the works fit for their purpose) are different from, and can be higher than, those for negligence (which are the reasonably foreseeable loss caused by the negligence). Further, a *'state of the art'* defence would not be available. A professional could not argue, for example, that a particular piece of knowledge was not available at the time the design was prepared.

The expression '*warrants*' indicates that the professional is promising that a condition will be fulfilled, and it is in this context that it also appears in non-standard professional services agreements. For example:

> *The professional warrants that all work performed on this project related to its design will conform to the drawings and specifications and be operable in accordance with the professional's design intent;*

and

> *The professional warrants that all services performed hereunder by itself, its employees or agents, will be performed by persons who are extraordinarily skilled in their profession and in accordance with the highest standards of workmanship in their field.*

Care must be taken to ensure that such warranties are only given where appropriate. A warranty can also be an undertaking as to the truth of a statement, for example '*the professional warrants reasonable skill and care has been used*'. The risks attached to making statements whether in an appointment, in reports or to third parties is considered in chapter 11.

The professional indemnity insurance arrangements of professionals usually reflect the obligation imposed at common law, that is, to exercise reasonable skill and care. Thus, insurance that is on a negligence only basis does not cover warranties for fitness for purpose. Insurance on a legal liability basis would cover such warranties because, once accepted, they become a legal liability. However, these types of policies can specifically exclude warranties for fitness for purpose, as the risk is considered too high. Giving such a warranty could therefore mean the professional is not insured. The risks must be very carefully assessed before a professional agrees to give one.

4.3 Absolute or strict obligations

Non-standard professional services agreements often contain absolute or strict obligations, for example the:

(1) *professional shall ensure the most efficient and cost-effective solution;*

or

(2) *professional shall ensure that the finished product meets/complies with the requirements of the Client in all aspects;*

or

(3) *professional shall comply with the client's requirements;*

or

(4) *professional's site staff shall procure that construction is in accordance with the plans and drawings.*

The effect of undertaking absolute or strict obligations are exactly the same in law as if a professional had signed a warranty for fitness for purpose.

'Ensure' means to guarantee and is an absolute performance obligation. *'Secure'* has a similar meaning. These words were considered by the Court of Appeal [*John Mowlem & Company* v *Eagle Star and Others* (1995)]; who upheld the judge's view that the words *'ensure'* and *'secure'* in obligations to *'ensure the regular and diligent progress'* of the works and to *'secure the completion of the same'* in a management contract meant exactly what they said and could not be watered down to an obligation to do no more than use best endeavours. As a result, Mowlem was not entitled to an extension of time for delays that were caused by sub-contractors beyond Mowlem's control.

Other words and phrases can be used to create absolutes, for example *'comply'* or *'procure'* in the foregoing examples.

The problem is that these obligations can either amount to warranties for fitness for purpose — because, for example, the client's requirements contain such warranties — or impose an obligation to achieve something that depends on matters outside the professional's control. Taking one of the above examples, the professional's site staff cannot *'procure'* (that is, ensure that something happens) that construction is in accordance with the plans and drawings because this depends on the contractor and/or sub-contractors over whom the professional has no control. There is no direct contract with them nor are they the professional's employees.

The same is true of promises to *'comply'* with something. This should be undertaken only if it is certain that compliance is possible.

A duty to assess, for example, whether the contractor's proposed materials are *'a satisfactory equal'* to those specified is an unnecessary absolute — the criterion should be *'satisfactory equivalent'*. A technical understanding of what is *'equal'* might be that material possesses similar performance characteristics and can fulfil the same function for the required length of time, but with no inference of being identical in all respects. However, *'equal'* could be interpreted as meaning material of exactly the same size, characteristics and so on without any difference at all. The word *'equivalent'* does not give rise to similar confusion.

Sometimes obligations to *'prove'*, *'show'* or *'ensure'* something are linked to the need for a professional to investigate and/or obtain samples. A professional can never be certain that investigations and sampling are indicative of the *'whole'* and thus no agreement should be given to any clause in a professional appointment that suggests otherwise, without adding an appropriate caveat.

Sometimes non-standard professional services agreements will qualify such strict or absolute obligations by reference to the duty of care, for example *'the professional will use reasonable skill and care to ensure that ...'.* It will depend on the wording in each case as to whether the professional will only be held by a court to be liable if it has failed to use reasonable skill and care, or whether the court will decide the professional undertook to ensure something happened. In the latter case, the professional could be in breach even if what is intended by the parties is that the professional would only be liable if, and to the extent that, negligence by the professional had arisen. The obligation should be expressly stated in these terms to avoid ambiguity.

4.4 Best endeavours

'Best endeavours' is an onerous obligation.

The court [*Sheffield District Railway Company* v *Great Central Railway Company* (1911)] has described *'best endeavours'* as *'broadly speaking [to] leave no stone unturned'* but that *'the limits of reason must (not) be overstepped with regard to the cost ...'* In other words, considerable effort including the expenditure of money, whether recoverable from others or not, must be expended.

The court [*IBM UK Ltd* v *Rockware Glass Ltd* (1980)] has also stated that *'best endeavours'* required non-owner land purchasers to *'take all those steps in their power which are capable of providing the desired results ... being steps which a prudent, determined and reasonable owner, acting in his own interests and desiring to achieve that result, would take'.*

Most recently the courts [*Midland Land Reclamation Limited and Leicestershire County Council* v *Warren Energy Limited* (1997) unreported] have confirmed that an obligation to use best endeavours imposes an obligation to do what can reasonably be done in the circumstances. Thus, a company should take action which, having regard to costs and the degree of difficulty, is commercially practicable. It is not required to take action which would lead to its financial ruin or undermine its commercial standing and goodwill. It must also incur such expenditure as is reasonable in taking such action and act in the interests of the company.

Professionals, therefore, should be careful to assess what might be involved in terms of time, additional costs, and the actions that might have to be taken before undertaking an obligation to use *'best endeavours'* in relation to a particular activity.

4.5 Timescale for professional services

If nothing is said in an appointment about the time for performing services, the law implies a term that they will be carried out within a reasonable time.

A proposed non-standard professional services agreement may include a specific requirement (that is, a strict or absolute obligation (see section 4.3)) for the completion of professional services within a certain timescale. This should only be agreed to where it can definitely be met, as a failure to comply can lead to a client (possibly a contractor) incurring losses which are claimable from the professional. This means that the services required of the professional must be precise, that resources can be guaranteed and that there is no liability for the actions (for example late supply of information, gaining approvals, etc.) of either the client itself or third parties which may not be under the direct control of the professional.

Where the professional has direct control of a third party, for example a sub-consultant, it will be responsible to the client for any default and delays caused by that third party. It may be possible to pass on claims from the client to the third party, particularly if there is a proper appointment in place. However, the client's claim will be against the professional, which will inevitably involve it in additional time and probably not wholly recoverable costs. Delays can be caused by a failure to perform when required or by other events (for example errors in drawings).

A client's late delivery of information (whether this is to be supplied by the client or the client's other professionals or contractors), instructions, or approvals to a professional can result in delays to the professional's timetable. Generally, it will be implied into a contract that such matters will be provided in a reasonable time and so as not to delay the professional. It is better, however, that this situation is dealt with expressly in the professional services agreement.

Extracts from the standard conditions of engagement dealing with the client's obligation to give decisions, information, etc., are set out in section 4.10.

If the obligation to comply with a programme is to be included in the appointment, the appointment should also cover all the matters which may delay the professional (and thus relieve the professional of this obligation) and state, if appropriate, how they should be dealt with. Formal provisions for claiming extensions of time are becoming prevalent in non-standard professional services agreements and need to be considered very carefully — do they cover all the possible circumstances which may arise, do they give a right to additional costs (and, if so, who decides those costs) and can the decision later be opened up and reviewed?

The ACE (Second Edition 1998) sets out the professional's duty in relation to the programme as follows:

B2.9   *All requests to the Client by the Consulting Engineer for information, assistance or decisions required in accordance with B3.1, B3.2 and B3.3 shall be made in a timely fashion. Subject always to conditions beyond his reasonable control (including acts or omissions of the Client or third parties), the Consulting Engineer shall use reasonable endeavours to perform the Services in accordance with any programme agreed with the Consulting Engineer from time to time.*

Neither the RIBA (CE/99) nor the RICS (1999) include anything about the time for performance of the services. The RIBA (CE/99) states expressly in clause 7.1 that *'the Architect does not warrant that the Services will be completed in accordance with the Timetable'*.

The APM (1998) provides:

2.4   *... The Project Manager shall use the skill care and diligence required by Clause 2.1 to perform the Services at such time or times as shall be appropriate having regard to the Programme.*

4.6 Reliance

A client will sometimes insert a statement into an appointment that it has or will rely or exclusively rely on the professional in respect of the project.

Such wording is not needed in order to establish a duty of care because the appointment already does this. Its origins lie in the law of tort where reliance on a third party needs to be established as part of determining whether or not a duty of care in tort is owed by that third party (see chapter 11).

It can also carry a risk to the professional because it could mean that the client or client's staff or other parties engaged by the client (for example to check the professional's work) do not have to take responsibility for their own decisions or for information provided, or that the professional will remain responsible for a particular aspect of the services notwithstanding that the client has taken separate professional advice on this matter and is relying on that advice.

The responsibility for decisions, information and advice in these circumstances should be determined by reference to the facts at the time — the professional should not agree in advance that reliance in all cases or for all matters has been placed on it. It may later be impossible to argue that it has not.

If such statements cannot be deleted it might be possible to amend them, for example delete words such as *'reliance in respect of the project'* and substitute *'reliance only in respect of those matters for which the professional is responsible and to the extent of that responsibility'*.

4.7 Deleterious/prohibited materials

Deleterious/prohibited materials clauses are now almost always included in non-standard professional services agreements. A professional is usually required to state that certain listed materials will not form part of the specification. A typical clause (as in the BPF warranties in chapter 17) is as follows:

The Firm warrants that it has exercised and will continue to exercise reasonable skill and care to see that, unless authorised by the Client in writing or, where such authorisation is given orally, confirmed by the Firm to the Client in writing, none of the following has been or will be specified by the Firm for use in the construction of those parts of the Development to which the Appointment relates:
(a) high alumina cement in structural elements;
(b) wood wool slabs in permanent formwork to concrete;
(c) calcium chloride in admixtures for use in reinforced concrete;
(d) asbestos products;
(e) naturally occurring aggregates for use in reinforced concrete which do not comply with British Standard 882:1983 and/or naturally occurring aggregates for use in concrete which do not comply with British Standard 8110:1985;

A professional already has a duty *'to exercise reasonable skill and care'*, and this will extend to the specifying of materials, so such a clause is not necessary. It is not included in the ACE Conditions, nor the RIBA (CE/99).

A professional may, however, be prepared to state such an obligation expressly, provided the list is acceptable. Some are very widely drawn. For example, references prohibiting the specification of materials *'generally known to be deleterious'* are unspecific and could be open to argument. They should be qualified by stating the time of such knowledge (that is, at the time of specification) and to whom this was known (that is, the professional concerned).

Words such as *'materials used will comply with all applicable codes'* or *'British Standards'* are often inappropriate because not every building material is covered by a British Standard and different national standards might conflict. If a reference to a British (or any other) Standard remains, it should refer to the Standard relevant at the time the specification was prepared.

The obligation is often extended so that it extends to *'ensuring'* or *'seeing that'* such materials are not used in the construction of the project. Such an obligation cannot be undertaken where there is no duty of supervision or inspection. Even if there is such a duty and the obligation is limited to those parts of the project with which the professional is concerned, it should not be accepted. It is an absolute obligation and therefore creates risks for the professional (see section 4.3). A professional may be able (depending on the nature of appointment) to undertake that the client will be notified immediately on becoming aware that any deleterious/prohibited materials are being used.

An additional problem can arise where deleterious/prohibited materials have not been referred to or listed in the appointment between the client and the professional, but are mentioned for the first time in a collateral warranty. It would be unfair to expect a professional to warrant that certain materials have not been included in any specification when such prohibitions were not notified to it at the time of preparing that specification. In such circumstances it would be entirely reasonable to require the deleterious/prohibited material clause to be deleted.

Some manufacturers are upset by the description *'deleterious materials'* and have threatened legal action on the basis that, while the materials in question may not be suitable in all applications, they are not inherently deleterious. As a result, it is preferable to refer to *'prohibited materials'*.

4.8 Confidentiality

It is a common requirement of professional appointments for the professional to be asked to agree not to disclose to others confidential information provided by a client unless authorised to do so.

It is an equitable wrong to breach confidentiality. As the law is based on equitable principles, compensatory damages will not normally be available for breaches of confidentiality, but the courts may order any offending material to be returned or it may issue an injunction to stop future breaches.

The court [*Coco* v *A N Clark (Engineers) Limited* (1969)] held that the doctrine of breach of confidence required three separate elements as follows:

(1)   The information must have the *'necessary quality of confidence'*.
(2)   The information was passed on in circumstances where there was an obligation of confidence.
(3)   There must have been some unauthorised use of the information.

The *'necessary quality of confidence'* test is satisfied if the information is of limited public availability and is distinguishable from any generally available information. It must therefore be possible to determine the limits of the confidentiality and separate out the confidential information from other public information. The information must be sufficiently important and involve some original thought.

The court [*Thomas Marshall (Exports)* v *Guinle* (1976)] also held that, in order for the information to be confidential, the owner must believe that disclosure of the information would either harm the owner or benefit the owner's competitors. The owner must also believe that the information is not generally available, and this belief must be reasonable.

The information must also be passed on in circumstances imposing an obligation of confidence. This obligation may arise expressly through a contractual term. Otherwise it could arise where it would be obvious to a reasonable person that the information being passed on was confidential. If the relationship between the parties is one of a fiduciary nature, the duty of confidentiality will be easily implied, but the duty must exist at the time when the information is disclosed. An employee, for example, will always owe a duty of confidentiality to the employer, as will doctors, solicitors and bankers to their clients.

There must also have been some unauthorised use of the information, and the courts have established that innocent use can give rise to liability, even though the remedies might be restricted in this situation.

As the law of confidentiality is unclear in certain areas, it is advisable for clients and professionals to have specific ways of protecting information, for example by marking documents as confidential in a sensible manner and by recording how information was received.

As to clients, the question of confidentiality is often so important that they do not wish to rely on this general duty and thus most standard conditions and non-standard professional services agreements contain an express definition of all the material that is to be regarded as confidential and an express duty not to disclose it.

The ACE (Second Edition 1998), in the Schedule of Services provides:

> B7.2   ... *The Consulting Engineer shall not disclose to any person any information provided by the Client as private and confidential unless so authorised by the Client.*

The RIBA (CE/99) and the RICS (1999) contain no express provisions concerning confidentiality.

The APM (1998) provides:

> 10.2   ... *The Project Manager shall not without the approval of the Client, such approval not to be unreasonably withheld or delayed, release to any magazine, newspaper, radio or television programme any confidential information regarding the Project.*

The provisions in non-standard professional services agreements can be much more lengthy and onerous. The main questions for the professional will be whether the provisions are practicable and whether they require the professional to ensure compliance by third parties not under their control (for example sub-consultants) and whether they put unreasonable restrictions on the professional's personnel and working procedures. If so, the provisions need amending.

The professional's insurers and professional advisers should be excepted from any prohibition on divulging confidential information to third parties. They are also bound by duties of confidentiality and the professional must be able to seek advice from them without having to seek the client's consent to the release of information.

The obligation concerning confidentiality may be coupled with an obligation to return all the client's documents on completion or termination. The professional, however, will need the right to retain copies both for the purpose of keeping records and against the possibility of future claims.

4.9 Key personnel

Proposals for professional services agreements often require details to be provided of the particular individuals who will be involved, on the understanding that those individuals would be made available if the proposal is accepted. There are then detailed provisions in the appointment itself dealing with those individuals. These need to be checked to ensure they are practicable. How can a commitment be made to keep key personnel on a project when they might become ill, relocate, leave, become engaged on other projects, be promoted, and so on?

Where possible the number of key personnel named should be kept to a minimum and otherwise only a general obligation included to provide '*an appropriately qualified/experienced member of staff*' instead of providing names.

Key personnel provisions should be practicable, so that if, for example, the client has a right to consent to any removal or replacement, this right must be qualified by '*such consent not to be unreasonably withheld or delayed*' if the professional's internal arrangements are not to be disrupted. There are sometimes provisions that the client can insist on the removal of an employee; if so, the cause must be stipulated and the client's opinion be qualified by '*reasonable*' so that it it is not possible to act in an arbitrary manner.

4.10 Client obligation to provide information and decisions

In addition to the obligation to pay, a non-standard professional services agreement should also deal with the client's obligation to give information and decisions, approvals, assistance, etc. This sort of obligation would often be implied into the contract as an implied term, except where the appointment has an '*entire agreement*' clause (see sections 3.6

and 3.7). However, it is better to have it included specifically, not only to remind the client but also to provide for the particular requirements of the commission. There may also be a need for specific provisions concerning the client's project manager or representatives.

The ACE (Second Edition 1998) provides:

B3.1   *The Client shall supply to the Consulting Engineer, without charge and in such time so as not to delay or disrupt the performance by the Consulting Engineer of the Services, all necessary and relevant data and information (including details of the services to be performed by any Other Consultants) in the possession of the Client, his agents, servants, Other Consultants or Contractors.*

B3.2   *The Client shall give, and shall procure that his agents, servants, Other Consultants and Contractors give, such assistance as shall reasonably be required by the Consulting Engineer in the performance of the Services.*

B3.3   *The Client shall ensure that his decisions, instructions, consents or approvals on or to all matters properly referred to him shall be given in such reasonable time so as not to delay or disrupt the performance of the Services by the Consulting Engineer.*

B3.4   *The Client shall not, without the written consent of the Consulting Engineer which consent shall not unreasonably be delayed or withheld, assign or transfer any benefit or obligation under this Agreement.*

B3.5   *The Client shall designate a Client's Representative who shall be deemed to have authority to make decisions on behalf of the Client under this Agreement. The Client shall notify the Consulting Engineer immediately if the Client's Representative is replaced.*

B3.6   *The Client shall appoint Contractors to execute and/or to manage the execution of the Project and the Works. The Client shall require that the Contractors execute the Project and the Works in accordance with the terms of the relevant contracts. Neither the provision of Site Staff nor periodic visits by the Consulting Engineer or his staff to the site shall in any way affect the responsibilities of the Contractors or any Sub-Contractors for constructing the Project and the Works in compliance with the relevant contract documents and any instructions issued by the Consulting Engineer.*

The RIBA (CE/99) is similar, providing:

3.1   *The Client shall name the person who shall exercise the powers of the Client under the Agreement and through whom all instructions shall be given.*

3.2   *The Client shall supply, free of charge, accurate information as necessary for the proper and timely performance of the Services and to comply with CDM Regulation 11.*

3.3   The Client, when requested by the Architect, shall give decisions and approvals as necessary for the proper and timely performance of the Services.

3.4   The Client shall advise the Architect of the relative priorities of the Brief, the Construction Cost and the Timetable.

3.5   The Client shall have authority to issue instructions to the Architect, subject to the Architect's right of reasonable objection. Such instructions and all instructions to any Consultants or Contractors or other persons providing services in connection with the Project shall be issued through the Lead Consultant.

3.6   The Client shall instruct the making of applications for consents under planning legislation, building acts, regulations or other statutory requirements and by freeholders and others having an interest in the Project. The Client shall pay any statutory charges and any fees, expenses and disbursements in respect of such applications.

3.8   Where it is agreed Consultants, or other persons, are to be appointed, the Client shall appoint and pay them under separate agreements and shall confirm in writing to the Architect the services to be performed by such persons so appointed.

3.9   Either the Client or the Architect may propose the appointment of such Consultants or other persons, at any time, subject to acceptance by each party.

3.10   Where it is agreed Site Inspectors shall be appointed they shall be under the direction of the Lead Consultant and the Client shall appoint and pay them under separate agreements and shall confirm in writing to the Architect the services to be performed, their disciplines and the expected duration of their employment.

3.11   The Client, in respect of any work or services in connection with the Project performed or to be performed by any person other than the Architect, shall:

    .1   hold such person responsible for the competence and performance of his services and for visits to the site in connection with the work undertaken by him;

    .2   ensure that such person shall cooperate with the Architect and provide to the Architect drawings and information reasonably needed for the proper and timely performance of the Services;

    .3   ensure that such person shall, when requested by the Architect, consider and comment on work of the Architect in relation to their own work so that the Architect may consider making any necessary change to his work.

3.13   The Client shall procure such legal advice and provide such information and evidence as required for the resolution of any dispute between the Client and any other parties providing services in connection with the Project.

The RICS (1999) provides:

2.1   *The Client shall supply such information to the Quantity Surveyor at such times as is reasonably required for the performance of the services.*

2.2   *The Client shall notify the Quantity Surveyor in writing of any agent appointed to act on behalf of the Client and of any change or dismissal of the agent.*

2.3   *The Client shall notify the Quantity Surveyor in writing of any instruction to vary the services.*

The APM (1998) provides:

2.3   *The Project Manager shall be provided with copies of all contracts between the Client and Consultants and Contractors relevant to the Project...*

2.4   *The Project Manager shall be provided with copies of all existing programmes, specifications, drawings, cost plans and any other information relevant to the Project as soon as practicable following commencement of the performance of the Services ...*

7.1   *The Client shall appoint his Representative to act on his behalf for the purposes of the Project and this Agreement, including for the purpose of issuing instructions to and receiving information from the Project Manager. The Client may appoint a replacement Client's Representative by notice in writing to the Project Manager.*

7.2   *Within 14 days of the date of this Agreement, the Client shall issue to the Project Manager or request that within a further 14 days the Project Manager prepares and issues to the Client a draft written statement of the Client's goals and objectives in relation to the Project. Following issue of such draft statement the parties will endeavour in good faith to agree the same within a further 14 days. The Client and the Project Manager shall initial a copy of the agreed statement which shall thereafter constitute the Project Brief.*

7.3   *The Client shall supply to the Project Manager within a reasonable time of any request, any approvals, responses, instructions or directions required by this Agreement and any relevant data and information in the possession of the Client or which may only be obtained by the Client and which is necessary for the performance of the Services.*

7.4   *The Client shall ensure that the Consultants and Contractors give such assistance to the Project Manager as shall reasonably be required by the Project Manager in the performance of the Services.*

Chapter 5

The services

5.1 Definition of tasks

A clear definition of the tasks involved in a professional appointment is essential in order to describe correctly what is being undertaken and to help make clear the respective responsibilities of all parties to the project. They will also be the duties against which a professional is judged in any later claim for breach of contract or negligence. If a professional has agreed to carry out something specifically, but has in fact done something else, that will be a breach of the professional's obligations under the appointment. Those tasks, if extensive or complicated, may need to be listed on an attached appendix to the letter of appointment and should be referred to in its text. It goes without saying that a professional should only agree to tasks that can be dealt with and in the timescale required.

Other clarifications may be necessary. If terms like 'as required' or 'as necessary' are used to describe the extent of any particular services, there could be a major difference of opinion as to what this was meant to encompass. 'Supervision' gives rise to particular difficulties and therefore is dealt with separately (see section 5.5). Even if the professional's tasks and role are perfectly clear between professional and client at the time of negotiation, over the period of a contract the individuals involved may no longer be available to deal with any question concerning these. Third parties who later become involved, such as funders, purchasers and tenants, will only be able to refer to the duties contained in the appointments attached to or referred to in their warranties. The same would be true of any client who later takes over by way of novation or via rights allowing it to step into the place of the original client. The statement of tasks should therefore be definitive and exhaustive. It would not be sufficient for the client and professional to agree that they understand the wording to mean something specific when the wording seems quite clearly to indicate something different or more extensive. The professional should not rely on a statement by the client's representative to the effect that *'you'll never be held to that'* or *'we won't expect you to do all that'* because the representative may not be around when the written obligation is later insisted upon. The professional would then be left to try to prove a variation by consent.

It may be necessary to state expressly any limitations that have been placed on a task or that something has been specifically excluded, again so that both parties are clear as to what is to be done.

If services can only be performed after information or assistance is obtained from third parties, this should be stated.

Generally, the role of each type of professional is self-evident, for example a structural engineer will provide structural designs and a quantity surveyor will undertake measurements and pricing. However, in some circumstances engineers might undertake the measurement of quantities, architects might provide some minor design and detailing, and so on.

It is therefore essential clearly to define in writing the respective tasks and services to be provided wherever there can be confusion. Non-standard professional services agreements often do not list comprehensively normal services to be provided and optimistically do not anticipate what might constitute additional services for which additional payment should be made to a professional. Even standard conditions are sometimes unclear in certain areas as to which professional is responsible for what.

Lack of clarity has led to disputes as to what the professional is responsible for. For example who is to check the elements of fire-proofing in a building (usually an architect but a structural engineer is typically involved in the fire-proofing of structural steelwork), flat-roof detailing and so on. Another area which should be clarified is the extent to which a professional has responsibility for designs carried out by specialist sub-contractors.

An area that needs specific clarification is the role of a project manager. The role of this relatively new type of professional can be a source of confusion for clients.

The following are examples of unacceptable wording or wording that imposes onerous obligations with particular reference to a professional employed by a contractor:

(1) *The professional shall determine any information which may affect the contractor's tender,* that is, be aware of all matters which might affect the contractor's tender price.

(2) *The professional shall advise the contractor on the need for any special conditions of contract and of the unsuitability of any of the goods, materials or plant which are specified within the Employer's Requirements,* that is, act as the contractor's contract advice specialist and take responsibility for the adequacy of the employer's technical specification.

(3) *The professional shall advise the contractor on a realistic overall contract programme*, that is, be responsible for the contractor's programme.

(4) *The professional shall visit the site as frequently as the professional deems fit to satisfy itself as to quality*, that is, guarantee the quality of the contractor's works.

(5) *The professional shall provide such design and specifications that will enable the contractor to prepare the most competitive tender and maximise the opportunities to obtain a contract award*, that is, the professional is responsible for considering every option to obtain the most economical design when priced by the contractor – it is arguable that if a competitor wins with a cheaper option, the professional has not done its job and the contractor could claim tender preparation costs (and loss of potential profit).

(6) *The professional shall provide advice to the contractor on the level of contingency to be included in the tender and also provide an assessment of the construction risk and uncertainty with regard to design development*, that is, the professional is responsible for assessing all construction risks and uncertainty associated with the design and for determining the contingency level to cover those risks and uncertainties.

5.2 Approving, checking, reviewing, etc.

It is important to realise that if a professional undertakes to approve, review, comment on, examine or otherwise check someone else's work and documents, etc., the professional will incur some responsibility for those tasks. The extent of that responsibility will depend on what was required to be undertaken as well as what was actually undertaken.

For example, if a professional undertakes to check another consultant's or sub-contractor's design and fails to find an error, it can become concurrently liable with that other consultant or sub-contractor (see section 9.6 on joint and several liability). It will not matter if that area of design was not within the professional's expertise. If, however, the purpose of the check is set out and correctly describes what the professional is to do, for example '*check that the design information ... is consistent and integrated where necessary*', it can only incur liability if it fails to make that particular check. If the design check is to be comprehensive — reviewing every document and detail, for example where a professional is being replaced — the duty should state this. It will then follow that the professional will become liable for all of that third party's design, unless any limitation or exclusion of liability applies. If it is a check of major elements of a structure, again this should be stated. The same is true for any other type of review or approval — always state what the exact nature and extent of the review is and its purposes and the purpose of any approval.

5.3 Review of shop drawings

FIDIC makes particular reference to approval with regard to shop drawings. It clearly identifies that approval of shop drawings is, in fact, only a review process and the word *'approve'* should be avoided since it recognises outsiders (presumably including clients and perhaps those with English as a second language) generally take approval to mean *'unqualified acceptance'*. It should therefore be excluded from a professional services agreement. Instead, FIDIC states that the professional should state unambiguously what is required from a contractor with regard to shop drawing submissions and hence clarify its own duties to its client at the same time.

The following wording which can be incorporated into a shop drawing specification clause is generally in accordance with FIDIC advice. With simple amendments, it could equally be used within a professional services agreement:

The Contractor shall design all connections, prepare all fabrication and erection detail drawings and calculations for the structural steelwork and shall submit [two] copies to the [Professional] for review at least [fourteen] days before being required. The detail drawings shall give all information necessary for the fabrication and erection of the component parts of the structural steelwork including the grade of steel, location, size and type of welds and the location, size, type and grade of bolts. The review is for checking general conformance with the requirements of the Contract Documents. The [Professional] shall, when appropriate, return one copy of the drawings or calculations with comments to the Contractor. The Contractor shall supply [two] amended copies of the drawings and calculations, again allowing [fourteen] days for further review by the [Professional].

Review by the [Professional] shall not relieve the Contractor of responsibility for any error subsequently discovered in the detail drawings'

There is even less risk if the following is added:

Corrections or comments made on shop drawings or calculations during this review will not relieve the Contractor from compliance with the requirements of the drawings and specifications. This check is only for review of general conformance with the design concept of the project and with the information given in the contract documents. The Contractor is responsible for confirming and correlating all quantities and dimensions; selecting fabrication processes and construction techniques; and performing work safely.

Having received the relevant information from a contractor, the professional should proceed with extreme care without using the words *'approval'* or *'approved'*. The following provides an example of the written notification that might be provided to a contractor:

We herewith return a copy of each of the shop drawings and/or shop drawing calculation sheets listed below. These have been reviewed in accordance with Clause ... of the Specification. Action, if any, is as noted.

DRAWING NO.	CATEGORY			
	1	2	3	4

CALCULATION SHEET NO.	CATEGORY			
	1	2	3	4

Note:
Category 1 – No comments.
Category 2 – Make corrections noted on the relevant copies and proceed without resubmitting.
Category 3 – Amend and resubmit.
Category 4 – Totally rejected – see endorsements [on drawings, calculations, separate letter]

The foregoing information could be (and frequently is) incorporated additionally and more briefly in the form of a pro forma stamp, with tick box, on each reviewed document.

5.4 'As-built' drawings

Professional appointments frequently require the preparation and issue of *'As-built'* drawings. However, *'As-built'* drawings may not fully represent the as-built condition, as a professional's site staff are not omnipresent nor able to measure and record in detail all of the works. There is a risk therefore that a client could rely upon incomplete or inaccurate information in an *'As-built'* drawing for, say, extension or remedial works, and incur additional costs which the client then attempts to recover from the professional.

To some extent in UK construction the words *'As-built'* may be recognised as being not quite precisely what they say. However, that might not always be the case, particularly overseas, and anyway, it is common for inverted commas to be left out.

'As-built' drawings are therefore best not referred to as such at all, nor any obligation undertaken in respect of them. For example, in recognition of the potential problem, there is no mention of them in the ACE (Second Edition 1998). The Schedule of Services C18.2 provides:

> *If so requested [we agree to] deliver to the Client one copy of each of the final drawings supplied to Contractors for the purpose of constructing the Project.*

If there is any possibility that the client believes it is receiving *'As-built'* drawings or the professional has had to agree to provide drawings which accurately reflect all that has been provided on site, the client should be made aware of their limitations when they are sent. For example:

> *We enclose copies of the 'As-built' drawings prepared in accordance with our Terms of Reference. Whilst we have taken reasonable skill and care in their preparation, we must warn you that 'As-built' drawings may not fully reflect the actual conditions on site as it is impossible to verify every item of work undertaken by the Contractor, and we have prepared them using only readily available information provided by others.*

5.5 'Supervision', 'inspection' or 'monitoring' on site

The matter which perhaps most frequently seems to give rise to misunderstanding between a client and a professional is what is meant by *'supervision'*, *inspection'* or *'monitoring'* of the contractor's works.

In practice it is never possible for a professional to *'supervise'* or *'inspect'* the works to the same degree and in the same manner as a contractor, however many site staff are provided, or to guarantee that works will be constructed in accordance with the drawings and specification. Further, the professional should not tell the contractor how to construct the works, what plant and labour to use, and so on. Indeed, it would be dangerous for a professional to attempt to do so because the professional or the client would then be responsible for those instructions and their consequences, and could become liable in respect of them. (In some circumstances, where the professional may have to give instructions to a contractor, it should be aware of the risks in doing so.) The responsibility for the works always rests with the contractor.

The perils of a general obligation to supervise are exemplified by the following example [*McKenzie* v *Potts and Dobson Chapman* (1995)]. A contractor built a house and engaged an architect who agreed to supervise. The floors cracked after the property was purchased and it transpired that the contractor had (*inter alia*) used some clay backfill instead of hardcore. Both the contractor and the architect were sued. The architect had visited site in accordance with the agreement, but had not been there when the contractor had put in the backfill. The contractor had covered the clay backfill with sand. The architect accepted the builder's assurance that the appropriate materials had been used and so did not uncover it to check. He was found concurrently liable with the contractor. Even worse, the judge found the architect 40% liable to the contractor's 60%. On appeal to the Court of Appeal against the apportionment, the Court found that although some other judges might have taken a more sympathetic view of the degree of culpability of the architect, it was within the spectrum of discretion of the trial judge to hold the architect 40% to blame and so the Court of Appeal would not interfere.

In order to avoid the misunderstanding *'supervision'* and perhaps *'inspection'* can cause, those words are excluded from the ACE (Second Edition 1998), the more correct description of *'monitor'* or *'monitoring'* being used instead, combined with a statement as to the purpose of such monitoring:

> *to monitor that the Works are being executed generally in accordance with the contract documents.*

The RIBA (CE/99) services include:

> *As Contractor Administrator, administer the terms of the building contract and monitor the progress of the works against the contractor's programme. Make Visits to the Works*

and clause 2.8 provides that *'the Architect shall in providing the Services make such visits to the Works as the Architect at the date of the appointment reasonably expected to be necessary'*.

The RICS (1999) includes nothing about site supervision or inspection.

It is appropriate to note at this point that the words *'monitor'* and *'monitoring'* have their own implications where there is a requirement in a professional services contract for a professional to monitor progress, performance or cost.

The court [*Chesham Properties Limited* v *Bucknall Austin Project Management* CILL (1996) p. 1190] held that, even if not expressly stated, a professional may have an implied duty to warn a client if other professionals in the team appear to be in breach of their contracts or are negligent. This does not apply to the professional's own default or that of the client. This duty appears to be more onerous in this respect than the duty to *'supervise'*. The latter is normally taken to be *'watching over the contractor'*, unless there is an express requirement to be responsible for those in a design team as well.

The question of site staff is, of course, linked to *'inspection'* or *'monitoring'*. Both the ACE and RIBA standard conditions include provisions whereby the professional recommends the appointment of site staff if appropriate and agrees details, scope, payment and so forth, as well as the question of site visits with the client. Both also deal with the responsibilities of the contractor (or any sub-contractors), notwith-standing the provision of the professional's site staff so that the respective responsibilities are made clear.

The ACE (Second Edition 1998) concerning site staff and visits to site provides:

> B4.1 *If in the opinion of the Consulting Engineer the execution of the Works including any geotechnical investigations warrants full time or part time Site Staff to be deployed at any stage the Client shall not unreasonably withhold consent to the employment and/or deployment of such suitably qualified technical and clerical Site Staff as the Consulting Engineer shall consider necessary. The Client and the Consulting Engineer shall discuss, agree and confirm in writing in advance of such deployment the number and levels of staff to be deployed to site, the duration of such deployments, the frequency of occasional visits and the duties to be performed by Site Staff.*

> B4.2 *Site Staff shall be employed either by the Consulting Engineer or by the Client directly. The terms of service of all Site Staff to be employed by the Consulting Engineer shall be subject to the approval of the Client, which approval shall not unreasonably be delayed or withheld.*

> B4.3 *The Client shall procure that the contracts of employment of Site Staff employed by the Client empower the Consulting Engineer to issue instructions to such staff in relation to the Works and shall stipulate that staff so employed shall in no circumstances take or act upon instructions in connection with the Works other than those given by the Consulting Engineer.*

> B4.4 *Where duties are performed by Site Staff employed other than by the Consulting Engineer, the Consulting Engineer shall not be responsible for any failure on the part of such staff properly to comply with any instructions given by the Consulting Engineer.*

> B4.5 *The Client shall be responsible for the cost and provision of such local office accommodation, furniture, telephones and facsimile apparatus and other office equipment, protective clothing and transport as shall reasonably be required for the use of Site Staff and for the reasonable running costs of such necessary local office accommodation and other facilities, including those of stationery, telephone and facsimile charges and postage. Unless agreed between the Client and the*

Consulting Engineer that the Client shall arrange for such facilities, the Consulting Engineer shall arrange, whether through Contractors or otherwise, for the provision of such local office accommodation and other facilities.

RIBA (CE/99) concerning site visits and site staff provides:

2.5   *The Architect shall advise the Client on the appointment of full- or part-time Site Inspectors, other than those named in Schedule 4, under separate agreements where the Architect considers that the execution of the Works warrants such appointment.*

3.10   *Where it is agreed Site Inspectors shall be appointed they shall be under the direction of the Lead Consultant and the Client shall appoint and pay them under separate agreements and shall confirm in writing to the Architect the services to be performed, their disciplines and the expected duration of their employment.*

The ACE (Second Edition 1998) concerning responsibility provides:

B3.6   *... Neither the provision of Site Staff nor periodic visits by the Consulting Engineer or his staff to the site shall in any way affect the responsibilities of the Contractors or any Sub-Contractors for constructing the Project and the Works in compliance with the relevant contract documents and any instructions issued by the Consulting Engineer.*

A client will sometimes attempt to dictate a professional's site staffing establishment. However, it is the professional's duty to recommend to a client the resources necessary to administer the contract.

If there is nothing in any appointment document concerning the terms on which site staff are to be employed, it is prudent for the professional to set this out specifically to the client and obtain the client's express agreement. All the matters set out in one or other of the standard conditions mentioned previously should be included.

Proposed staff should not be named initially if possible, unless at that early stage individuals can be firmly committed to the future work. It is usually better to refer to them by grade (for example resident engineer, assistant site engineer, quantity surveyor, or architectural assistant) and to give an indication of qualifications and experience for the most senior staff, for example:

A Member of the [appropriate institution] with not less than [xx] years of relevant experience.

After the recommended level of site presence is agreed, the names (with relevant short CVs) of proposed staff can be provided with salaries and budget estimates of costs, as well as the professional's conditions of employment for site staff on which budget costs have been based.

Inspection or '*supervision*' by professionals appointed by design and build contractors is discussed in section 5.6.

5.6 Services for a design and build contractor

As a professional can be directly employed by a contractor as a sub-contractor, it is necessary to ensure that the obligations and the services agreed to be provided are clearly stated. The contractor is likely to have a wide-ranging specification and it is important that the professional's brief is clearly defined and where necessary limited exactly to that which it is prepared to undertake. It must not be left vague or ambiguous, especially if there is a fixed fee appointment.

Particular attention needs to be paid to any requirement to inspect the contractor's work. A contractor's supervisory work is assumed to be that necessary to enable the contractor to meet its obligations under the building contract, which may be a '*fitness for purpose*' obligation (see section 4.2). '*Inspection*' or '*supervision*' by a professional on behalf of a contractor may be seen by an unsophisticated third party (such as a contractor's employer) to be part of the contractor's supervision obligations. To agree to '*inspect*' or '*supervise*' could involve a professional in any claim that is made relating to its work. If the professional is found to be concurrently liable with the contractor for the loss suffered by the employer, and the contractor has gone out of business, the professional could be liable for 100% of the damages, for example, see *McKenzie* v *Potts and Dobson Chapman* (1995) in section 5.5. This is on the basis that each is responsible for the whole of the employer's loss.

Even where the main design and build construction conditions of contract limit a contractor's design obligations to '*skill and care*', the site works will almost certainly still need to be '*fit for purpose*' and all associated supervision and inspection by, or on behalf of, the contractor will relate to those '*fitness for purpose*' obligations. In addition, a contractor's supervision (as opposed to a professional's '*inspection*') is outside a professional's normal business and is not usually covered by professional indemnity insurance.

Occasionally for commercial reasons (for example a valued contractor/client relationship or generous terms of payment) it might be considered appropriate to accept a more detailed site services role. Typical wording might be:

> *We shall of course, be pleased to deal with site queries regarding design matters and we have allowed for reasonable attendance at progress meetings for administrative purposes during the course of the works. Should additional meetings and services be required we propose that we be reimbursed on a time basis.*

As discussed earlier, *'supervision'* by a professional is not an appropriate word, and this is particularly so in a design and build appointment. The design and build contractor is the professional's employer, and one does not supervise (that is, control) one's employer. Therefore it might be appropriate to state specifically the following:

The [Professional] shall not be responsible for the Contractor's implementation or supervision of the works.

Frequently, design and build contractors wish to restrict the services provided during the construction phase in order to minimise the professional's fees.

A professional engaged by a contractor will often visit site only to:

(1) Obtain/confirm information (for example, ground conditions) related to the professional's design services.
(2) Attend site meetings which are reasonably requested, in order to clarify written information previously provided by the professional to the contractor relating to the works.

For its own protection relating to any provision of site services, the professional should:

(1) Keep a detailed record of all events related to any site visits.
(2) Not comment on any aspect of construction on site (except obviously hazardous construction, and then in writing).

Care must be taken in any report given to a contractor (see chapter 11).

There is a need for the professional to clarify, define and limit its task and related services. A general reference to *'ensure compliance with the specification in the contractor's main construction contract'* (which could include, for example, all works to ensure obtaining planning consents, and temporary works design) is an absolute obligation and is not acceptable (see section 4.3).

Advice should preferably not be given on the *'adequacy'* of an investigation or to describe additional works which would ensure *'adequacy for the contractor's purposes'*: only give a conservative interpretative opinion on the results of investigation information provided and avoid taking on contractor's ground condition risks.

Responsibility for the totality of the main *'construction contract'* must not be accepted. Obligations should be limited solely to those contained in the professional services agreement. The contractor should state which main contract clauses are proposed to be specifically applicable to the professional so that they can be reviewed.

If professional services include the production of a specification (or the supply of a standard specification), which is to relate to any portion of the contractor's work, the specification should be checked to see that it does not place an obligation on the professional to '*inspect*' or '*approve*' work on site.

Limit any interpretation by the professional of the results of any investigations to its effect on the professional's design and not to the contractor's method of construction.

Professional services agreements often require a professional to provide an indemnity (see chapter 14) in respect of '*any loss that may be suffered by the contractor*' resulting from a breach by the professional under the appointment. The professional should be aware that such a clause may extend exposure into areas where damages would not normally be recoverable.

Claims against professionals from contractors are more likely because:

(1) Design and build contractors usually have to commit themselves to fixed prices. If a professional's error or miscalculation results in the design and build contractor incurring additional expense, the contractor is likely to claim those costs from the professional. If a professional is providing services so that the design and build contractor can price a tender, it is essential that suitable qualifications and caveats are stated regarding information or materials provided — for example, the possibility that trial pits or samples may not be representative of site conditions as a whole. If providing less detail or a less rigorous investigation than would normally be recommended because the professional is working on a speculative basis, this should be recorded in the professional's appointment or in the relevant report.

(2) The contractor is more likely to claim against a professional because of the latter's professional indemnity insurance, than to claim against a sub-contractor with, possibly, a design responsibility. This would apply also to the ultimate holder or beneficiaries of collateral warranties (see chapter 17), and particularly because a contractor is generally more likely to be, or become, insolvent than a professional.

5.7 Contractors' obligations

As already discussed (see chapter 4) contractors' obligations are very different from professionals' obligations (for example absolute obligations, warranties for fitness for purpose and duties of supervision). As a general rule, such obligations should not be taken on by a professional. Further, the insurance arrangements for contractors are very different and a professional's professional indemnity insurance should be checked before such obligations are assumed.

A detailed study of a contractor's obligations is outside the scope of this text.

5.8 Hired-in plant operators

Where hired-in plant is required to enable a professional's agreed tasks to be carried out, it will probably be by means of an agreement with a hire plant company using the company's own terms or some nationally agreed standard form. The agreement should, wherever possible, be arranged by a professional acting as an agent for a client (see section 2.2). Where this is not possible, and the professional has a direct contract with the hire company, the professional should be aware that under some conditions of hire it can become responsible for additional risks such as:

(1) Loss (for example theft) or damage to the plant.
(2) Consequential losses (for example loss of hire charges) of the owner/supplier while the plant is not available because of loss or damage.
(3) Damage or injury to third parties arising out of the use of the plant.
(4) The actions of operators/drivers, even if wages are paid by the owner/supplier.
(5) Ensuring the plant is legal if using public roads.

Any relevant insurance held by the owner/supplier should be checked and, where there are gaps in cover, further insurance agreed or arranged. This may require a new insurance policy or extensions to existing policies. In addition to insurances, roadworthiness and taxation certificates must be valid in order for the plant to be used on public roads, and the professional should clarify who is responsible for these.

Chapter 6

Payment of fees

6.1 Offers, estimates and quotations

It is important when making a fee proposal for a professional to distinguish between whether an offer is being made to do the work for a certain amount, or whether it is an estimate only which is therefore subject to review and possible amendment. If it is an estimate, it must be clearly stated as such. For example:

> *As discussed you will appreciate that it is not possible for us to predict the level of fees and disbursements that we would incur in undertaking the above Services but for budgetary purposes we currently estimate a total in the order of £xxx inclusive of fees and disbursements but exclusive of VAT.*

or:

> *Our fees and disbursements will of course reflect the actual services undertaken but you may wish to allocate domestic budgets now for those services. We advise for that purpose that we currently estimate a total of £xxx (fees plus disbursements) excluding VAT. Should the Services develop so as to need revision of this estimate we shall advise you.*

In the second example it is imperative that if the estimate is going to be exceeded the client is informed promptly or it may be able, quite properly, to argue that, as no revision was indicated, the estimate has become the fee payable.

There is no principle in contract law that a document describing itself merely as an estimate cannot be treated as an offer to contract [*Croshaw* v *Pritchard* (1899)]. The acceptance of an estimate can create a binding contract.

It would, of course, be open to the professional to argue that it did not intend to be bound by the estimate, or that the estimate was not an offer as it was only a statement of price to be used as the basis for further negotiations. The distinction between an estimate and an offer can be a fine one, and the individual circumstances must be considered. The courts, however, have held that there is no binding contract where the parties have only agreed a price for the work where other terms are still to be determined.

If an offer or quote for a specified sum is given in relation to a specified piece of work, and that is accepted, the agreement is binding and no revision to the fee will be permitted unless the offer itself makes clear the circumstances in which that will happen. It is also useful in those circumstances to set out how fees will then be charged – for example, on a specified hourly rate.

If any fee proposal is to be related to the *'Cost of the Works'* or *'the Cost Plan'*, always check the definition and the provisions as to what is to happen if the cost of the works or cost plan is exceeded, and that the final settling up provisions are satisfactory.

6.2 Lump sums and fixed fees

The principles in relation to offers are particularly important where a client wishes to pay a professional on a lump sum or fixed fee basis. Further, and subject to the provisions of the Construction Act 1996 relating to instalments (see section 6.6), unless payment intervals are also agreed a client can insist on the services being completed before the lump sum fee is paid to a professional for services rendered. If these stage payments are based on, say, a regular percentage of the total being paid monthly, there is a danger that those accumulative percentages will lag behind the actual amount and costs of input of the professional. If the client should then cease trading the professional would make a disproportionate loss. The court [*Bosky v Shearwater Property Holdings* (1992)] held that a quantity surveyor was entitled only to that part of the agreed lump sum remuneration which had accrued at the date of termination, rather than the value of work carried out at that date. A better solution therefore is to agree stage payments based on the actual input of the professional at the end of each stage.

6.3 Disbursements

The basis on which disbursements and expenses are to be paid and whether or not they are included in the fee should be made clear.

6.4 Conditional payment and speculative work

Clauses relating to payment need to be reviewed to see whether any condition has been placed on payment, for example, *'subject to the* satisfactory performance by the professional of the services and its other obligations the client shall pay ...'. Such clauses would allow the client to withhold payment if the client believes the services to be unsatisfactory. This would be a subjective test. If a professional is prepared to accept such a condition it would be better to make the test objective, that is, '*if in the reasonable opinion of the client the performance by the professional of the services is satisfactory the client shall pay ...*'.

There have been some non-standard professional services agreements which make the payment of fees conditional on the signing of collateral warranties. This would clearly be unacceptable if some or all of those warranties could be signed after the completion of the services — is the professional to receive no fee until the last warranty is signed?

Especial care needs to be taken with the terms on which any speculative work is done or conditional fees are undertaken. For example, if work is undertaken in order to obtain planning permission, is the professional to be paid whether or not the planning application is successful or only if the planning permission is obtained? If the latter, is it clear what constitutes '*obtained*'? Is the professional to do all the work in connection with any appeal within the original fee, regardless of how long this takes or how far the appeal is taken?

If payment is dependent upon '*funding*', for example, is it clear what will trigger the payment? Is it the signing of the funding agreement? Is it when any or all conditions attached to the funding have been fulfilled, even though these may not affect the professional, or is it when monies are released to the client? Does the fee agreed reflect the length of time the professional may have to wait to be paid?

Similar considerations apply to competition work, for example, are the fees only payable if the competition is won? What if the scheme is not then implemented?

The terms of the licence of any copyright work produced by the professional in these circumstances also need particular consideration. Is the client to have a licence in any event, only on the payment of fees, or only if the project goes ahead?

6.5 Payment of fees by instalments

It is assumed that a professional can ascertain the appropriate fees required for the scope of the work concerned, so that aspect is not considered further in this text. The sequence of payments needs to be considered also, that is, if the provision of services extends over several months or years a professional will inevitably require periodic payments for work done to date or certain landmark points being achieved. Non-standard professional services agreements may have no provision for this, or provisions may not be considered to be adequate. Such matters need to be agreed in the appointment.

Dealing with the effect of delay on instalments or stage payments is always difficult but any provisions concerning this should be fair. If fee payment is related to stages, there needs to be some provision to protect the professional if a stage becomes very delayed, especially if this is due to default by others. This will be of less importance if there is an entitlement to additional fee payment for the costs of delay and disruption.

The ACE (Second Edition 1998) provides for payment in instalments by reference to a schedule or at monthly or quarterly intervals or by references to stages of the works.

RIBA (CE/99) provides that the intervals are to be those set out in clause 5.10 unless otherwise agreed as follows:

> 5.10 *The Architect's accounts shall be issued at intervals of not less than one month and shall include any additional fees, expenses or disbursements and state the basis of calculation of the amounts due.*
> *Instalments of the fees shall be calculated on the basis of the Architect's estimate of the percentage of completion of the Work Stage or other Services or such other method specified in Schedule 3.*

The RICS (1999) provides for instalments to be set out in clause 4 of the Fee Offer, where they can be fixed by reference to the stage of services, date or other criteria; the amount or basis of calculation is also to be set out.

The APM (1998) provides for the instalments of the fee to be set out in the Fee Schedule and for invoices to be submitted from time to time but not more frequently than monthly. The invoices are to show the sums currently due and all sums previously paid and invoiced.

6.6 Instalments under the Construction Act 1996

The Construction Act 1996 applies to professional services agreements that are *'construction contracts'* (see section 21.4). Section 109 of the Act provides:

(1) A party is entitled to payment by instalments unless the contract specifies the duration of the work is to be less than 45 days or the parties agree the duration is estimated to be less than 45 days.

(2) The parties are free to agree the amounts of the payments and the intervals at which, or circumstances in which, they become due.

(3) In the absence of such agreement the relevant provisions of the Scheme for Construction Contracts (England and Wales) Regulations 1998 (the Scheme) apply (see section 21.4).

However, the use of the Scheme by adoption or default should be avoided if possible because the Scheme has been drawn up with contractors, not professional services agreements, in mind. The basis of calculation is by reference to aggregate amounts over periods and relates to the *'value of any work performed'* plus *'an amount equal to the value of any materials manufactured on site or brought on to site'* plus *'any other amount or sum which the contract specifies'*. It is not clear what the *'value of any work'* means or how that relates to an agreed fixed sum or hourly basis of payment, etc.

It would be much safer, therefore, for the parties to agree the intervals and the amount to be paid at each interval or a mechanism for deciding the same.

The instalment period prescribed by the Scheme is 28 days — which may prove helpful in negotiations with clients. There is nothing, however, in the Act itself which would stop a client from attempting to impose longer (or very long) instalment periods, and the difficulty then would be in deciding whether or not to agree to the client's proposal or let the Scheme apply. The Scheme would, however, automatically bring with it the method of calculating the amount due at each interval.

6.7 Additional fees

It is surprising how many non-standard professional services agreements do not contain provisions for additional fees, or set out a basis of payment for certain specified additional services only. The terms should generally include a specified list of additional services, the basis of fees for those additional services and provide for additional payment for such matters as changes by the client, or contractor changes accepted by the client, and for delays or for additional work caused by reasons beyond the professional's control. It may also be appropriate to have a provision allowing for the annual or other revision of hourly rates if the project is to go on for a long period. Again, the basis of the additional payment should also be set out. Such matters are variously covered by the standard conditions as follows.

The ACE (Second Edition 1998) provides:

> *6.7 If the Consulting Engineer has to carry out additional work and/or suffers disruption in the performance of the Services because:*
> - *the Project or the Works or Brief is or are varied by the Client; or*
> - *of any delay by the Client in fulfilling his obligations or in taking any other step necessary for the execution of the Project or the Works; or*
> - *the Consulting Engineer is delayed by others (or by events which were not reasonably foreseeable); or*

- *the Project or the Works is damaged or destroyed; or*
- *of other reasons beyond the control of the Consulting Engineer*

the Client shall make an additional payment to the Consulting Engineer in respect of the additional work carried out and additional resources employed (unless and to the extent that the additional work has been occasioned by the failure of the Consulting Engineer to exercise reasonable skill, care and diligence) and/or the disruption suffered. The additional payment shall be calculated (unless otherwise agreed) on the basis of time based fees as set out in A20.2 with payment by instalments in accordance with A21.1 save that the instalments shall start at the next instalment date provided by A21.1. The Consulting Engineer shall advise the Client when he becomes aware that any such additional work shall be required or disruption shall be suffered and shall if so requested by the Client give an initial estimate of the additional payment likely to be incurred. Where the Client requires that payment for such additional work or disruption is to be in the form of lump sums, these lump sums and the intervals at which instalments shall be paid and the amounts of each instalment should be agreed prior to the additional work being commenced. For the avoidance of doubt it is hereby agreed that if the Consulting Engineer carries out any work which subsequently becomes redundant the Client shall (unless otherwise agreed) pay the Consulting Engineer therefore on the basis of the time based fees as herein set out.

The RIBA (CE/99) provides:

5.6 *If the Architect, for reasons beyond his control is involved in extra work or incurs extra expense, for which he will not otherwise be remunerated, the Architect shall be entitled to additional fees calculated on a time basis unless otherwise agreed. Reasons for such entitlement include, but shall not be limited to:*

   .1 *the scope of the Services or the Timetable or the period specified for any work stage is varied by the Client;*

   .2 *the nature of the Project requires that substantial parts of the design cannot be completed or must be specified provisionally or approximately before construction commences;*

   .3 *the Architect being required to vary any item of work commenced or completed pursuant to the Agreement or to provide a new design after the Client has authorised the Architect to develop an approved design;*

   .4 *delay or disruption by others;*

   .5 *prolongation of any building contract(s) relating to the Project;*

   .6 *the Architect consenting to enter into any third party agreement the form or beneficiary of which had not been agreed by the Architect at the date of the Agreement;*

> .7 the cost of any work designed by the Architect or the cost of special equipment is excluded from the Construction Cost.
>
> This clause 5.6 shall not apply where the extra work and/or expense to which it refers is due to a breach of the Agreement by the Architect.

The RICS (1999) provides:

> 4.7 The Quantity Surveyor shall notify the Client in writing as soon as it becomes reasonably apparent that any work additional to the subject of this Agreement will be required.
>
> 4.8 Where the Quantity Surveyor is involved in additional work because of:
>
> - changes in the scope of the works, and/or
> - changes in the programme of the works, and/or
> - changes instructed to the services, and/or
> - the commencement of adjudication, arbitration or litigation
>
> the Client shall pay to the Quantity Surveyor additional fees calculated (unless otherwise agreed) on the time charge basis on Clause 2 of the Fee Offer.

The APM (1998) defines 'Additional Services' as '*any Services other than the Basic Services which the Client may from time to time require the Project Manager to carry out including those specified in Section 2 of the Scope of Services*'. Clause 3 then provides:

> 3.1 The Project Manager shall notify the Client if at any time the Project Manager considers that Additional Services are required, specifying what he considers are required and why. The Client may at any time (and notwithstanding that a requirement may have been issued under Clause 3.2) require the Project Manager to perform Additional Services which the Project Manager is competent to perform.
>
> 3.2 The Client may at any time before issuing an instruction under Clause 3.1 provide the Project Manager with a description of Additional Services which the Client may require the Project Manager to perform. In that event, the Project Manager shall provide his assessment to the Client as to whether and to what extent the performance of such Additional Services would have an impact on the Programme and provide an estimate of the Additional Fees which he would require for performing the Additional Services.
>
> 3.3 If the Client accepts the Project Manager's estimate under Clause 3.2, or the parties agree a revised estimate and the Client issues an instruction under Clause 3.1 in respect of such Additional Services, the amount of such estimate or revised estimate shall for all purposes be the Additional Fees to which the Project Manager shall be entitled in respect of such Additional Services.

3.4 *In the event that no requirement is issued under Clause 3.2 or no agreement on an estimate is reached under Clause 3.3, the Additional Fees in respect of Additional Services instructed by the Client shall be a fair and reasonable sum agreed between the Client and the Project Manager.*

6.8 Date for payment of fees

Non-standard professional services agreements may make no, or no adequate, provision for the period within which a professional's fees must be paid. This is obviously unacceptable and needs to be negotiated to the professional's satisfaction.

6.9 Due date and final date for payment of fees under the Construction Act 1996

The Construction Act 1996 applies to professional services agreements that are *'construction contracts'*. Section 110 of the Act provides that any construction contract must include the following.

(1) An adequate mechanism for determining what payments become due and when.
(2) A final date for payment of any sum which becomes due.
(3) The parties are free to agree the period between the date on which a sum is due and the final date for payment.

It does not necessarily follow that providing for intervals for payment such as the first of each month, also means that the payment is due on that first day of the month. It is more usual, and probably better practice, for the appointment to state when an amount is due. The ACE (Second Edition 1998) provides that *'payments ... shall become due for payment on submission of the Consulting Engineer's invoice ...'* and the RIBA (CE/99) states that *'payment under the Agreement shall become due to the Architect on issue of the Architect's accounts'*. The ACE (Second Edition 1998) provides for the final date for payment to be 28 days thereafter and the RIBA (CE/99) for 30 days from the issue of an account. The RICS (1999) provides for payment to become due seven days after the date of submission of the invoice and the final date for payment to be 21 days thereafter. Under the APM (1998) payments become due by reference to the instalment schedule and the final date for payment is to be the number of days after receipt by the client of the project manager's invoice specified in the Schedule of Particulars.

The statutory Scheme for Construction Contracts (see section 21.4) is incorporated if no mechanism is included in a *'construction contract'* for establishing the due date and the final date. It provides a rather complicated formula for establishing those dates.

(1) The *'due date'* is the later of *'the expiry of seven days following the relevant period'*, that is, the 28 day period prescribed by the Scheme for instalment periods (if the *'construction contract'* fails to provide for this) or the instalment period fixed by the appointment itself or *'the making of a claim by the payee'*. An invoice or an application for payment would qualify as *'making a claim'*, provided it contains the information prescribed by the Scheme. *'Making a claim'* is *'a written notice given by the party carrying out the work under a construction contract to the other party specifying the amount of any payment or payments which he considers to be due and the basis on which it is, or they are, calculated'*.

(2) The *'final date for payment'* is 17 days thereafter. This makes a total of 24 days.

(3) If the contract is so short that there are no instalments, or where it is the last payment, the Scheme provides that payment becomes due on the expiry of 30 days following completion of the work or the making of a claim by the payee, whichever is the later, and the final date for payment is again 17 days thereafter.

6.10 Interest payments and Late Payment of Commercial Debts (Interest) Act 1998

At common law, interest is not payable on late payment of debts unless there is an express agreement to that effect or an agreement can be implied from a course of dealing. Most non-standard professional services agreements make no provision for interest. Various statutes, however, now provide that payment of interest should be made on outstanding payments. Section 35A of the Supreme Court Act 1981 provides that simple interest is payable on debts or damages in the High Court, and Section 74 of the County Courts Act 1984 makes similar provisions in relation to county court debts or damages. Section 35A of the Supreme Court Act 1981 gives the court power to award interest at such rates *'as it thinks fit'* on all or part of a debt between the date on which the cause of action arose and the date of the judgment. Such interest only applies if a claim form has been issued.

Where no rate of interest is fixed, there is no rule as to the amount of interest that will be allowed by the court, and the rate may vary according to the practice of the court and the circumstances of the case. Long ago, the courts allowed a rate of 5% for commercial transactions or where the rate of interest is designed to be a penalty and in other cases interest at a rate of 3 to 4%. Nowadays the courts award interest at more commercial rates. The statutory interest on judgment debts is currently 8%.

The Late Payment of Commercial Debts (Interest) Act 1998 provides that from 1 November 1998 there is a statutory right to interest on late payments. Initially, the Act only applies to debts owed by a large business or the public sector to a small business supplier. Businesses include those of professionals. The Act applies to any debt resulting from an agreement made between two businesses for the supply of goods or services. A large business is one that employs more than 50 people and a small business is one that employs 50 people or fewer. There are complicated rules for calculating the number of employees which is outside the scope of this text.

From 1 November 2000 the provisions cover debts owed to small businesses by all other businesses and the public sector. From 1 November 2002, the provisions cover debts owed to all businesses and the public sector can use the Act against all other businesses and the public sector.

The statutory rate of interest is the Bank of England's base rate plus a percentage (currently 8%). It may be claimed from the date the debt becomes overdue (that is, the first day after any agreed credit period has ended or, if none, 30 days after the performance of services or after notice of the debt has been given, whichever is the later) to the date of judgment. Thereafter, interest accrues at the current statutory rate of interest. If, however, a contractual rate of interest has been agreed, that will apply instead, provided it is 'substantial'.

The ACE (Second Edition 1998) provides for interest to be paid on amounts unpaid after the final date for payment at a rate to be identified in the Memorandum and the RICS (1999) has a similar provision. The RIBA (CE/99) provides for interest at 8% over Bank of England base rate current at the date of issue of the account once the 30 days for payment has expired. The APM (1998) provides for interest to be paid after the final date for payment at a rate to be specified in the Schedule of Particulars.

6.11 Payment of undisputed portions of invoices

Non-standard professional services agreements should contain provision for the payment of non-disputed portions of invoiced fees. An express provision is required stating that the undisputed portion must be paid (in accordance with the agreed time for payment provisions), and also that interest is due on the payment of disputed amounts later agreed and paid.

Where the professional services agreements are *'construction contracts'* the provisions concerning notices of withholding described in section 6.14 will apply and no monies can be withheld unless such a notice has been given. There is therefore no need to have an express provision dealing with disputed invoices in a *'construction contract'*.

The ACE (Second Edition 1998), RICS (1999), RIBA (CE/99) and APM (1998) all incorporate the payment provisions of the Construction Act 1996, whether or not the appointment is a *'construction contract'*, and therefore they no longer contain express provisions concerning disputed invoices.

6.12 Notice of payment under the Construction Act 1996

The Construction Act 1996 applies to professional services agreements that are *'construction contracts'*.

Section 110(2) of the Act provides:

Every construction contract shall provide for the giving of notice by a party not later than five days after the date on which payment becomes due from him under the contract, or would have become due if:

(a) the other party has carried out his obligations under the contract and

(b) no set-off or abatement was permitted by reference to any sum claimed to be done under one or more other contracts specifying the amount (if any) of the payment made or proposed to be made and the basis on which that amount was calculated.

If a *'construction contract'* does not contain such a provision the relevant provisions of the Scheme apply. The Scheme simply repeats the foregoing provisions.

The reason for the rather convoluted provision about set-off is to stop payers arguing, when payment is due, that no notice was necessary either because nothing is due because the work or services are, for example, defective, or because under the contract (or any other contract between the same parties) monies/damages were owed by the payee to the payer. The payer must give a notice which specifies the amount, if any, of the payment made or proposed to be made and the basis on which that payment has been calculated. The notice therefore is needed even if payment is to be made in full or if no payment will be made. (Set-off is also discussed in section 6.13.)

Failure to give the notice of paying is a breach of contract (although it is difficult to see what loss a payee suffers in the absence of such a notice if the amount asked for was received before, or on, the final date for payment).

The 5-day notice of payment period in Section 110(2) is the only mandatory period stipulated in the Act. The parties cannot alter it, but they can arrange *'the due date'* so that it minimises administrative inconvenience.

Although it is not necessary to set out the requirement for giving notice of payment, because if omitted it will be imported into every *'construction contract'* by the Scheme, the ACE (Second Edition 1998), RIBA (CE/99), RICS (1999) and APM (1998) have incorporated it expressly.

It should be noted that if any appointment document contains these notice provisions even though the appointment is not a *'construction contract'* within the Act, the client has to give the notice of payment (and, if necessary, notice of withholding (see section 6.14)) because these will then be express terms of the contract.

6.13 Set-off generally

The common law has complex and sophisticated rules as to what can and cannot be withheld or set-off against monies due, such as professional fees.

The courts have recognised, for example, that a defendant to a claim for payment has the right to reduce or eliminate the amount claimed by using any debts which it is owed by the claiming party.

This right of set-off is therefore a cross-claim, acting as a defence to the original claim, although it is only available in certain circumstances. The cross-claim must be for a monetary amount, and that amount must be quantifiable at the time the right of set-off is claimed.

There is no requirement that the original claim and the cross-claim are linked to the same transaction, although the claims must be between the same parties *'in the same right'*. This last requirement merely means, for example, that a personal claim could not be used to set-off a contractual claim.

There are also equitable rights to set-off in relation to the same contract — for example, a client has an equitable right to set-off a claim for negligent work by a professional against a claim for fees made by that professional.

It is not necessary, therefore, for an appointment to have specific provisions concerning set-off. If it does, the provisions normally give a client wider rights than the common law, so need to be considered carefully.

RIBA (CE/99) provides:

> 5.11 *The Client may not withhold payment of any part of an account for a sum or sums due to the Architect under the Agreement by reason of claims or alleged claims against the Architect unless the amount to be withheld has been agreed by the Architect as due to the Client, or has been awarded in adjudication, arbitration or litigation in favour of the Client and arises out of or under the Agreement. Save as aforesaid, all rights of set-off at common law or in equity which the Client would otherwise be entitled to exercise are hereby expressly excluded.*

Neither the ACE (Second Edition 1998) nor the RICS (1999) contains any reference to set-off, although the RICS (1999) refers to set-off in relation to enforcement of adjudicators' decisions. The only reference to set-off in the APM (1998) is in relation to the notice of withholding under Section 111 of the Construction Act 1996.

6.14 Notice of intention of withholding payment under the Construction Act 1996

The Construction Act 1996 applies to professional services agreements that are *'construction contracts'*. Section 111 of the Act provides:

(1) *A party to a construction contract may not withhold payment after the final date for payment of a sum due under the contract unless he has given an effective notice of intention to withhold payment.*

(2) *To be effective such a notice must specify:*

   (a) *the amount proposed to be withheld and the ground for withholding payment, or*

   (b) *if there is more than one ground, each ground and the amount attributable to it,*

   (c) *and must be given not later than the prescribed period before the final date for payment.*

(3) *The parties are free to agree what that prescribed period is to be.*

As usual, if the appointment does not set out what the prescribed period is to be, the Scheme applies. That stipulates that the prescribed period is not later than *'seven days before the final date for payment determined either in accordance with the construction contract or, if there is no such provision, in accordance with the provisions of the Scheme'*.

Section 111 of the Act also states the notice of payment can be used as the notice of withholding (although it would have to be given earlier under Section 110 if the Scheme applied) if it contains the information prescribed in Section 111.

If there is a dispute as to the amount withheld or the grounds for withholding, the matter can be referred to adjudication. The Act then provides for a final date for payment once the adjudicator has decided what amount should be paid. It is *'seven days from the date of the decision or the date which apart from the notice would have been the final date for payment, whichever is the later'*.

The ACE (Second Edition 1998), RIBA (CE/99), RICS (1999) and APM (1998) all incorporate the notice of withholding provisions of the Act, although they do not all use the exact wording of the Act.

The Act also includes a right to suspend performance if there is non-payment. This is dealt with in section 7.5.

6.15 Pay when paid clauses

Non-standard professional services agreements may contain *'pay when paid'* clauses, that is, the professional's client will pay the professional's fees only after the client has received them itself from whoever is paying the fees. However, a professional will not want to be dependent for payment of fees on a third party with whom there is probably no direct contract, who might become embroiled in a dispute with the professional's client, become insolvent, or otherwise be slack or difficult payers.

Pay when paid clauses should thus be rejected except for the strongest commercial reasons.

Pay when paid clauses must be considered carefully and amended where possible. For example, the professional might be able to persuade the client to accept a requirement that the client will apply promptly for any payment due to the professional, will pay it over within a short time of receipt and will give access to documents or records so the professional can verify that those requirements are being followed. An obligation for the client to make an application to its funder for any additional payment due to the professional and to recover it on the professional's behalf might also be required.

6.16 Pay when paid clauses under the Construction Act 1996

The Construction Act 1996 applies to professional services agreements that are *'construction contracts'* and it severely restricts the rights of parties to make any payments conditional on the receipt of monies from a third party.

Section 113 of the Act provides:

> *(1)   A provision making payment under a construction contract conditional on the payer receiving payment from a third person is ineffective, unless that third person, or any other person payment by whom is under the contract (directly or indirectly) a condition of payment by that third person, is insolvent.*

This will particularly affect contractors and professionals taking on sub-contractors and sub-consultants, where to date they have to be able to employ them on a *'pay when paid'* basis. The risk of the client not paying or paying late will now pass to the contractor or the professional.

If a pay when paid clause is rendered ineffective by the Act, the Scheme will imply into the appointment all the payment provisions of the Act — the right to payment in instalments, a due date and final date for payment, the notice provisions, as well as the mechanisms for determining the amount due.

The only time such a provision is allowed is when the third person upon whom the pay when paid provision relies is *'insolvent'*. This is defined in the Act and the definition should be checked by anyone seeking to take advantage of Section 113, because some commentators suggest the definition is incomplete.

There is also the difficulty of how this might be expressed in an appointment by a professional or a sub-consultant. Payments to the sub-consultant during the contract cannot be on a pay when paid basis but there could be a general provision relieving the professional from the obligation to pay immediately the client is insolvent within the meaning of the Act. If the professional's contract with the client contains a provision for termination if one of the parties is insolvent and if the sub-contract or sub-consultancy appointment contains a provision that that appointment terminates if the professional's contract with the client terminates, this will be sufficient to relieve the payer of any obligation to make future payments. What has to be paid up to that date will be governed by the contract with the sub-contractor or sub-consultant. (See also section 9.3 with reference to sub-consultancy appointments.)

Chapter 7

Termination and suspension

7.1 Termination generally

A professional services agreement should describe how a professional is to terminate the agreement, what documents are to be delivered to the client, as well as stipulating the payment to be made in that event.

There should be an express provision to the effect that:

the termination of the engagement shall be without prejudice to the rights and remedies of either party in relation to any negligent act or omission or breach of this Agreement [or 'accrued rights or claims'].

This is necessary to ensure that, notwithstanding termination, either party can bring a later claim, for example for additional fees or for negligence. In the absence of such a provision, the termination of a contract would bring to an end all the parties' rights and obligations.

7.2 Client's right to terminate

Up until the mid 1980s the right of a client to terminate a professional's appointment for anything other than breach of contract or insolvency rarely appeared in non-standard professional services agreements. Clients were prepared to employ their professionals on the basis of a *'whole appointment'* — that is for the whole project. The professional, as a result, could plan work and fee accordingly. This attitude was reflected in the standard conditions. For example, the ACE Conditions prior to the 1995 Edition were on the basis of a whole appointment with limited rights to terminate. This meant that if a client terminated the appointment for any reason not stipulated in the appointment, that contract had been terminated wrongfully, the client was in breach and the professional would be entitled to the losses which flowed from that breach. These could include unavoidable expenses such as redundancy costs and loss of profit.

Non-standard professional services agreements almost invariably contain an express right to the client to terminate at any time. Standard forms have tended to contain the same right.

The entitlement to payment in these circumstances is often very restricted. Generally, the professional will be entitled to that part of the fee that has accrued due up to the date of termination (or perhaps only up to the last interval on which any instalment is due) with no compensation for the professional's work being disrupted, and staff possibly being reassigned or made redundant. Further, if the structure of the fee payments has not been considered carefully, the amount of work undertaken at the date of termination may exceed the fee payable.

There will often be an express stipulation that termination will not give rise to any claim for any damages against the client for loss of profit or other losses arising out of termination.

The client may also be given the express right to terminate if the professional is in breach of its obligations. This may be tempered by the inclusion of a time limit for putting things right. Such a right is unexceptionable, except perhaps if it is exercised when the breach is very minor and has no adverse effect on the client or the project. For this reason, the reference to breach is often qualified by it being required to be a '*material*' breach.

The professional has to consider the implications of such a breach and what the client may or may not be entitled to claim. Common law has sophisticated rules for assessing the damages payable if there has been a breach of contract, and any express provisions setting out what losses or damages the client will be entitled to in these circumstances will usually be intended to improve the client's position. This could also mean that the professional's professional indemnity insurers may not cover the full amount payable to the client because the indemnity provided by insurance may only extend to the damages properly recoverable in law.

Some non-standard professional services agreements state that if the appointment has been terminated because of the professional's breach, the breach will be deemed to be a '*repudiatory breach*'. Such a provision has to be deleted. The law determining when a breach is a repudiatory breach is very complex. Briefly, this will be where the breach is so serious that, if the repudiation is accepted by the other party to the contract, it relieves that party of the obligation to complete performance of the contract. If the breach by the professional is repudiatory, the client is not only entitled to recover all its losses flowing from the breach, but also the losses incurred by the client because the contract has come to an end. These could include the costs of any delays to the project while the client finds a new professional and any additional monies it has to pay to that professional over and above those that would have been paid to the original professional.

If a client and professional cannot agree whether a breach is repudiatory, the courts will decide. This should not be prejudged in an appointment and again professional indemnity insurers may not provide a full indemnity for the damages payable.

There may also be an express provision that the professional is not entitled to any outstanding fees when the appointment has been terminated for breach. Again, this needs to be considered carefully. The common law has established rules as to whether or not a breach is such that no fees or no outstanding fees should be paid. Any express provision about this could adversely alter those rules in favour of the client and so should be resisted.

Otherwise, the right to terminate should only generally be agreed where there is insolvency of a professional or acts leading up to its insolvency, such as the appointment of a receiver.

Some recent cases have indicated that a right to terminate at will can only be exercised in good faith or for good cause. This depends on the circumstances of each case and advice would be needed to see if these principles would apply to any particular termination.

7.3 Professional's right to terminate

A professional's right to terminate should mirror the client's rights. Often, however, there are no rights for a professional to terminate, not even if there has been non-payment of fees after a certain length of time. This leaves the professional with the difficult task of deciding how long the professional should continue to work and whether the non-payment amounts to a repudiatory breach, as described in the preceding section 7.2.

7.4 Suspension

The right of the client to suspend is usually tied in with the right to terminate and generally the client reserves the right to suspend at any time. This may be essential because of the nature of the project. However, the professional needs to consider how many times the client can do this and how long the period of suspension should be before the fee and/or the services are reassessed. Non-standard professional services agreements often do not recognise the disruption that can be caused to a professional's work by many or lengthy suspensions, and payments to cover the costs of starting up again are almost never included. It is prudent, therefore, to consider whether there should be an aggregate period of suspension, after which the professional should be given the right to terminate the appointment. This at least would provide an opportunity to renegotiate the fee if the client wished the professional to continue. Otherwise, the fee would remain the same however many times the client exercised the right to suspend.

The entitlement to payment of fees on suspension needs to be checked in the same way as for termination.

More rarely, the professional is given a right to suspend for a certain period, rather than terminate if, for example, there have been problems in paying fees or if the professional has been prevented from carrying out services.

7.5 Suspension under the Construction Act 1996

The Construction Act 1996 applies to all *'construction contracts'*. What constitutes a *'construction contract'* is considered in section 21.4. The Act has provisions relating to payment and suspension, the subject of this chapter, and adjudication (see chapter 21).

The Act gives a statutory right to suspend performance if there is non-payment of any sum due under a construction contract.

Section 112 of the Act provides:

> (1) *Where a sum due under a construction contract is not paid in full by the final date for payment and no effective notice to withhold payment has been given, the person to whom the sum is due has the right (without prejudice to any other right or remedy) to suspend performance of his obligations under the contract to the party by whom payment ought to have been made ('the party in default').*
>
> (2) *The right may not be exercised without first giving to the party in default at least seven days' notice of intention to suspend performance, stating the ground or grounds on which it is intended to suspend performance.*
>
> (3) *The right to suspend performance ceases when the party in default makes payment in full of the amount due.*

It should be noted that the right is *'to suspend performance of his obligations under the contract'*, not simply to suspend the carrying out of the construction works. This would indicate that such matters as the contractors' obligations regarding insurance and security of the site can also be suspended.

The right cannot be exercised unless a notice of intention to suspend has been given and this notice has to be of at least 7 days *'stating the ground or grounds on which it is intended to suspend'*. The only ground given in the Act is a failure to pay *'a sum due under the contract by the final date without giving the proper notice to withhold.'* It is difficult to see, therefore, what other grounds there could be, but perhaps the legislators were anticipating multiple non-payments.

The right to suspend arises in respect of '*a sum due*'. There could be an argument about whether a payment is due because, for example, the payment is in respect of work that is alleged to be defective. It would be unlikely for such an argument to succeed, however, because it would defeat the object of the Act — which is to provide clear grounds for whether and in what circumstances a payee can suspend.

Once the payee is paid in full, it must recommence work.

As to the consequences of suspension, the Act provides that:

Any period during which performance is suspended in pursuance of the right conferred by this section shall be disregarded in computing for the purposes of any contractual time limit the time taken, by the party exercising the right or by a third party, to complete any work directly or indirectly affected by the exercise of the right.

Where the contractual time limit is set by reference to a date rather than a period, the date shall be adjusted accordingly.

There is a right at common law and under most standard conditions to stop work if a payee has not been paid. However, the payee takes the risk that it may eventually be held by the courts or arbitration that the payer was justified in not paying, and the payee would then be liable for the costs incurred by the payer as a result. The Act helps to make it clear when a payee is entitled to suspend performance, that is, when the final date has passed without the proper notice of withholding payment having been served at the correct time. This relieves the payee of the cost consequences of suspension so long as the payee in turn has given the requisite notice.

The effect of the Act is that any period of suspension is disregarded in calculating the date for completion, with the result that an '*automatic*' extension of time is obtained. The extension does not extend, however, to the time taken for demobilisation and remobilisation but only to the strict period of suspension.

There is no right under the Act to recover any loss or expense incurred during the suspension. If this is to be recovered it is thought that the appointment must specifically provide for it, although it could be argued that such loss and expense flows from the client's breach of the payment requirements.

It is not clear whether the parties to a construction contract may be able to contract out of the right to suspend. They might be unwise to do so, however, until this point has been tested in the courts. A client could, however, make it difficult to exercise the right. The notice of intention to suspend has to be at least 7 days before the right of suspension is to be exercised. This can be extended by an express term in an appointment and so should be checked.

Some non-standard professional services agreements include suspension provisions in accordance with the Act, but sometimes it is not clear how the statutory provisions will interact with other provisions in the appointment concerning suspension.

It should be noted that there is no need expressly to include the Construction Act provisions concerning suspension within appointments. Equivalent provisions to the suspension provisions in the Act will be implied automatically into an appointment which is a *'construction contract'* by operation of the Scheme (see section 21.4).

The RIBA (CE/99), RICS (1999) and APM (1998) all include the Act's provisions concerning suspension, but the ACE (Second Edition 1998) does not.

7.6 Provisions for termination and suspension in standard conditions of engagement

The ACE (Second Edition 1998) gives a client a right to terminate and postpone a professional's appointment at any time. It provides for the services to be ceased in an orderly manner and for an aggregate period of suspension of 12 months before the professional is entitled to treat the project or works as abandoned and the appointment terminated. Either party may terminate for breach (with a 2-week period in which the breach can be repaired) or in the event of insolvency. The professional is given a right to suspend performance if prevented or significantly impeded in the performance of services for a period up to 26 weeks. Finally, there is the usual provision concerning accrued rights.

The fee to be paid is different in different circumstances. Where the client determines by notice at any time, or suspends, or where the professional suspends or determines, the fee must be a reasonable amount commensurate with the services performed to date (not just the amount due to date), together with a sum for loss and costs of disruption, calculated on the basis set out. Where the client has determined the appointment because of the professional's breach or insolvency, the amount to be paid is a reasonable amount commensurate with the services performed.

The RIBA (CE/99) provisions are shorter — both the client and the architect can suspend performance of the services — the client on 7 days' notice and the architect if any period of suspension exceeds 6 months. Either party can terminate on 14 days' notice and the appointment is also terminated if either party is insolvent or the architect is unable to act because of death or incapacity. Again, termination is without prejudice to accrued rights and remedies.

Where the client or architect suspend or determine, the architect is entitled to any part of the fee then due. Where the suspension or determination is because of a breach by the client, the architect is entitled to all expenses and other costs necessarily incurred as a result.

The RICS (1999) allows the client to suspend performance of any or all of the services on 7 days' notice. After 12 months' suspension, either party may terminate the appointment. A further right to suspend or terminate is given to either party on bankruptcy, liquidation, insolvency or any arrangement with creditors.

The client can terminate the appointment at will on 7 days' notice and the quantity surveyor can terminate on notice if the client has been in material breach of obligations and has failed to remedy the breach within 28 days.

The APM (1998) also allows the client to terminate or suspend the appointment on 1 calendar month's notice. The project manager can terminate if the suspension lasts longer than a period to be set out in an attached Schedule of Particulars. The project manager can also terminate for breach by the client and the appointment is automatically terminated if either party becomes bankrupt, goes into receivership, etc.

Chapter 8

Intellectual property rights

8.1 Copyright

Intellectual property can cover anything which is the result of mental labour — drawings, specifications and other documents of any kind, books, manuals, software programs, articles, inventions, information, ideas. The main intellectual property rights are copyright, patents, design rights, trade marks, confidentiality and database rights.

Broadly speaking, the purpose of intellectual property rights is to confer on their owner the exclusive right to use the particular intellectual property concerned. These rights can then be commercially exploited by the owner, by being licensed on appropriate terms to others.

However, not all intellectual property can be protected by all these rights. It depends on the nature of the intellectual property.

For example, an idea, by itself, can only be protected by confidentiality, that is, by ensuring that, if it is imparted to another party, it is done so only on a confidential basis (see section 4.8). The same applies to information, on its own. However, information may be effectively protected by copyright if it is in a form which can be protected by copyright, for example if it is in a document or a drawing.

Copyright protects literary and artistic works (among others). They do not have to be works of any quality — any document is a literary work and any drawing is an artistic work. A software program is a literary work.

In the absence of any special agreement, copyright in a literary or artistic work belongs to the author or artist of that work. However, if the author or artist is an employee producing the work in the course of his or her employment, copyright belongs to the employer, in the absence of any agreement to the contrary.

A work in which there is copyright may consist, for copyright purposes, of a number of different works, the copyright in which could belong to different owners. Thus, in the case of a book containing a compilation of writing and illustrations by different people, the various writers and illustrators may own the copyright in the parts that they have contributed, and the compiler of the book may own the copyright in the compilation. This is typically the case with a software program, which often consists of bits and pieces originating from various parties, some of which may have had to be licensed to the compiler of the program itself.

Likewise, a work in which copyright subsists can (with the copyright owner's permission) be adapted or modified by another person and the other person will then own the copyright in the adaptation or modification.

Infringement of copyright in a work by another party includes copying it (that is, reproducing it or a substantial part of it in any material form) or making an adaptation of the work or selling an infringing copy. Copying includes storing the work in any medium by electronic means. The transient reproduction of any work on a computer screen will amount to copying. In the case of a drawing, copying can include constructing the subject matter of the drawings, that is, reproducing the drawing in three-dimensional form.

In the UK, no formalities are necessary to own and protect copyright. A copyright owner can enforce his rights against any infringer through the courts. However, in some countries (though not now in the USA), it is necessary for the work to bear the international copyright symbol (©) followed by the name of the author or artist and the year of first publication. There is no harm, therefore, in putting this symbol on UK copyright work, and this is frequently done.

Protecting copyright is, therefore, straightforward, as long as it is clear who the copyright owner is and that no licence (express or implied) has been granted to the infringer.

Having established in which documents the professional has copyright, the provisions concerning copyright in the appointment need to be checked. Is copyright to remain with the professional or is it to be vested in the client? The latter should be resisted if at all possible (although the Crown and other statutory bodies will insist on having copyright in all the professional's materials). If copyright is vested in another party, all the rights belonging to the author also pass to that party who can then copy and as a consequence use the documents for any purpose and not necessarily for the project for which they were prepared. Further, the professional will be infringing the client's copyright if the professional copies its own documents. It is essential, therefore, in these circumstances that a licence back to the professional is included in the appointment and that this extends, if necessary, beyond the particular project.

The ACE (Second Edition 1998), RIBA (CE/99) and RICS (1999) all provide that copyright in drawings and/or documents remains with the professional. The ACE (Second Edition 1998) defines the documents so that they include '*all drawings, reports, specifications, bills of quantities, calculations and other documents and information prepared by or on behalf of the Consulting Engineer in connection with the Project for delivery to the Client* ...'. It is best to be as specific as possible so there is no misunderstanding as to the extent of the copyright claimed.

For reports and documents produced in circumstances in which there is no formal agreement about copyright, it can be helpful to include a statement concerning copyright and the extent, if any, of the licence given (see section 8.3).

Copyright belonging to a third party, for example to a sub-consultant, can only be vested in the client by that third party. Therefore, if it is a condition of the professional's appointment that all copyright, including that belonging to third parties, be vested in the client, the professional must ensure each third party agrees in its contract either to vest copyright in the client direct or in the professional so the professional may in turn vest copyright in the client.

Indemnities in respect of any infringement by a professional of a third party's copyright are frequently requested by clients. Whether or not the professional agrees to give an indemnity will depend upon factors such as those set out in chapter 14.

8.2 Remedies for infringement of copyright

The main remedies for infringement of copyright include payment of damages or the granting of an injunction.

An award of damages is usually based on any lost profits or licence fee, and it is not always necessary to prove actual loss — nominal damages may be awarded if the infringement only affects the claimant's reputation. No damages will be payable if the defendant did not know that there was copyright in the work at the time of the infringement. The court may, however, award additional damages depending on the circumstances of the case and the flagrancy of the breach.

The court may also consider any benefits obtained by the defendant through the infringement, and the claimant may claim any profits made by the defendant as an alternative to damages.

Injunctions are a discretionary remedy, and the court may not issue an injunction where it appears that the claimant is only interested in financial compensation. The grounds for granting an injunction to protect copyright have been set out by the courts [*American Cyanamid Co* v *Ethicon* (1975)] — for example an injunction will not be issued where the harm to the defendant is disproportionate to the benefit to the claimant.

Other remedies for breach of copyright include delivery up and seizure. The owner of copyright can apply to the court for an order that infringing articles or copies of copyright works be delivered up to the owner or to a third party, and any infringing copy of a work which is put on sale in public premises may be seized by the copyright owner. There is no need for a court order before exercising the remedy of seizure, but the copyright owner must follow detailed rules before seizing the infringing article, such as notifying the local police station of what is intended.

8.3 Licences

A licence in copyright works sets out the terms on which someone other than the copyright owner (the licensee) can copy or use the copyright works. The licence agreement will, for example, deal with the right to copy, which includes building the subject matter of a drawing, adapting documents and, perhaps most importantly, the purpose for which the documents can be used. Care needs to be taken to ensure that the purpose is correctly identified and does not, except in appropriate circumstances, extend beyond the particular project or purpose for which the information was provided.

If nothing is agreed in writing, when the copyright owner releases copyright work a licence may well be implied, but the terms of that licence may be unclear — for example is it restricted to use by the client and project team or does it extend to purchasers and tenants? It is better, therefore, to have express licence terms included in the appointment documents. It should be noted that a grant of a licence does not automatically carry the right to grant sub-licences.

The provisions in ACE (Second Edition 1998), concerning the licence to be given to the client are as follows:

> B7.1 ... the Client shall have a licence to copy and use such drawings and other documents and information for any purpose related to the Project including, but without limitation, the construction, completion, maintenance, letting, promotion, advertisement, reinstatement, refurbishment and repair of the Project. Such licence shall enable the Client to copy and use such drawings and other documents and information for the extension of the Project but such use shall not include a licence to reproduce the designs contained therein for any extension of the Project. In the event of the Client being in default of payment of any fees or other amounts due under this Agreement the Consulting Engineer may revoke the licence granted herein on giving seven days' Notice. Save as above, the Client shall not make copies of such drawings or other documents or information nor shall he use the same in connection with any other works without the prior written approval of the Consulting Engineer which shall not unreasonably be withheld and upon such terms as may be agreed between the Client

> *and the Consulting Engineer. The Consulting Engineer shall not be liable*
> *for the use by any person of any such drawings or other documents or*
> *information for any purpose other than that for which the same were*
> *prepared by or on behalf of the Consulting Engineer.*

Taking various elements of the foregoing ACE clause: the phrase '*a licence to copy and use*'. A licence should not be qualified by such words as '*irrevocable*', '*exclusive*', '*freely assignable*', all of which alter the nature of the licence given and need therefore to be assessed individually. An '*irrevocable*' licence would mean that whatever the circumstances, such as a breach of its obligations by the client, the licence will not cease. The professional is thus giving away any rights to argue that the licence has come to an end. It is rare to see an '*exclusive*' licence, but this is tantamount to handing over copyright because it would confer on the licensee sole rights to copy and use the documents, etc., and this would prevent the other consultants, contractor, sub-contractor, etc., having this facility. It would also prohibit the professional from exploiting the professional's copyright work freely. If a licence is '*freely assignable*' or the licensee is permitted to grant further sub-licences, the professional could lose control of the number of people who have the right to copy the professional's documents, and the uses to which they can be put, and so again such a right needs to be considered carefully.

The phrase '*such drawings and other documents and information*' refers back to the items listed at the beginning of the clause, that is, '*the copyright in all drawings, reports, specifications, bills of quantities, calculations and other documents and information prepared by or on behalf of the Consulting Engineer in connection with the Project for delivery to the Client shall remain vested in the Consulting Engineer but . . .*'. The licence is therefore being given only in the drawings and other documents and information. If the client wishes to copy and use '*reports, specifications, bills of quantities and calculations*', it would be necessary to agree the terms of a licence specifically for these with the professional. This is because the client does not actually need to have the right to copy and use these. Often the documents in respect of which a licence is to be given are defined elsewhere in the appointment document. The list should be checked to see if it is appropriate for that project.

A licence in respect of '*calculations*' can be particularly contentious. As a general policy, the release of calculations should be refused, as one purpose, whether stated by the client or not, can be to use them in litigation against the professional. Many calculations, if meticulously checked, could be found to contain an arithmetic error. This could have had no effect on the overall design nor amount to negligence, but the finding of such an error could give a client ammunition in a claim. If the client can supply a valid non-contentious reason, it may be considered commercially valid that calculations can be released. It is suggested that the following requirements be met.

(1) The calculations are final calculations and not working drafts.
(2) The calculations are in a satisfactory state for release (calculations which are of unsatisfactory appearance are a poor reflection on the professional and their release could be counter-productive in terms of the impression made on the client).
(3) The costs of copying, etc., should, if possible, be reimbursed by the client.
(4) The calculations should be accompanied by an appropriate licence agreement.

Hence '... *use ... for any purpose related to the Project* ...', it is essential to define the use to which the documents can be put. It would not be advisable for the client to have the right to use them for *'any purposes'* because the documents may not be appropriate for any purpose and the professional may have no opportunity to review and advise concerning their use for other purposes. Further, the fee will not generally cover the preparation of documents of general application, say, to several projects. The phrase in the ACE licence clause assists in emphasising to clients that documents prepared for one project are not necessarily suitable for another.

In '... *use ... for the extension of the Project but such use shall not include a licence to reproduce the designs contained therein for any extension of the Project* ...', a distinction is drawn between a right to use them for any extension (for example to see where services are, what the structure of the original was) but not to reproduce the design, that is, build something identical to the original. This is particularly important to architects (see RIBA (CE/99) following).

'... *In the event of the Client being in default of payment of any fees or other amounts due ... the Consulting Engineer may revoke the licence granted herein on giving seven days' notice* ...'. It can often be very difficult, in the absence of an express provision, to determine whether a licence to use drawings or similar documents is revocable if the client is in arrears with the fees due to a professional. There is some authority to the effect that if the client is in repudiatory breach (see section 7.2) a licence is revoked. However, it is much clearer if this is dealt with in the appointment. It is also clearer to express it as the revocation of licence, rather than making the licence *'subject to the payment of fees'*. This is because drawings and documents are often released before payment is due and there will be no doubt that, at the time of their release, the client was given an implied licence, if not an express one, to copy and use them. It will then be a question of whether that licence could be said to be *'subject to the payment of fees'* and thus revoked if subsequent fees are not paid.

'*Save as above the Client shall not make copies of such drawings or other documents or information ... without the prior written approval of the Consulting Engineer.*' This is again a useful reminder that any extension or variation to the licence expressly given must be agreed with the professional.

'*The Consulting Engineer shall not be liable for the use by any person of any drawings ... for any purpose other than that for which the same were prepared and provided by or on behalf of the Consulting Engineer.*' Although the professional may not be liable in such circumstances, this statement is again a useful reminder of this fact to clients and, perhaps more importantly, to anyone to whom a further licence may be given.

The RIBA (CE/99) states:

6.1 *The Architect owns the copyright in the work produced by him in performing the Services ...*

6.2 *The Client shall have a licence to copy and use and allow other Consultants and contractors providing services to the Project to use and copy drawings, documents and bespoke software produced by the Architect in performing the Services ... for purposes related to the Project on the Site or part of the Site to which the design relates.*

The licence in clause 6.2 includes '*its operation, maintenance, repair, reinstatement, alteration, extending, promotion, leasing and/or sale but shall exclude the reproduction of the Architect's design for any part of any extension of the Project and/or for any other project unless a licence fee in respect of any identified part of the Architect's design is stated in Schedule 3.*'

Clause 6.2 also provides that '*the Architect shall not be liable if the Material* (that is, the documents) *is modified other than by or with the consent of the Architect, or used for any purpose other than that for which it was prepared or used for any unauthorised purpose.*'

The RICS (1999) provides:

6.1 *The copyright in all documents prepared by the Quantity Surveyor in providing the services shall remain the property of the Quantity Surveyor. Subject to payment by the Client of the fees properly due to the Quantity Surveyor under this Agreement the Quantity Surveyor grants to the Client an irrevocable non-exclusive royalty-free licence to copy and use the documents for any purpose related to the project.*

6.2 *The Quantity Surveyor shall not be liable for any use of the documents for any purpose other than that for which they were prepared and provided by the Quantity Surveyor.*

There is no definition of '*the documents*', although the Form of Enquiry attached provides a table of documents so that the quantity surveyor can indicate which tender documents it will produce and the services could also include for the provision of certain documents.

The APM (1998) provides:

10.1 *Copyright in any documents prepared by the Project Manager in connection with the Project shall remain vested in the Project Manager. The Project Manager hereby grants to the Client a non-exclusive licence to copy and use such documents for any purpose whatsoever relating to the Project including, but without limitation, the execution, completion, maintenance, extension, marketing, reinstatement and repair of the Project. The Project Manager shall not be liable for any use of such documents for any purpose other than that for which they were prepared by the Project Manager.*

8.4 Design right

A '*design right*' is created by and defined in the Copyright, Designs and Patents Act 1988 (*the 1988 Act*) as a property right which subsists in certain original designs. Design in this context means the design of any aspect of the shape or configuration (whether internal or external) of the whole or part of an article, and there is no requirement for aesthetic quality. There are various statutory exclusions, such as any method or principle of construction. It will, in the main, subsist in designs of functional articles, such as chairs or spare parts for cars, which it is intended should be manufactured. There may be some overlap between these rights and the copyright protection previously referred to, but this, and a detailed consideration of '*design rights*' themselves, is beyond the scope of this text.

Design rights prevent the copying of any original three-dimensional design. In order to qualify for protection, the original design must either be recorded in a design document or an article must have been made to the design.

8.5 Identification as author

The Copyright, Designs and Patents Act 1988 (the 1988 Act) also created several '*moral rights*', including in Section 77 the right to be identified as the author of (or person who created) a copyright work.

For a professional, this would mean the right to be identified as the author of the drawings for a building, for example. Section 78 of the 1988 Act requires that such a right must be positively and formally asserted either on the copyright work or by an instrument in writing, for example the appointment document, before it can be enforced.

The right is infringed if certain acts are done without the author's consent, for example if the work is published commercially. As far as architects are concerned, there are special provisions giving architects the right to be identified whenever copies of a graphic work of their building or of a model for a building are issued to the public. Also, where the building the architect designed is being constructed, the architect has the right to be identified on the building as constructed.

The RIBA (CE/99) includes in clause 6.1 that the architect *'generally asserts the right to be identified as the author of the artistic work/work of architecture comprising the Project.'*

The 1988 Act also gives a right to object to a derogatory treatment, which includes in Section 80 the adaptation of copyright work.

Any infringement can give rise to an action for breach of statutory duty owed to the person entitled to the right.

These rights can cause administrative problems for a client and many non-standard professional services agreements include a provision that all the professionals agree not to assert the right to be identified as the author by expressly waiving this right or by agreeing not to assert the right and usually do this by reference to the relevant sections of the 1988 Act, for example:

> *The Consultant agrees not to assert against the Client or any other person who, with the permission of the Client, publishes commercially, exhibits in public, films, broadcasts, includes in a cable programme service, photographs or otherwise copies or deals with any image of the Project or any of the [copyright work] any right which the Consultant may have to be identified as author of the Project or any part of it or the [copyright work] pursuant to Section 77 of the Copyright, Designs and Patents Act 1988 ('the 1988 Act') or any other legislation which may supplement the 1988 Act. The Consultant also waives any rights it may have pursuant to Section 80 of the 1988 Act or any legislation which may supplement the 1988 Act.*

Whether such a waiver can be accepted by a professional will depend on the nature of each particular appointment.

Other intellectual property rights may also be applicable, such as those concerning patents and trademarks, but these are beyond the scope of this book.

Chapter 9

Liability for work carried out by others

9.1 Privity of contract

Under the doctrine of privity of contract, the general rule is that only parties to a contract (and not third parties) can acquire benefits under a contract or be subject to liabilities arising under the contract. A third party cannot therefore be responsible for the actions of one of the contracting parties unless it is also a party to the contract. This general rule is, however, subject to certain specific exceptions. A principal is responsible for the actions of its agent taken with its authority where the agency has been disclosed (see chapter 10), and an employer is responsible for its employees' negligent acts and omissions which are within the scope of the employment contract. Case law may affect the position and statutes may also create exceptions to the rule, particularly in the context of transactions relating to land or under the Contracts (Rights of Third Parties) Act 1999 which gives rights in certain circumstances to third parties to enforce terms of contracts that are for their benefit (see section 2.3).

The effect of the rule is often avoided by the use of collateral contracts, where the main contract is accompanied by an ancillary contract with a third party relating to the same subject matter (see chapter 17).

9.2 Responsibility for the work of others

The circumstances in which a professional can become responsible for the work or actions of others can vary. Such a responsibility can arise out of the appointment — for example where a professional is instructed to check another professional's design — or arise through the sub-contracting of some of its work to another when the professional will remain fully responsible for the work of that third party sub-contractor. A professional can become liable for the acts of another party through joint liability, such as a joint venture.

While contracts do not usually impose liability on third parties, it is possible for a third party to be liable for another party's actions under the law of tort. In particular, a party is liable for torts which it has authorised or ratified, and it can also be liable for the actions of others which it has not authorised, such as the actions of employees, as long as they are within the course of the employee's duties. An employer is, however, not generally liable for the acts of an independent contractor, where for example a person employs an independent person or organisation to carry out cleaning or refurbishment work.

Some non-standard professional services agreements may seek to make the professional responsible for (or *'guarantee'* or *'warrant'*) the work or design of third parties with whom the professional has no contractual relationship and over whom therefore it has no control. This must be resisted.

It is essential to make clear in the appointment what the professional is, and is not, responsible for.

This can be usefully coupled with a statement of what the professional will do, especially where there may be a misapprehension on the part of a client as to the professional's duties, for example in relation to coordination. For example, the ACE (Second Edition 1998) regarding other consultants, provides:

> B2.5 ... *The Consulting Engineer acting as Lead Consultant shall coordinate and integrate the services of such Other Consultants as the Client may appoint. The Consulting Engineer shall not be responsible for the detailed designs of any Other Consultant or liable for defects in or omissions from them;*

and in relation to the design of sub-contractors:

> B2.7 *The Consulting Engineer may recommend to the Client that the detailed design of any part of the Works should be carried out by a Contractor or Sub-Contractor and the Client shall not unreasonably withhold consent to such recommendation. The Consulting Engineer shall examine ... that detailed design and integrate it into his own design. The Consulting Engineer shall not be responsible for such detailed design or liable for defects in or omissions from it.*

The RIBA (CE/99) also includes statements as to the matters for which the architect is not responsible. It provides:

> 3.11 *The Client, in respect of any work or services in connection with the Project performed or to be performed by any person other than the Architect, shall:*
>
> > .1 *hold such person responsible for the competence and performance of his services and for visits to the site in connection with the work undertaken by him;*

.2　ensure that such person shall cooperate with the Architect and provide to the Architect drawings and information reasonably needed for the proper and timely performance of the Services;

.3　ensure that such person shall, when requested by the Architect, consider and comment on work of the Architect in relation to their own work so that the Architect may consider making any necessary change to his work.

3.12　The Client shall hold the Principal Contractor and/or other contractors appointed to undertake construction works and not the Architect responsible for their management and operation methods, for the proper carrying out and completion of the Works in compliance with the building contract and for health and safety provisions on the Site.

9.3　Sub-contracting of services by a professional

A professional cannot pass on obligations under a contract, such as to perform the services specified to be undertaken, to a third party such as a sub-contractor, without consent from the client (see chapter 16).

Where a professional does sub-contract or sub-let some obligations or services, the professional remains fully responsible to the client for all the acts and omissions of the sub-contractor, exactly as if the professional had performed the sub-contract services or work. The client can therefore recover from the professional all the loss or damage to which it is entitled, regardless of whether or not the professional can recover those from the sub-contractor.

The ACE (Second Edition 1998) states the position clearly in relation to sub-consultants:

B2.6　The Consulting Engineer may recommend to the Client that the Consultant Engineer sub-lets to a specialist sub-consultant the performance of any of the Services. The Client shall not unreasonably withhold consent to such recommendation and the Consulting Engineer shall integrate such sub-consultant's services with his own. The Consulting Engineer shall be responsible for the performance and the payment of any such sub-consultant.

In some contracts a client may not be too concerned who undertakes the provision of professional services as long as those services are undertaken to at least the same standard and cost to the client and no more. Indeed, most main construction contracts permit sub-contracting of building or civil engineering activities, albeit consent of the client is usually required. However, there will be circumstances where a client has expressly chosen a professional and therefore specifically prohibits the professional from sub-contracting some or any of its services. The professional should be aware that this may be a serious requirement of a client, not to be ignored as a peripheral issue, when it considers whether it intends to sub-contract.

In RIBA (CE/99) Conditions, there is an express reminder about this:

> 4.2 *The Architect shall not appoint any Sub-Consultants to perform any part of the Services without the consent of the Client, which consent shall not be unreasonably withheld. The Architect shall confirm such consent in writing.*

The RICS (1999) contains a similar provision:

> 3.2 *The Quantity Surveyor shall not subcontract any part of the services without the consent of the Client in writing.*

If it is important to the professional to sub-contract some part of the services agreed, this must be specifically agreed at the beginning with the client, and preferably included in terms in the appointment. The latter may well want to impose some special conditions on its consent, such as the provision of direct collateral warranties by the sub-consultant.

9.4 Professional as lead consultant

There are special considerations relating to sub-consultancy appointments. First, the employer (the *'lead consultant'*) of the sub-consultant has to remember that it is responsible to the client for all the acts and omissions of the sub-consultant. It is therefore very important for the lead consultant to:

(1) Sort out the contractual arrangements between the lead consultant and the sub-consultant.
(2) Be satisfied as to the standing, assets and professional indemnity insurance arrangements of the sub-consultant.
(3) Obtain the express consent of the client before any work is undertaken by the sub-consultant, and to comply with any conditions imposed by the client.
(4) Check there are no restrictions in its professional indemnity policy concerning sub-contracting.

If there is negligence by the sub-consultant, the lead consultant will be responsible to the client for any damages that result. The lead consultant will be able to pass on those damages to the sub-consultant if the sub-contract is *'back to back'*, but whether or not it will be able to recover them will depend on whether the sub-consultant is still in business and/or solvent at the time of the claim (which can be many years after the event giving rise to the claim) and on whether the sub-consultant has sufficient assets or professional indemnity insurance to cover them.

Any contract with the sub-consultant should therefore contain an obligation by the sub-consultant to maintain adequate professional indemnity insurance for whatever period is applicable for that particular contract, although the risk that this may not be done must also be considered.

The lead consultant needs to ensure that its agreement with the sub-consultant is *'back to back'* with its own if it is to be fully protected. Otherwise, it could find it was liable under its appointment with the client for something that the sub-consultant has done and is unable to pass it on to the sub-consultant. Thus, if the lead consultant's appointment is under seal or signed as a deed, so should the sub-consultant's contract. If copyright is to be vested in the client, the sub-contract must provide that copyright vests in the consultant or directly in the client. If the duty of care is higher than *'reasonable skill and care'* that, too, must be included.

The most important matters, however, concern the services and payment. It is essential that the particular lead consultant services which are to be performed by the sub-consultant are clearly and fully identified and set out in the sub-consultant's contract. Lines of responsibility should be made clear so that, for example, the sub-consultant knows from whom instructions are to be taken.

It is the lead consultant who is responsible for the payment of the sub-consultant's fees, usually regardless of when or if the client pays the lead consultant. The lead consultant will also be responsible for any additional payment due to the sub-consultant for work undertaken on instructions of the lead consultant, for example work outside the stipulated services, regardless of the fact that the lead consultant may or may not be able to recover this from the client. The sub-contract payment provisions and any entitlement to additional payment should therefore mirror those in the lead consultant's appointment, as far as reasonably possible, so that the lead consultant only has to pay the sub-consultant if the latter is entitled to such payment. This will not protect the lead consultant, however, against the risk of the client becoming insolvent or refusing to pay.

Further, the lead consultant does not want to find itself committed to the sub-contract when its own appointment could be terminated, so the termination provisions should also be *'back to back'* (with the same provisions about payment in those circumstances) and with an overriding provision that if the lead consultant's appointment is terminated, so is the sub-contract.

9.5 Professional as sub-consultant

In the past, lead consultants usually dealt with the risk of late, partial or non-payment of fees by the client by making the sub-consultant's entitlement dependent on the receipt by the lead consultant of the amount due for the sub-consultant's work (*'pay when paid'*) (see section 6.15). The Construction Act 1996 has outlawed such provisions in construction contracts (see section 6.16). If the sub-contract is a *'construction contract'* and contains a pay when paid clause (except where the client is insolvent) this will be of no effect and the Scheme will apply, bringing an entitlement to payment by instalments (if the contract is of sufficient duration), a calculation of the amount due, a 'due date' and 'final date' for payment and the notice requirements (see sections 6.9, 6.12 and 6.14).

It is reasonable for a sub-consultant to see the lead consultant's appointment (except perhaps the provisions specifically concerning the amount of the lead consultant's fees). Then it can check the provisions which may affect the sub-consultant's services and fee, for example if it is asked to perform and comply with some or all of the lead consultant's obligations.

Provisions in the sub-contract should not be more onerous than those in the lead consultant's appointment and, if collateral warranties are to be given by the sub-consultant to third parties such as tenants, this (and the form of the warranties) should be agreed with the client at the beginning. Collateral warranties by sub-consultants to the client should be resisted, however, because the reason for having a lead consultant who employs all the other consultants as sub-consultants is that the client need only look to one party for the performance of the obligations or in the event of any default (assuming the lead consultant still exists and has adequate professional indemnity cover and/or funds).

9.6 Joint and several liability

If there is more than one party performing a contract, the party commissioning the works will often not be concerned as to how the responsibility for the work is divided up between the other parties; one of its main concerns will be that the work is completed as specified in the contract. If the works are delayed or disrupted, the commissioning party will want to be able to seek compensation from the other parties (which might include a professional organisation) rather than to carry out an extensive investigation to determine which party is at fault. This is achieved through the principles of joint and several liability.

If the liability of co-parties is joint, they have all jointly promised to carry out the contract. There is therefore only one contractual obligation and performance of the contract by any one party will relieve the other parties from possible liability. This can happen, for example, where there are joint guarantors. Several or concurrent liability arises where each party separately contracts with the commissioning party in respect of the contract obligations. There will be separate contracts, so each contracting party can be sued independently. An example of this would be where two or more parties enter into two or more separate contracts with the same party − the client with the engineer, the client with the contractor, the client with the architect, etc.

Joint and several liability arises where all the parties performing a contract jointly contract with the commissioning party to perform their obligations, for example where a partnership enters into a contract. The effect of several liability is that any or all of the contracting parties may be sued by the commissioning party in respect of any breaches of contract, and separate actions may be brought against any of them.

The death of an individual who is one of the contracting parties will not affect liability because the personal representatives of that individual will become jointly and severally liable with the remaining parties.

There is a presumption that an obligation taken on by two or more persons is joint, so that express words are necessary to create several liability. For several liability to be implied the courts will look for words of severance or an indication that the parties only intended their potential liabilities to be restricted to their own acts.

It has already been noted that where two or more parties are jointly and severally liable for contractual obligations, the party seeking compensation for breach of these obligations can sue any or all of the contracting parties. If one party only is sued it may be able to recover a contribution from one or more of the other contracting parties through the Civil Liability (Contributions) Act 1978. The Act states that *'any person liable in respect of any damage suffered by another person may recover contribution from any other person liable in respect of the same damage (whether jointly or otherwise).'*

The Act goes on to provide that the amount of the contribution is to be determined by the courts, having regard to the extent of the person's responsibility for the damage. The court makes the assessment on equitable principles, with the result that the court may hold that the cost should be shared unequally, or that one party should pay nothing at all. There is uncertainty as to whether the courts should consider a party's overall blameworthiness or relative blameworthiness in relation to others, but the court cannot consider the fault of parties not involved in the proceedings.

Concurrent liability should therefore be avoided if at all possible in any non-standard professional services agreement.

If avoidance is not possible for commercial reasons, a way to reduce concurrent liability risks is to have a clause in the professional services agreement which accepts concurrent liability, but only on the basis that the client warrants that all other professionals (and, if relevant, the contractor) have similar arrangements with the client which are to remain valid during the period when a claim could be made. In these circumstances the onus is placed on the client to ensure that there are similar liability clauses in its appointments with other professionals, otherwise the liability clause with the professional may not be contractually effective.

Another way to reduce the impact of joint and several liability is for the professional to require each of the other jointly or concurrently liable parties to provide it with indemnities (see section 9.7 and chapter 12) backed up by insurance or other evidence of ability to meet long-term claims against them.

The inclusion of a *'net contribution'* clause can also assist (see section 9.8).

9.7 Joint ventures

Professionals may sometimes be asked to join with other organisations to create a joint venture.

There are several different sorts of joint venture arrangements. The most usual is known as a *'horizontal joint venture'*, where the parties to the venture are relatively equal as regards their involvement in the enterprise (irrespective of their economic power) and the venture has been set up for a common and related purpose.

There is also the *'conglomerate joint venture'*, which describes an entirely new enterprise for all of the participants.

There are three forms of joint venture: a corporate joint venture, a partnership (unincorporated) joint venture set up through the medium of a partnership, and a consortium.

(1) *A corporate joint venture* is effected by setting up a company, most commonly a private, limited liability company. It is most used where the intended venture is significant, either in terms of the resources to be committed by the parties, the number of parties or the likely duration of the enterprise. The principal reason for choosing a company structure is the fact that the company can be registered with limited liability. Thus, unless individual guarantees are given, the participants in the joint venture, as shareholders, will be protected from liability for the company's losses and therefore from the liabilities that can arise during the operation of the joint venture. The company can be used to hold assets and incur contractual commitments of its own and has a defined management structure. The relations between the parties are governed by a memorandum and articles of association, but the most important document is the shareholders' or joint venture agreement which regulates and determines the relationship and rights of the participants.

(2) *A partnership joint venture* can be set up under the Partnership Act 1890, but whether a joint venture arrangement is actually a partnership will depend on a mixture of fact and law. The definition of a partnership is *'the relationship which subsists between persons carrying on business in common with a view of profit.'* If it is a partnership, some provisions of the Act will apply to the joint venture, irrespective of any contrary intention or any agreement drawn up by the joint venture parties. Special care is needed to ensure that the joint venture is not inadvertently constituted as a partnership unless that is the specific intention. Under a partnership arrangement, each partner is deemed to be the agent of the other and each participant can therefore bind the enterprise and all the participants in respect of any act or transaction carried out by any of them in the ordinary or usual course of business. The main difference between a corporate and partnership joint venture relates to liability. Under a partnership arrangement the participants are jointly liable to the full extent of their assets for all the debts and obligations of the joint venture and are liable jointly and severally for all the tortious acts and omissions of any of the participants in the joint venture. This means one of the participants could find itself liable to the full extent of its assets for the liabilities of another participant (see section 9.6). It is for this reason that many professional indemnity insurers require professionals to tell them specifically if they are proposing to enter into a joint venture arrangement.

Insurers will only usually provide cover for the consequences of acts of their insured. They will be concerned if any Joint Venture agreement does not include *'subrogation'* clauses that permit their insured to claim a contribution from the other liable partners in the Joint Venture agreement towards any money insurers might have to pay out for a claim. There may be express clauses inserted deliberately that waive subrogation rights against the other parties. Other clauses may be more obscure but refer to *'joint-named'* insurance which results in the parties being co-insured: as an insurer normally cannot sue a party it is insuring this has the same effect as waiving subrogation rights. In the latter case those rights can be re-established by means of cross-liability clauses which enable insurers and the joint-named insureds to treat the insureds as if they were separately insured for subrogation purposes.

(3) *A consortium* is the simplest structure for a joint venture, and it is based upon a specific contract drawn up between the participants. This contract is generally described as a consortium or cooperation agreement. Under this agreement the parties to the joint venture

agree to form their association solely as independent contractors, as opposed to being partners under the Act or shareholders in a company registered under the relevant Companies Acts. The consortium agreement should define the rights and duties of the members and determine the rights and duties between the members of the consortium and the third parties who will deal with the consortium, for example the client.

A consortium agreement is most frequently used to avoid having to set up the more formal arrangements necessary for a joint venture company or to avoid incurring joint and several liability under a partnership. The consortium contract usually provides the members with a direct interest in the assets and revenue of the venture. It is an arrangement commonly used by parties seeking to tender on a joint basis for a substantial contract or for a business enterprise which is of short duration or consists of a single undertaking or venture.

A consortium agreement should:

(1) Set out the scope and duration of the joint venture.
(2) Define the specific and detailed obligations of the individual members.
(3) Devise the machinery for financing the venture.
(4) Provide a mechanism for determining the sharing of profits or bearing of any losses which may result from the running of the enterprise.

The consortium agreement should also contain particular provisions to deal with any property to be used by the members and should determine, for example, which assets remain the exclusive property of the members and which assets are to be joint property.

Because the members are not partners, they do not owe any statutory duty to the other members and are not subject to any joint responsibility for the liabilities and obligations of the consortium, nor are they liable for the other members' acts or omissions. Nevertheless, a member of a consortium can be exposed to claims (which may be unlimited) by third parties and for liabilities incurred by the consortium on the basis that a member has expressly assumed responsibility or is vicariously liable under the consortium agreement. This arises through the general presumption that each member of a consortium is the agent of the other. It is, therefore, important that the consortium agreement should define the extent to which each member will be responsible for the acts and omissions of the other members and also define the areas where they have no authority to bind the other members. Each member should indemnify the others against liabilities that member has incurred because it has acted outside any expressed authority. Such indemnities are, however, only of any value if they are, and will continue to be, backed up by sufficient assets.

Where a project is undertaken by all the members of a consortium, their liability for that contract will be joint. This will occur, for example, where the client enters into a contract with all the consortium members. Where an individual member of a consortium assumes sole responsibility for a liability undertaken on behalf of the joint venture, for example where the client contracts with only one member of the consortium, the agreement should contain indemnities to protect that particular participant.

9.8 'Net contribution' clauses

It follows from the principles of joint and several liability (see section 9.6) that professionals and contractors who become *'liable in respect of the same damage'* are taking the risk of another member of the construction team becoming insolvent or having no (or insufficient) assets and/or professional indemnity insurance. This was perceived as unfair when liabilities to people other than the client were incurred through collateral warranties and it was in collateral warranties that *'net contribution'* clauses first started to appear. Even where the client is concerned, there is the argument that the client should take this risk because it alone chooses the contractor and the professionals and can therefore choose reputable organisations with financial standing and proper professional indemnity arrangements, and who are likely to be in business if and when a claim is made.

The objective of these clauses is to try to ensure that each party *'liable in respect of the same damage'* only has to pay to the client (or holder of the collateral warranty, as the case may be) that proportion of the damages for which it is responsible. Thus, if a contractor is held 70% responsible for some damages and a professional 30% responsible for the same damage, each will pay their respective 70% and 30% only, even if the other is not able to pay its full proportion.

The main elements of such clauses where included in an appointment would consist of:

(1) Limiting liability to a sum which it would be just and equitable for that party to pay, having regard to the extent of its responsibility for the damage in question (this echoes the words of the Civil Liability (Contribution) Act 1978).

(2) Identifying the other parties who could have contributed to the same physical damage. In the case of a professional, this could comprise the other professionals, the contractor and any sub-contractors responsible for detailed design or construction of the parts of the project to which the professional's services relate.

(3) Deeming those other parties to have undertaken contractual obligations to the client no less onerous than those of the party who has contracted with the client. If they were less onerous the other party could escape responsibility for '*the same damage*' and therefore not be brought in to any assessment of contribution. As this is to be '*deemed*' it will not matter whether or not their contractual obligations are less onerous and the professional would not have to check them.

(4) Deeming those other parties to have paid such contribution to the client as it would be just and equitable for them to pay. Thus, again, it will not matter whether or not the other parties have actually been able to pay their respective proportions.

At the time of writing, there have been no cases to determine whether or not such clauses are effective. The risk is that a judge will find it impossible to determine what proportion any of the parties should be deemed to have paid without going through a trial to establish what the actual proportions are. Further, such clauses would also have to pass the '*reasonableness*' test which applies to clauses used in seeking to limit liability (see chapter 13).

The BPF forms of collateral warranties in favour of future purchasers and tenants have contained '*net contribution*' clauses for some time. More recently, their funders' collateral warranties have also included such clauses (see chapter 17). Non-standard professional services agreements more rarely include a '*net contribution*' clause but some of the standard conditions incorporate them.

The ACE (Second Edition 1998) includes a net contribution clause within limitation of liability clauses which provides:

B8.2 *Subject to B8.1 but notwithstanding otherwise anything to the contrary contained in this Agreement, such liability of the Consulting Engineer for any claim or claims shall be further limited to such sum as the Consulting Engineer ought reasonably to pay having regard to his responsibility for the loss or damage suffered as a result of the occurrence or series of occurrences in question, on the basis that all Other Consultants and all Contractors and Sub-Contractors shall be deemed to have provided contractual undertakings on terms no less onerous than those set out in B2.3 to the Client (whether or not they shall have been so provided to the Client) in respect of the carrying out of their obligations and shall be deemed to have paid to the Client such proportion which it would be just and equitable for them to pay having regard to the extent of their responsibility.*

The RIBA (CE/99) provides in its Memorandum of Agreement:

7.3 *In any action or proceedings ... the Architect's liability for loss or damage in respect of any one occurrence or series of occurrences arising out of one event shall be limited to whichever is the lesser of [a sum to be stated] or such sum as it is just and equitable for the Architect to pay having regard to the extent of his responsibility for the loss and/or damage in question when compared with the responsibilities of contractors, sub-contractors, consultants and such other persons for that loss and damage. Such sum to be assessed on the basis that such persons are deemed to have provided contractual undertakings to the Client no less onerous than those of the Architect under the Agreement and had paid to the Client such sums as it would be just and equitable for them to pay having regard to the extent of their responsibility for that loss and/or damage.*

Thus, on the principle set out above, other parties with responsibility for design will be brought into the calculation if they are '*liable in respect of the same damages.*'

The RICS (1999) also has a net contribution clause which provides:

13.1 *The liability of the Quantity Surveyor shall be limited to such sum as it would be just and equitable for the Quantity Surveyor to pay having regard to the extent of the responsibility of the Quantity Surveyor for the loss or damage suffered on the basis that all other consultants, the contractor and any subcontractors who have a liability shall be deemed to have provided contractual undertakings to the Client on terms no less onerous than those applying in the case of this Agreement and shall be deemed to have paid to the Client such sums as it would be just and equitable for them to pay having regard to the extent of their responsibility for such loss or damage.*

Chapter 10

Agency

10.1 Appointment as agent

The situation in which a professional is appointed by an agent on behalf of a client is discussed in chapter 2. In this chapter the situation in which a client asks a professional to act as its agent (that is, to undertake matters on the client's behalf) is considered. Where a professional acts as an agent for a client in respect of the client's CDM Regulations particular considerations arise (see section 19.4). More usually the matter of agency arises when a client asks the professional to engage a third party, for example a materials testing house, a contractor or another professional. The ACE (Second Edition 1998) contains examples of several services, such as site investigations, which the professional is to *'arrange as agent for the Client'*.

It is clearly important to establish whether the intention of the client is for the professional to act as an agent for the client or as a principal. If there is any doubt at all, the professional should immediately clarify this with the client — the question being: *'Is the client the person who is in fact the employer [of the contractor or plant operator] and is therefore responsible for their payment, or is it the professional?'*

If the professional is to be an agent for the client, the professional needs to ensure that the third party is aware of this and should also protect its own position.

10.2 The extent of the agency

The professional should ensure that it confirms to the client what is going to be done, stating it is being done on the client's behalf as its agent and giving brief details of the contract that is going to be organised and the arrangements to be made about payment.

In most cases, it is usual for payment to be made direct by the client to the third party. In some cases, however, the client may wish the professional to pay and then the client will reimburse the professional. Professionals should be wary about entering into an arrangement on this basis in case the client becomes insolvent or does not honour payment commitments in good time.

It is also important to establish the extent of the authority given by the client, for example to what extent the professional can give directions or instructions to the third party, change the nature of the work, add to the scope of the work, or do anything that might result in additional payment. If in doubt about any of these, the professional should obtain clarification from the client before proceeding further. This is because any contract entered into as agent for the client must be in accordance with the instructions given by the client.

10.3 The contract with a third party, such as contractor, plant operator, etc.

It is essential that the professional makes it clear to the third party that the contractual arrangements are being made '*on behalf of*' the client. If the contract is formed by an exchange of letters between the professional and the other party, the professional should confirm the terms '*on behalf of the client*', make it clear that the contract is directly with the client and that the client will be responsible for payment.

If there is a formal contract, the parties to that contract should be the client and the third party. Although the professional can sign the contract on behalf of the client if given authority to do so, it should be stated after signing that it is being signed '*for and on behalf of [the client]*'.

Copies of any contractual arrangements should be sent to the client immediately they have been entered into, with a statement that this has been done on the client's behalf. The client should also be reminded of such things as when payment is due and how much.

10.4 Duties of an agent

An agent has to use reasonable skill and care in carrying out the tasks undertaken for the client.

An agent should act only within the extent of the express authority given by the client, but this will extend to subordinate acts which are necessarily and ordinarily incidental to the exercise of that express authority, for example giving information to a contractor which it may need, even though this has not specifically been referred to between the client and the professional.

An agent is expected to carry out the tasks agreed to be undertaken in person, or through the agency's organisation. If given a definite instruction by the client as to how to carry out the commission, that must be followed strictly, provided it is lawful; if the agency does not do so it could be liable. The agent has no discretion to disregard express instructions from a client, even if the agent believes that it is acting in good faith in the interests of that client. Further, the agent must not delay unreasonably in carrying out instructions.

Where an agent has been given expressly a discretion as to how to carry things out, the agent must be guided by '*the honest exercise of its own judgement and the interests of the client*', or in accordance with the ordinary usages of that business.

In negotiating a contract on behalf of a client, an agent must take all reasonable precautions to protect the client. The form of the contract must be capable of being enforced by the client.

Once the contract negotiations are completed and signed, an agent is not entitled to rescind the contract or vary its terms unless it has express authority to do so.

An agent must disclose any conflicts of interest between itself and the client, and it cannot enter into any transaction that is likely to produce that result unless it has given full disclosure to the client and obtained consent.

As the nature of the client–agent relationship is fiduciary, if an agent receives money for or from the client for a specific purpose, the agent becomes a trustee of that money and has to keep accounts, or account for the monies received, and take no secret commission or bribe.

If, in the course of a transaction or contract, an agent receives notice, or acquires knowledge, of material facts (for example defects in work being carried out), it is the agent's duty to communicate this immediately to the client.

10.5 An agent's rights against a client

A professional acting as an agent will have a right to an implied indemnity from a client for any liability incurred and any losses suffered which were in contemplation when the agency was undertaken, together with any expenses occasioned by the agent's employment. Thus, if the client does not reimburse the professional for any sums paid by the professional to the contractor, or for any expenses incurred, the professional can rely on this implied indemnity in order to obtain payment from the client. It is better, however, if an express indemnity from the client is included in the professional's agency agreement. Whether an indemnity is implied or expressly stated, money may not be recoverable if the client has become insolvent in the interim.

10.6 The relationship between the client and the third party

A client is responsible for all the acts of the agent which were authorised by the terms of the agency agreement between them. If, however, the professional did something that was not within the scope of its express or implied authority from the client, the client would not be bound. For example, if the professional instructed some extra work which had not been specifically authorised by the client, the client would be able to recover the extra costs of that work from the agent.

Where a contract with a third party has been made by the professional on behalf, and with the authority of, the client, this can be enforced by the third party against the client directly — for example if payment has not been made, the contractor can go straight to the client. If the contractor were successfully to pursue the professional for payment, the professional can rely on indemnity from the client to recover that payment from the client.

If a third party, say a contractor, contracts with the professional, honestly believing the professional to be the principal and not an agent, the real principal (that is, the client) cannot sue the contractor direct (for example if there were allegedly defective works and the client did not want to pay the amount due under the contract). The professional, however, could be sued by the client if it has acted outside the terms of its authority.

10.7 The agent's liability in tort

If a client should give the professional express authority to do a particular act which is wrongful in itself, or necessarily results in a wrongful act, the client would be jointly and severally liable with the professional to a third party for any loss or damage. The professional should clearly refuse to undertake anything that it thought might have this result.

Similarly, a professional has to be careful when making representations or statements on behalf of the client, because the professional could become liable for negligent misstatement or fraudulent misrepresentation. In this situation the client would be liable jointly and severally with the professional to the third party if the professional was acting with express authority.

10.8 Criminal liability of an agent

As a general rule no criminal liability can be imposed on a client as a result of any criminal act by an agent. However, professionals should

the professional owed it a duty to take reasonable care. The third party can in such cases generally only recover damages for personal injury or damage to third party property, such as chattels and building contents [*Murphy* v *Brentwood District Council* (1991)]. This is consistent with the general principle that economic loss is not normally recoverable in tort.

One of the important exceptions to that principle relates to negligent misstatements.

11.4 Negligent misstatements

Statements made by a professional in reports, surveys and similar advice, as well as in certificates, could be negligent misstatements if a duty of care was owed to the person to whom the statement was made and the statement was made without the proper care.

The courts [*Hedley Byrne* v *Heller* (1963)] have defined what must be established in order for a duty of care to exist in connection with the making of a statement:

(1) There must be a special relationship between the maker of a statement and its recipient.
(2) There must have occurred a reasonable reliance by the recipient on the statement.
(3) It must be proved that the maker of the statement must have, or ought to have, known that the recipient would rely on the statement.

If these criteria are met the professional can become liable to the third party for economic loss in addition to being liable for damages for personal injury and damage to third party property.

11.5 Those to whom the professional can become liable

Clearly, a professional would be liable to the client. However, what constitutes a *'special relationship'* (or sufficient *'proximity'*, as the cases often refer to it) to a third party and *'reliance'*?

It has been established that a relationship of proximity cannot exist between the maker of a statement put into general circulation and a recipient who has relied on the statement for a purpose not anticipated by the statement maker. For a third party to succeed in a claim for breach of duty of care against the maker of a statement, the following four conditions must be satisfied:

(1) The maker must know the statement made is being communicated to a person or class of a specific nature. If, for example, a client has agreed with a professional that the professional's report can be

shown to its funder, the client cannot use it in a prospectus for the sale of land, for example, and make the professional potentially liable to future purchasers.

(2) The communication must have occurred in connection with a specific transaction or transaction type. So, in the example just given, it can be relied on for the purpose of lending money but not for the purpose of a sale.

(3) The communication must have been made to a person or class likely to rely on it in determining if it or they should enter into a certain transaction without making a separate independent enquiry. The courts have been fairly lenient in their interpretation of this and have not only included domestic purchasers but also fairly sophisticated third parties, such as bankers and other lenders, within the category of people who were not considered as having to make separate enquiries. This is perhaps surprising.

(4) The person or class that has relied on the statement must have suffered some loss as a result.

The Law Lords [*Caparo Industries plc* v *Dickman* (1990)] have restricted the liability of professional advisers to those third parties with '*reasonably close proximity*'. Otherwise, they thought this would '... *confer on the world at large a quite unwarranted entitlement to appropriate for their own purposes the benefit of the expert knowledge or professional expertise attributed to the maker of the statement.*'

If a statement or report is prepared for someone and then altered by that person and incorporated into another document, no proximity or special relationship will occur between the original writer and any third party relying on the altered document.

The court [*ADT Limited* v *BDO Binder Hamlyn* (1995)] considered the consequences for a professional of a negligent misstatement. A firm audited a company's accounts. A prospective purchaser of that company asked the audit partner about those accounts and the partner stated that he stood by his firm's audit opinion. It was found that the audit partner had made a negligent misstatement. It led to a judgment against the firm of £65 million plus £40 million in interest and costs. The firm appealed and the case settled before the hearing of the appeal.

11.6 Necessary expertise of the maker of a statement

The duty of care only arises where the statement maker holds himself or herself out as '*possessing the necessary skills/competence to give advice and the necessary diligence to give reliable advice.*' A professional will fall within this category and will therefore be a person who has responsibility to make any statement with reasonable skill and care.

11.7 Circumstances in which there can be a breach of the duty of care

A professional will be in breach of duty of care if the professional does something a reasonable person would not do, or fails to do something such a person would do.

The courts have established that a professional, in writing a report, should display and apply reasonable care and a reasonable standard of professional competence, but this does allow for a margin of differing opinion and even a degree of error. Evidence of what is acceptable practice within the profession or what standards are laid down by its professional bodies is crucial in determining the standard of care to be exercised by a professional.

11.8 Gratuitous advice or statements

A professional can be liable even if it had not been paid for the advice or statement or if the fee is a very small one. The question of payment is immaterial.

11.9 Disclaimers

Disclaimers are the means by which clients or third parties are notified that the professional does not accept liability to them and that they cannot rely on the report or statement for their purposes.

Disclaimers, like other limitations of liability, are subject to the test of *'reasonableness'* (see chapter 13). A general disclaimer for the whole of the content of a report is not likely to be effective against a claim by a client.

Disclaimers can, however, be effective against third parties. The courts [*Omega Trust Company Limited and Banque Finindus* v *Wright Son & Pepper and Barker & Co* (1998 3 PNLR 337)] had to consider a disclaimer in the case of a valuation of three leasehold properties that a firm of surveyors was asked to send to a bank which was providing a loan to the owner. The valuation, which had originally been prepared for another lender, was readdressed to the bank and a nominal fee was paid, making that bank the surveyor's client. The valuation contained a disclaimer that:

> *This report shall be for the private and confidential use of the clients for whom the report is undertaken and should not be reproduced in whole or in part or relied upon by third parties for any use whatsoever without the express written authority of the surveyors.*

Unknown to the surveyors, another bank had been asked to participate in the loan and the valuation was passed to it. When the security was found to be insufficient, both banks sued the surveyors. However, the Court of Appeal held that no duty of care was owed to the undisclosed bank and that it was fair and reasonable for the surveyor to rely on the disclaimer. It drew a clear distinction between commercial transactions and those with domestic householders and considered that it would have been reasonably practicable for the bank to have obtained a separate valuation, or to have asked the surveyors directly whether they were prepared to assume responsibility to the bank.

11.10 Certificates

Certificates which have to be given by professionals under construction contracts (for example as to the value of the work carried out by the contractor) are outside the scope of this text. This chapter deals with certificates required by non-standard professional services agreements in relation to the professional services, often to be given to third parties, describing what the services may or may not have achieved. Clients such as government departments often require such certificates. They are usually in a fixed form and may contain statements describing a level of performance different from, or beyond, what can reasonably be expected from the professional. Examples include:

'The [professional] will certify on completion of the works, that the works have been constructed in accordance with the drawings and specification. The [professional] will further certify that all calculations, designs, drawings and contract documents prepared by the [professional] are to the highest standard utilising staff well experienced in works of this type.'

'The resulting structure, if constructed as designed, will be capable of meeting the Client's requirements of the scheme made known in writing.'

'The said Design Data comply with the Construction Requirements, as amended ... and comply in all other respects with the Agreement.'

'The Temporary Works are satisfactory for the safe and proper discharge of the Client's obligations.'

'The resulting engineering services, if installed as designed and correctly serviced, will be capable of meeting the Client's environmental criteria and policies which have been made known to [the professional] in writing and upon which the design has been based, and will provide proper access for safe operation and maintenance purposes.'

'[The professional] has exercised reasonable skill, care and diligence in performing the services required by its commission in relation to inspection *of the work to see that the Contractor has generally fulfilled its obligations with regard to the Building Regulations, Codes of Practice (including the Department of Health Firecode) and British or European standards specification or European technical approvals or common technical specifications, as appropriate, relevant in the design calculations and drawings, subject to any alterations or modifications made by [the professional] under its commission.'*

The latter two quotations have been taken from the Department of Health's Agreement for the Appointment of Architects, Surveyors and Engineers for Commissions in the National Health Service.

Claims usually arise out of such certificates (and this does not include any other claims the client might be able to bring for breach of contract or in tort) under what is known as the Hedley Byrne principle (see section 11.4). The claim arises when financial damage results to the person relying on the statement, if that statement is not correct but was acted upon.

A problem for professionals in relation to certificates can arise if a statement made about fitness for purpose turns out to be untrue, even though the professional used reasonable skill and care. (See sections 4.1 and 4.2 on the principles concerning the duty to use reasonable skill and care and warranties for fitness for purpose.) Certificates such as the foregoing often blur the distinction between professionals' and contractors' duties. For example, in one of the foregoing examples the words *'Construction Requirements'* were used. *'Construction Requirements'* will generally include matters which are, or amount to, warranties for fitness for purpose. So, if the professional makes a statement such as *'the said Design Data comply with the Construction Requirements'*, and if, in fact, the professional's design does not achieve the criteria set down in the *'Construction Requirements'*, the professional could be in breach even though *'reasonable professional skill and care'* might have been exercised in the preparation of the design. The professional would then be liable. Worse, the professional indemnity insurers would not be liable to indemnify the professional if the policy excluded such warranties, as they often do.

On the other hand, the statements in the NHS certificates are expressly qualified so that the test is whether the professional has exercised reasonable skill and care. The statements include:

'[The professional] has exercised reasonable skill care and diligence in performing the Services to see that ...'

or similar wording, and there is an opening paragraph in each NHS certificate which provides:

'Notwithstanding anything to the contrary contained in this certificate this Firm is obliged to exercise reasonable skill and care in the performance of the services required by that commission and this Firm shall not be liable except

to the extent that it has failed to exercise reasonable skill care and diligence and this certificate shall be read and construed accordingly.'

It is thus clear that the intention is that the professional's duty is limited to exercising reasonable skill and care.

If certificates must be given, the professional should be able to adjust the wording if required. The professional should therefore try to ensure:

(1) The terms of appointment do not compel the giving of a certificate in a certain form to a certain person, regardless of the actual circumstances at the time. Otherwise, the professional will be in breach of contract if the professional then refuses to give or tries to qualify the certificate, even though the professional may have good reasons for wishing to do this.

(2) The wording of the certificate should be such that it accurately records only what the professional has or has not done and does not amount to a statement of what others have done or what they or the works will achieve.

(3) Express wording to limit liability to reasonable skill and care should be agreed, if possible. Wording similar to that in the NHS certificates could be used (although it has not been tested in court and thus it is not known for certain how effective it is).

11.11 Particular contract considerations for reports, surveys, etc.

All the principles concerning professional services agreements discussed in this text apply equally to contracts to undertake reports, surveys, and so on. However, in relation to these, the professional should consider the following in particular:

(1) Who is entering into the contract on the professional's behalf and the nature of the report. For a very risky project it might be wished to establish a separate limited liability company and use what is known as *'ring fencing'*, that is, confine all the liabilities and risk to that particular company. There are practical considerations about this which would need to be looked at carefully.

(2) Whether the terms of reference are fully understood and any ambiguities or limitations on the enquiries discussed, agreed and recorded, preferably in, or at least referred to specifically in, the contract.

(3) Whether the services are defined, that is, whether they set out what the professional will be doing in detail and the extent to which, for example, the professional may be inspecting or monitoring any contractors' work or other third parties and, if so, for what purpose.

(4) Whether the contract includes all that the professional needs and whether, for example, the client is going to provide it or whether the client will be arranging for something to be done by someone else. For example: is there any information which is needed from the client or third parties, will it be sufficient, is more needed, will the client obtain it, is there anything else the client should undertake to do?

(5) Whether the end-product (for example, the report) is defined in detail.

Other matters which may arise in non-standard professional services agreements relating to reports and surveys, etc., could include the following, which also need careful consideration:

(1) The client requiring the professional to give guarantees or specific assurances directly or indirectly to third parties. This could result in the professional becoming liable to the third party.

(2) Statements of future uses of the premises or site, for example by third parties; whether third parties are to be entitled to copies of the report and/or there is a statement that the professional must have *'due regard'* to the interests of third parties, such as future owners/occupiers in preparing the report. This should alert the professional to the possibility that third parties could be given, and therefore be relying on, the report and, if so, this should be clarified. Remember that to be liable to third parties the professional has to know a statement is being communicated to a person (or class) in connection with a specific transaction. If a professional includes such a statement in the appointment, it will be considered to have such knowledge.

If the professional agrees that the third party should have a copy, the professional should also be told for what purpose so that the report can be limited to that purpose. The professional should not agree to include a provision which would allow anticipated uses or purposes to be changed, for example to things notified to the professional at a later date. It might then be impossible to amend or qualify the report to take account of this.

(3) Statements that third parties will *'rely'* on the professional exercising reasonable skill and care in the preparation of the report. These should be deleted. They are designed to pre-empt any arguments that the professional may have of whether a third party did rely on the report. It will be remembered that for third parties to succeed in suing a professional they must show not only that they relied on the statement but that the professional knew or ought reasonably to have known that they would.

(4)   Provisions which allow the client to disregard any matters in other reports or advice and to rely instead totally on the professional's report where someone else is being asked to advise on aspects which overlap with or complement the professional's terms of reference. This could inhibit any arguments the professional may have about the extent to which the client or third parties should have relied on the professional's report.

    If third parties should obtain their own advice (for example a survey) this should be stated either in the appointment or in the report.

(5)   The professional's right to the copyright in the report and the ability to restrict or prohibit licences should be used to protect the professional. The professional may not always know what use the client is going to make of the report or to whom it will be given. This should be discussed and agreed with the professional. If not, the professional should consider prohibiting any licence to copy the report, or make the copying of the report subject to the express consent of the professional, so that it is known to whom it is going and whether anything in particular needs to be said to those persons about the nature and extent of the report.

A limitation of liability ought to be considered in appropriate cases, for example where the risk is out of all proportion to the fee, or where the fee for the report is, say, £1000 but if the professional gets it wrong the claim could be for millions (see chapter 13). Limiting or excluding liability may be particularly necessary where environmental site investigations are being carried out and there is the possibility of pollution and contamination claims. Liability for such claims could be excluded or limited to clean-up costs or to a monetary amount.

11.12 Guidance on report writing

The professional should make the report as self-contained as possible. If a claim arises against a professional, it is the report itself that will be scrutinised by the court, possibly many years later, when some of the details of what happened at the time have become vague, warnings or discussions with the client may not have been recorded, a covering letter forgotten or misplaced, and so on. It is on the report itself that the professional might be judged and it is therefore vital that it is comprehensive.

Some matters that should be included are listed below. They may overlap and are not exhaustive because this will depend very much on circumstances.

(1) Identify the client for whom the report is prepared and its purpose, so there is no doubt to whom it is addressed and who should be using it.

(2) State the scope of the report as defined by the brief or terms of reference, including any limitations or restrictions on that brief. In particular, the specific transaction or transaction type in connection with which the report is being prepared should be identified. So, make sure there is no doubt or ambiguity about the scope, or any likelihood that it could be interpreted more widely than was intended.

(3) State what was done, what was not done, what could only be done to a limited extent and what should be done in the future.

(4) Describe the data and information received from the client or others, the nature of it, its adequacy or otherwise and say what effect it has had on the work undertaken and what reliance has been placed on it. Set out, if relevant, what information others are, or should be, providing.

(5) State what has not been received, and if and where this has been requested or promised.

(6) Record any restrictions imposed on the professional or the professional's enquiries by the client, outside agencies or circumstances.

(7) State the limitations on the information/advice contained in the report if, for example, it is preliminary or based on limited information. Spell out any risks inherent in the advice or in any reliance that is placed on it. Put in all necessary caveats and limitations. Expressly state any warnings.

(8) Detail any assumptions implicit in the report.

(9) Do not be generally reassuring. Be specific.

(10) Qualify any conclusions appropriately within the report, not only in any accompanying letters. Do not assume that any limitations, warnings or qualifications given to the client about the report will be remembered or recorded elsewhere.

(11) Make it clear that the report is not for the use of, or reliance on, by third parties.

(12) Prohibit any copying of the report for third parties without express consent. Then, if the client says it is needed for a third party, the professional can discuss the terms on which a copy of the report is released and whether any further caveats or limitations are needed so that the third party does not use it for purposes for which it was not intended.

(13) Date it so that anyone reading it later can be alerted to the fact it may be out of date.

The object is to make the report's purpose, the limitations of any advice or conclusions and the nature of that advice or conclusions, so clear that no one reading it could possibly mistake its purpose, content or rely on it for things that it simply was not reasonable for them to do.

Chapter 12

Insurances and liability

12.1 Professional indemnity insurance generally

Professional indemnity insurance policies are a form of liability insurance taken out by professional people to protect themselves against liability in respect of negligence. Such policies may either be on a *'negligence'* basis where they cover the insured's negligent acts or omissions, or on a *'civil liability'* basis where they cover any civil liability of the insured. The latter have become more common and the Architects' Registration Board has recently imposed mandatory professional indemnity insurance for architects on a civil liability basis. Cover may be on an *'each and every'* basis or *'in aggregate'*. The former provides cover for each claim up to an agreed limit of indemnity for each claim. The latter provides cover up to a maximum fixed sum in respect of all claims made during the policy period.

A number of insurers have introduced a form of hybrid cover — indemnity is provided on an *'each and every'* basis generally but with an aggregate limit for environmental and pollution claims. Some insurers treat date recognition problems in the same way. A few introduced an *'exclusion and buyback'*; under these policies, cover is excluded but can be bought back if certain conditions are fulfilled. The majority, however, decline to provide any cover for date recognition problems.

Most professional indemnity policies will indemnify the insured against loss resulting from any claim which is made against the insured by a third party in respect of any negligent act, error or omission by the insured or an employee or partner of the insured which arises in the course of the insured's business. The policy will not usually provide cover in respect of any negligence of the insured's clients, or any losses suffered by the insured itself because of its own negligence.

The policy is an indemnity policy, so that the insured cannot recover anything under the policy or make a monetary claim against the insurer until it has been found liable and suffered a loss. Proof of payment to a third party is not usually required unless this is stipulated in the policy.

In some insurance policies, the insurer will agree to provide a full indemnity to the insured against all claims within the scope of the policy. In the case of professional indemnity policies, however, it is usual for the insurer to impose a limit on the amount of the indemnity recoverable, so that the insured will be responsible for bearing some of the loss. The usual requirement is for the insured to bear the losses up to a specified amount, called the *'excess'* or *'deductible'*, in the case of each individual claim under the policy. The insurer therefore only has to bear the remainder of the losses.

There is, however, a difference between an excess and a deductible. In a policy for £1 million cover and a £250 000 excess, the £1 million cover comes into play once the excess is reached. If there is a deductible of £250 000, the maximum payable by insurers would be only £750 000. It is possible with some professional indemnity policies to agree an aggregate limit to the total excess within certain specified time periods.

12.2 No general duty to prevent liability

The Court of Appeal [*Yorkshire Water* v *Sun Alliance* (1996)] held that unless there was an express provision in the policy, the insured was not under a duty to take reasonable steps to avoid or mitigate a loss. If the insured did take steps to avoid such a loss and incurred expense as a result, the insurer would not be responsible for meeting that expense. The policy in question did, however, contain a clause requiring the insured to take steps to prevent losses *'at his own expense'* and the court held that the insured could not therefore be made to pay for preventative steps.

Where the insurance policy requires the insured to take reasonable steps to avoid incurring liability, it has been held that the insured would have to be at least reckless as to the action which is required before the policy becomes inoperative. The insured is not under a duty to take measures to avoid any liability which it did not foresee, nor take measures which a reasonable insured party would take.

12.3 Definition of 'claim'

A definition of what constitutes a single *'claim'* for the purposes of an insurance policy can be more difficult, that is, when is a claim in fact two or more claims each with its own excess? For example where a building development suffered various defects in different houses [*Trollope & Colls* v *Haydon* (1977)] the courts held that each defective house constituted a different claim. But what happens if each house suffered from the same defect (for example settlement from the same primary cause) or if the damage varied and could be allocated to separate breaches of duty by a professional such as poor design, poor specification and poor *'inspection'* all brought under one legal action?

It would appear from cases to date that the answer is that the courts will decide on the wording of the insurance policy concerned and on the facts of the individual case. (This is not very reassuring for the professional or his or her insurers.)

12.4 'Claims made' basis

Professional indemnity insurance is on a *'claims made'* basis, that is, the insurance policy that covers the claim is the one that is in operation when the claim is notified. The policy that is in force at the time an appointment is entered into, or when the breach occurs, will therefore be immaterial, unless the claim is made (notified) within the same period of insurance.

12.5 Limitations of professional indemnity insurance

Some of the most significant risks to professionals are those arising from claims that are outside insurance cover, or which might arise because certain obligations of the insurance contract between the professional and the insurer have not been met.

The following features relating to typical indemnity insurance policies should be noted.

(1) *Fines and penalties*: insurers will not indemnify an insured against illegal acts or non-compliance with certain statutory requirements (for example the Health and Safety at Work, etc., Act).

(2) *Liquidated damages*: insurers will not indemnify an insured against liquidated damages (or penalties) as such. It is possible under some policies for an indemnity to be provided if the liquidated damages payable do not exceed the damages that would have been payable if assessed by the courts on the usual common law basis.

(3) *Deliberate acts and omissions*: insurers will not indemnify an insured against the consequences of deliberately risky actions. They must be fortuitous events.

(4) *Legal liability*: insurers are not concerned with events for which an insured is not legally liable. Legal liability is a matter determined by law and proving liability will be a matter for whoever is making the claim against the insured.

(5) *The course of business*: insurers will generally only consider claims arising out of the insured's pre-agreed recognised business. This is because insurers will have one set of rates, terms and conditions for, say, consulting engineers, and another for a firm undertaking contracting activities. Therefore, a professional should obtain the insurer's approval, usually through the insurance broker, for any proposed work outside what could be considered normal activities. Examples might be the direct hiring of plant, or works usually undertaken by civil engineering or building contractors such as the physical opening up of a structure by the professional for inspection purposes. The alternative is to act as an agent for a client in the engagement of such services, or for the client to employ contractors directly. Insurers will normally require notice to be given of any joint venture arrangement and will decide in each case whether or not they are prepared to cover the arrangement. (Joint ventures, agency risks and vicarious liability are discussed elsewhere in the text. See also section 12.5.7 on subrogation rights.)

(6) *Warranties for fitness for purpose*: clients (a term which here can include design and build contractors) can seek to impose on professionals a warranty for '*fitness for purpose*' (see section 4.2). For the reasons explained in that section, professional indemnity insurers usually exclude such warranties specifically from cover. In '*soft*' insurance market conditions (that is, when business is slack and insurance premiums are low) it may be available for certain professionals, but there is never any guarantee that it will be included in future annual renewals, particularly if insurance market conditions harden. This does not mean that a professional cannot sometimes accept an uninsured risk, but that would be a commercial decision.

(7) *Subrogation rights*: a subrogation clause permits an insurer which has paid a claim (up to the limit of its indemnity to an insured) to pursue recovery of its payment from any third party it considers partially or wholly responsible for the claim arising in the first place. Such a clause can arise in any indemnity policy held by professionals, not only professional indemnity. A potential problem can arise for professionals in joint name policies where the parties are called '*co-insured*', or when they are joint venture partners, because the respective interests of, say, a main contractor and a professional are different (as opposed to '*joint insured*' parties, for example as joint mortgagees of a house, when the respective interests are the same). The problem arises because in theory co-insureds are parties to the insurance contract, not third parties, and so subrogation clauses could not be applied: one co-insured, say the professional,

cannot sue another co-insured, say the contractor or joint venture partner. This is usually circumvented by a *'cross-liability'* clause inserted into a joint name insurance policy which permits the co-insureds to be treated as separately insured, that is, one can be treated as if it were a third party to the other. In such circumstances subrogation rights will apply. Attempts to delete or omit cross-liability in joint name policies arranged by a contractor or other joint venture partner in order to prevent the professional's insurers seeking recompense from them for monies paid out to the professional, should be recognised as unusual and advice should be sought from insurers before accepting such a deletion or omission.

(8) *Pollution and contamination*: construction activities may result directly in creating pollution or, more indirectly, in disturbing natural pollution, or pollution from earlier activities which is already in the ground. There may be no risks, or another party other than the professional may accept the risks and/or a client may indemnify the professional. Where that is not the case, the professional should seek insurance cover. Unfortunately, there can be difficulty in professionals obtaining full cover for what is quoted typically as *'injury, damage or loss of use of property arising from seepage, pollution or contamination (including the costs of removing, neutralising and cleaning up afterwards), arising out of professional activities.'* Professional indemnity policies, if they do not exclude pollution and contamination claims, often include a specific aggregate annual limit on indemnity for claims relating to such matters. This is unlike normal professional and public liability policies. The professional therefore needs to be careful not to accept liability under an agreement for a particular project for an amount which, when combined with earlier liability exposures for similar projects that year, would exceed the annual aggregate liability insured under the policy. This requires careful management. What is called an *'evaporation clause'* can sometimes be incorporated into professional services agreements. This seeks to limit the professional's contractual liability to whatever remains of the aggregate cover at the time of any claim. The ACE (Second Edition 1998) includes such an *'evaporation clause'* as an option which limits liability for pollution and contamination claims, *inter alia*, to *'the amount, if any, recoverable by the Consulting Engineer under any professional indemnity insurance policy taken out by the Consulting Engineer.'*

12.6 Liability of partners

The liability of partners is unlimited and joint and several (see section 9.6.)

12.7 Liability of directors

There is no joint and several liability between directors.

An individual director cannot be liable in contract because contracts are made by clients with the director's company. However, if a director gives a personal guarantee in respect of the company's obligation under any contract, the director could, of course, become personally liable.

A director can be sued individually in negligence but the claimant would have to show that the director himself owed a duty to take reasonable skill and care in the actions he performed. It would therefore be necessary to establish a close relationship or direct contact between the director and the events resulting in the negligent act.

12.8 Liability of limited liability partnerships

An Act to allow the creation of limited liability partnerships (LLPs) may be passed in early 2001. LLPs will lie between a company, with its relatively inflexible structure and elaborate rules, but with limited liability, and a partnership, which has much more flexibility but where liability is unlimited. LLPs will be new legal entities which will carry on professional practice. The partners will be '*members*', and each will be an agent of the LLP. They will be able to organise their business on any basis they agree.

Measures to safeguard creditors will be included. For example, although neither a bond nor a guarantee will be required from the LLP, there will be a '*clawback*' provision against members similar to the one used where wrongful trading or fraudulent claims are brought by liquidators against the directors of a limited company. Knowledge of the insolvency or imminent insolvency of the firm will be required to show liability, so if a firm has been well run but meets an unexpected end, the risk of members having to contribute to the assets of the LLP through the operation of clawback should be limited.

The minimum number of members is two, which is the number also needed to create a partnership.

There is no requirement in the draft legislation for compulsory professional indemnity insurance, nor is there to be compulsory professional regulation. LLPs will therefore be available to any two individuals wishing to carry on a profession or trade together.

LLPs, like companies, will have to make public certain financial information, including the filing of audited accounts. Auditing of accounts will also be compulsory.

The partners will remain self-employed and continue to benefit from PAYE not operating on drawings and there will be no deduction of the

10% national insurance contribution. LLPs will also be allowed to create floating charges.

Members of LLPs will have limited personal liability. Thus, creditors and claimants will only have access to the assets of the business, which will include any professional indemnity insurance taken out by the LLP, but not to the personal assets of any members, unless that member has been personally negligent. This is comparable to the position of directors.

12.9 Public liability insurance

Public liability insurance policies are indemnity policies. They provide protection to the insured against any liability to the members of the general public, as opposed to employees of the insured, and cover claims resulting from physical actions causing accidental injury and damage. They are usually written on a *'claim occurring'* or *'occurrence'* basis: the relevant insurance cover will be that in existence at the time the event occurred.

It is again usual for such policies to contain limitations on the indemnity provided, so that the policy could stipulate a pecuniary maximum payment in relation to any claim or any period.

A public liability insurance policy will, typically, restrict the cover by reference to the business carried on by the insured, so that if an accident occurs the insured will only be covered if the accident arises out of the insured's stated activities. The policy will also typically specify the particular liability covered so that an insured incident must be of the specified type.

The importance of specifying liabilities in the policy is that the premiums payable under the policy depend on the probability of accidents occurring and the occupation and size of the insured's business.

Claims brought by an insured's employee when acting in the course of business will usually be covered by employer's liability insurance. If, however, an employee is not carrying out any identifiable professional activity when he is injured or injures a member of the public, the professional organisation's public liability insurance will cover the liability.

It is common for professional indemnity insurance and public liability insurance to be taken out at the same time through the same broker, which, taken in conjunction with statutory compulsory employer's liability insurance, will assist to ensure there are fewer gaps or overlaps in the liability cover provided.

An accident occurring to a third party while an employee is driving a company vehicle in working hours would be covered by a motor policy, not by professional indemnity or public liability insurance.

However, an employee of a professional organisation monitoring work on site, and who in the course of that monitoring causes injury to a contractor's employee or a member of the public, may be covered by professional indemnity insurance, as the professional's employee was engaged in professional activities at that time.

12.10 Insurance requirements of standard conditions of engagement

All main standard conditions now contain obligations to maintain insurance. The ACE (Second Edition 1998) includes both professional indemnity insurance and public liability insurance. It provides:

> B8.4 *The Consulting Engineer shall maintain professional indemnity insurance in an amount not less than that stated in A12 for any one occurrence or series of occurrences arising out of this Agreement and for the period stated in A13, provided that within that amount any annual aggregate stated in the relevant insurance policy in respect of claims for pollution and contamination shall be not less than the amount stated therefor in A14, and provided always that such insurance is available at commercially reasonable rates. The Consulting Engineer shall immediately inform the Client if such insurance ceases to be available on the terms required by this Condition at commercially reasonable rates in order that the Client and the Consulting Engineer can discuss means of best protecting their respective positions in the absence of such insurance.*
>
> 8.5 *The Consulting Engineer shall maintain public liability insurance covering the Consulting Engineer, his employees, agents and sub-contractors from the effective date of this Agreement until the completion of the Services in the sum stated in A15, provided always that such insurance is available at commercially reasonable rates.*
>
> 8.6 *As and when reasonably requested to do so by the Client, the Consulting Engineer shall produce for inspection brokers' certificates to show that the insurance cover required ... is being maintained.*

The RIBA (CE/99) deals only with professional indemnity insurance but in similar terms, providing:

> 7.4 *The Architect shall maintain Professional Indemnity Insurance cover in the amount stated in the Letter of Appointment for any one occurrence or series of occurrences arising out of any one event until at least the expiry of the period stated in the Letter of Appointment from the date of the last Services performed under the Agreement or (if earlier) practical completion of the construction of the Project provided such insurance*

is available at commercially reasonable rates and generally available in the insurance market to the Architect.

The Architect, when requested by the Client, shall produce for inspection documentary evidence that the professional indemnity insurance required under the Agreement is being maintained.

The Architect shall inform the Client if such insurance ceases to be available at commercially reasonable rates in order that the Architect and Client can discuss the best means of protecting their respective positions in respect of the project in the absence of such insurance.

The RICS (1999) in relation to professional indemnity insurance provides:

5.1 *The Quantity Surveyor is required to comply with the regulations of the Royal Institution of Chartered Surveyors in respect of the maintenance of professional indemnity insurance. He shall use reasonable endeavours to take out and maintain such Professional Indemnity Insurance above RICS limits, provided that it is available at commercially reasonable rates, as defined by reference to an amount and for a period in Clause 8 of the Form of Enquiry. Such insurance shall be with an insurer who is listed for this purpose by the RICS.*

5.2 *The Quantity Surveyor shall on the written request of the Client provide evidence that the insurance is properly maintained.*

5.3 *The Quantity Surveyor shall immediately inform the Client if the insurance referred to in Clause 5.1 above ceases to be available at commercially reasonable rates in order that the best means of protecting the respective positions of the Client and the Quantity Surveyor can be implemented.*

The APM (1998) also only deals with professional indemnity insurance, providing:

6.1 *The Project Manager shall effect a professional indemnity insurance policy with a limit of indemnity of not less than the sum stated in the Schedule of Particulars and shall maintain such insurance for the period stated in the Schedule of Particulars provided that cover remains available at that level on reasonable terms and at reasonable premium rates.*

6.2 *The Project Manager shall inform the Client if the Project Manager believes that insurance could not be maintained at the level required by Clause 6.1 in order that the Client and the Project Manager can discuss means of best protecting their respective interests in such circumstances.*

6.3 *As and when reasonably requested to do so by the Client, the Project Manager shall produce for inspection documentary evidence to the reasonable satisfaction of the Client that the insurance referred to in Clause 6.1 is being maintained.*

As can be seen, all obligations in the standard conditions (and also in the BPF forms of collateral warranties) are limited so that the insurance is provided '*as long as such insurance is available at commercially reasonable rates.*' This protects the professional against swings in the professional indemnity market when premiums could become prohibitively expensive, or even not available at all.

Professional indemnity policies held by many professional firms are usually professional '*group*' policies underwritten by several lead insurers covering a pool of similar insureds. The policy is not available for inspection by those outside the pool. It is normal to satisfy clients and others by means of a broker's certificate — the policy should rarely, if ever, be shown to third parties.

12.11 Insurance obligations in non-standard professional services agreements

Many clauses obliging the professional to maintain insurance in non-standard professional services agreements are loosely worded, often with no reference to the size of indemnity or for how long cover must remain in existence. The professional should require certain requirements to be spelt out and agreed between the parties.

Alternatively, some non-standard professional services agreements insurance clauses may be very specific and if unacceptable, may require negotiated amendment. For example, an insurance clause in a proposed non-standard professional services agreement might require an unreasonable length of time that insurance must be in place, and the production of a policy as the only apparently acceptable evidence of satisfactory insurance. The following are typical responses which can be amended as required that might be used by a professional, to attempt to delete or reduce such specific requirements:

We would like to clarify the position regarding our professional indemnity cover. Our professional indemnity and public liability insurance policies are arranged under the Group Scheme operated by [_____ (Insurance Brokers)] for members of [the name of the trade/professional group]. They provide cover on conditions which we believe are at least equivalent to those generally available to other [professionals] with the usual exclusions common to professional indemnity policies. Such insurance is renewable each year on terms which may be varied, and cover claims which are notified in that year. We cannot guarantee that the insurance will continue to be available, nor do we know the terms which the insurers may impose. We can only undertake to use reasonable endeavours to renew the insurance [for a period of X years from [practical completion, prior termination] of this agreement], providing it is available to us on reasonable commercial terms. Clearly we would wish to do so because professional indemnity insurance is taken out for our benefit.

And:

As there is one policy document which covers all the [professionals] in this Scheme, we are not allowed to produce the policy document itself for inspection. However we have professional indemnity and public liability cover for £x million and relevant certificates from our Brokers endorsing this are enclosed herewith. We trust that this assists you. Should you require further information or confirmation, we can request that from our Brokers.

The limit of indemnity included in the clause should be as low as is possible, commensurate with the risks for that particular project if a professional should be found to have been negligent, for example the risks of poor design on a short length of estate road are different from those on several miles of motorway. The limit of indemnity should not be the amount that the professional happens to carry at the time of the appointment. That is irrelevant and, indeed, it may not be the amount available when the claim is made. Notwithstanding the fact that the professional may be covered for higher amounts, that information should not be offered to a client if a claim arises as it would only increase the client's tendency to sue for those higher amounts. Further, providing information to the client or a third party as to the amount of cover available under a professional indemnity policy may well be prohibited by the terms of the insurance policy.

An obligation to maintain insurance cover to a certain level for a project is not the same as limiting liability to that amount. If liability is to be limited, this needs to be agreed and recorded separately in the appointment (see chapter 13).

Other potentially onerous elements of clauses requiring insurance to be maintained are:

(1) *Those stipulating the amount of excesses.* These can vary and are a matter of negotiation between the insured and the insurer. If an excess is required lower than that which the professional would normally agree with insurers, this could result in a higher premium.

(2) *Those requiring different cover from that normally contained in the insurance policy.* The professional will be obliged to find and pay for such insurance or be in breach of contract.

(3) *Those stipulating the use of a particular insurer or requiring the client's consent to an insurer.* This might restrict a professional's ability to find the most suitable and economic professional indemnity insurance. The same is true of a prohibition on obtaining insurance from outside the UK, for example.

The Act applies to terms which could affect liability (and these terms must therefore be *'reasonable'*), for example conditions:

(1)   As to time limits within which to make claims (see section 13.6).
(2)   Excluding or restricting other rights, for example to reject goods.
(3)   Excluding or restricting evidence or procedure, for example *'if you accept these goods this is conclusive evidence as to their fitness for purpose'*.

Terms in professional appointments which may be assessed for *'reasonableness'* in accordance with the Act include:

(1)   Terms which exclude or restrict liability in negligence − this will cover both a contractual term *'to use reasonable skill and care'* (this is not restricted to where a party is dealing with a consumer or on standard terms) and where there is a common law duty to use reasonable skill and care.
(2)   Indemnities by a person dealing as a consumer to indemnify another party in respect of a liability which may be incurred by that other party for negligence or breach of contract. However, indemnities given by persons who do not deal as a consumer are unaffected by the Act.
(3)   Terms which limit liability to a certain amount.

The Act says that such a term has to be *'a fair and reasonable one to be included having regard to the circumstances which were or ought to have been known or in contemplation of the parties when the contract was made.'*

It is therefore very important that such clauses are considered at the time the appointment is being negotiated.

Certain criteria have been laid down for establishing whether or not a clause restricting or excluding liability is *'reasonable'*.

(1)   It has to be clear because, if it is not, it is construed very strictly against the party relying on the clause to restrict or exclude its liability.
(2)   A clause is more likely to be considered *'reasonable'* if it restricts liability rather than excludes it. Liability, therefore, should be totally excluded only in rare cases (see section 13.5). However, a clause limiting liability to a small sum may be treated by the courts as if it was an exclusion clause.
(3)   A clause restricting or excluding liability should be discussed with a client before an appointment is finalised. The risks and the level of limitation proposed need to be discussed and it is prudent to document the discussions. This will help to establish that the client understood the sort of liability the professional could incur when agreeing to the limitation and therefore accepted that the clause was reasonable.

(4) The availability and amount of insurance is very important. In some cases it has been thought that if there was a correlation between the limitation clause and the insurance available, this would demonstrate that the clause was reasonable. For example, the courts held [*George Mitchell* v *Finney Lock Seeds* (1983)] that: '*Breathtaking sums of money may turn on professional advice for which it is impossible to obtain adequate insurance cover and which would ruin him personally if liable.*' As explained in Section 13.2, the availability of insurance will be considered by the court in assessing the reasonableness of a clause limiting liability to a specific monetary sum. Thus, it helps if a clause limiting liability is combined with an obligation to maintain professional indemnity insurance for that sum.

13.2 Limiting liability by reference to a monetary amount

It is perfectly permissible to limit liability by reference to a monetary amount, but in determining whether or not the limit is '*reasonable*' the courts are required by the Unfair Contract Terms Act 1977 (Section 11(4)) to have regard to:

(1) The resources that the professional could be expected to have available for the purpose of meeting the liability should it arise, for example the assets of the company or partners.
(2) How far it is open to the professional to be covered by insurance.

As it is usually open to a professional to obtain professional indemnity insurance, a failure to do so would probably make any clause limiting that professional's liability '*unreasonable*'.

It is important that the amount to which liability is to be limited is not calculated by reference to a formula, such as twice the fee, or to the same amount for every appointment. Each project needs to be considered separately on its merits and the amount should be an agreed monetary amount appropriate for that project. It also needs to be remembered that an aggregate limit for all claims under that contract will only apply if this is expressly stated in the limitation clause.

The validity of specific limitation clauses was considered in detail by the Court of Appeal [*St Albans City and District Council* v *International Computers Limited* (1996) 4 All ER 487]. In that case, the St Albans council ordered a computer system from International Computers Limited to calculate the level of community charge that should be set by the authority and to carry out the administration and collection of the charge. Due to an error in the system, the computer over-estimated the number of chargepayers in the region with the result that the council collected through the community charge significantly less than required, but still had to pay out the amounts that should have been recovered. The council claimed damages, although a limitation clause in the contract purported to restrict the level of damages payable by International Computers to £100 000.

At first instance the court applied the provisions of Section 3 of the Unfair Contract Terms Act 1977 and, as the contract was made on the defendant's written standard terms of business, the limitation clause would only be valid if it was '*reasonable*'. The court applied the Section 11(4) guidelines to assess this, noting that the defendant was a substantial company with ample resources to meet any liability, and that the defendant held product liability cover of £50 million worldwide. The court further noted that the defendant had called no evidence to show that it was fair and reasonable to limit its liability under this contract to £100 000. It therefore appears that any monetary figure used in a limitation clause cannot simply be chosen at random; it must be a figure that can be justified objectively.

The court, when considering whether it was better that the loss should fall on a local authority or on an international computer company, stated:

> *The latter is well able to insure ... and pass on the premium cost to the customers ... I do not think it unreasonable that he who stands to make the profit should carry the risk.*

The court therefore decided in favour of St Albans City and District Council and the Court of Appeal refused to interfere with this finding.

In deciding the maximum liability it is prepared to accept, a professional should assess the nature of the risks for each particular project and also the damages that could be payable if the professional is in breach of contract or is negligent. These will include not only the costs of putting things right but could also include all the other losses that could be caused to the client, for example inability to use or rent its building. An assessment would also need to be made of the damages that could flow from any particular matters, such as pollution and contamination claims.

The amount of professional indemnity insurance cover is a relevant factor but this does not mean that if the professional has £5 million insurance cover, the limit of liability for every appointment should be £5 million. The monetary amount included in the limitation clause should be appropriate for the type of commission being undertaken.

An obligation in an appointment to maintain professional indemnity insurance does not limit a professional's liability to the amount of cover provided by that insurance. A separate, express clause is needed, agreeing that liability should be limited. It needs to be remembered also that it is the policy in force when a claim is made that will provide the indemnity (if any) for that claim, not the policy in force at the time of making the original agreement with a client (see chapter 12).

The courts [*Moores* v *Yakeley Associates* (1998)] have considered the effect of a monetary limitation in the RIBA's standard conditions SFA/92. The court held that a limit of £250 000 was reasonable because it was not an arbitrary figure but based on the architect's assessment of the likely cost of the works; the fees were in the order of £20 000 and the ceiling was 10 times that amount; the client was in a stronger bargaining position than the architect — he could have instructed any architect; the client and his solicitor had both been aware of the clause and had had an opportunity to object and a comparison of their respective resources showed that the architect had none and the client was very wealthy. This decision was upheld on appeal.

13.3 Limiting liability by reference to 'net contribution'

Net contribution has been described earlier, in section 9.8. There is no reason why a clause limiting liability cannot use the amount of the professional's net contribution as a means of establishing a maximum that should be paid in relation to a claim. It needs to be remembered, however, that such clauses have not been tested by the courts, either as to their efficacy or their '*reasonableness*' and that they can only apply where the claim is such that two or more parties have been '*liable for the same damage*'. If the professional is found to be solely responsible for the damage arising out of that claim, such a clause will not be effective in limiting liability at all.

13.4 Limiting liability by reference to other matters

Limiting liability by reference to other matters can be effective if the limitation is reasonable. For example, liability could be limited to the costs of repair or of cleaning up a site, or to the amount recoverable under professional indemnity insurance (an '*evaporation clause*' (see section 12.5)). Certain types of damages can be excluded or limited, such as relocation costs, loss of profits or consequential losses.

If the liability is to be limited by reference to the sort of damages payable, this needs to be done carefully with appropriate advice. Two cases have dealt with '*direct*' and '*consequential*' losses. The courts [*British Sugar plc* v *NEI Power Projects Limited and Another* (1997)] decided that '*consequential*' losses were those other than '*normal*' losses, that is, the '*normal*' loss is that which every claimant in a like situation will suffer, and '*consequential*' loss is that loss which is special to the circumstances of the particular claimant. Thus, '*consequential*' losses would cover indirect damages and, therefore, might not cover loss of profits or loss of rent, for example. If a professional agreed with its client that *'consequential'* losses would be excluded, indirect damages only would be excluded.

This approach was confirmed by the courts [*Deepak Fertilizers & Petrochemical Corporation* v *Davy Kee* (1) *ICI Chemicals* (2) (1998)], when loss of profits and wasted overheads were found to be *'direct'* damages and not indirect or consequential damages.

A full discussion of the damages that may flow from any breach of a professional's appointment is outside the scope of this text.

13.5 Exclusion of liability

In exceptional cases it can be *'reasonable'* to exclude liability in respect of some particular claims or matters. For example, if a professional has not been asked to consider pollution or contamination in relation to a particular project because the client is taking separate specialist advice about this, it could be reasonable to state in the appointment that the client is doing this and any liability of the professional for any claim arising out of, or in connection with, pollution and contamination is excluded. It might also be *'reasonable'* to exclude liability for pollution and contamination claims where the client asks a professional to carry out a preliminary site investigation for a small fee, but where the clean-up costs could run into millions of pounds if the professional negligently failed to discover the site was contaminated. In such a case, the risks to the professional would be out of all proportion to the fee paid. (The ACE (Second Edition 1998) contains such an exclusion option.)

13.6 Limiting the time within which claims can be brought

Time limits must also satisfy the requirement of *'reasonableness'* and this may prove difficult because there are different time periods for bringing claims in contract and in negligence.

Time limits which relate only to claims in contract will more readily satisfy the test of reasonableness — 6 or 12 years might be reasonable, depending on whether the contract is under hand or executed as a deed (see section 3.14) because such claims can only be brought within 6 or 12 years from the date the cause of action accrues. It is possible for claims in negligence to be brought after a claim in contract would be time-barred. A limitation to bringing claims in negligence to, say, 6 years from completion of the services might not be considered *'reasonable'* as it could be a sizeable reduction in the position under the law at present, which is:

(1) Six years from the date of the accrual of the cause of action; or

(2) If longer, 3 years from the date when the claimant knew or should reasonably have known of the damage and its being caused by the defendant's negligence; with

(3) A long stop of 15 years from the date of the last act of negligence to which the damage is attributable (except in relation to fraud or deliberate concealment).

Thus, if a client only became aware of the defects in year 12 after completion of a project and it had been agreed that claims could only be brought at the end of year 6, that claim would be excluded before the client had any chance of knowing about it. (However, 15 years is itself an arbitrary time limit and it may not be unreasonable to reduce the length of time within which claims can be brought if the long-term availability of certain types of insurance, including professional indemnity insurance, is in doubt.)

Where claims involve fraud or deliberate concealment discovered many years later, the long stop provision would not apply. So if a professional sought to apply a 15 year (or similar) long stop on claims involving fraud or deliberate concealment, this would almost certainly be considered unreasonable.

One way of allowing claims based on fraud or deliberate concealment to be brought, regardless of any time limit, while limiting the time for bringing claims under the appointment for negligence, could be to exclude any concurrent claims in negligence. It has been confirmed by the courts [*Henderson v Merrett* [1995] 2 AC 145] that a party can contract out of a specific tortious liability while retaining contractual liability for negligence and liability for claims in tort for deceit. If this type of exclusion is used, it would mean that in most cases claims could only be brought within 6 years (provided the appointment was signed under hand). The wording to achieve this would be along the following lines: '*any cause of action for negligence which would otherwise lie against the professional in respect of its obligations under this agreement is hereby excluded.*' The disadvantage, however, when compared with a clause which clearly states an end date for bringing any claims, is that its effect is not readily apparent to non-lawyers.

13.7 The Unfair Terms in Consumer Contracts Regulations 1994

In addition to the provisions of the Unfair Contract Terms Act 1977, the terms of contracts entered into by consumers are governed by the Unfair

Terms in Consumer Contracts Regulations 1994, which came into force on 1 July 1995. For the purposes of the Regulations a consumer is defined as a *'natural person who is acting for purposes which are outside his business'* when making the relevant contract. The Regulations will furthermore only apply to standard conditions which have been drafted in advance, so that individually negotiated contracts are excluded. The Regulations only apply to contracts for the supply of goods and services.

The purpose of the Regulations is to strike out any term which is held to be unfair, and the rest of the contract is interpreted without the offending term unless the contract then makes no sense. The Regulations define an unfair term as any term which causes a *'significant imbalance in the rights of the parties to the contract to the disadvantage of the consumer.'* There is a schedule containing terms which might be considered to be unfair, but it is emphasised that the list is for illustrative purposes only, and the test for unfairness must therefore be applied to every contract.

The Regulations are wider in scope than the Unfair Contract Terms Act 1977 since they can potentially apply to every term of a contract which could be argued to be unfair, whereas the Unfair Contract Terms Act 1977 only applies to certain terms, for example unreasonably limiting liability or limiting the time in which a claim can be made. The Regulations are furthermore concerned with the unfairness of terms, whereas the Act only invalidates terms if they are unreasonable. A term could be reasonable and yet be unfair, so the Act will not necessarily invalidate unfair terms.

It is, however, unlikely that the Regulations will be of concern to many professionals, given that they would only apply to the professional's standard form contracts for services to consumers. Most contracts concerned with building and construction projects will be made with people in the course of their business, so the Regulations would not apply.

13.8 Limitation of liability in standard conditions of engagement

The ACE (Second Edition 1998) contains a net contribution clause (see section 9.8), a limitation of time within which claims are to be brought, and obligations in relation to maintaining professional indemnity and public liability insurance.

Two options for limiting liability are included in the Memorandum which is part of the ACE (Second Edition 1998). The first option provides that the liability of the Consulting Engineer for each claim shall not exceed a sum to be set out in the Memorandum. However, without prejudice to that, the total liability of the Consulting Engineer for claims arising in connection with pollution and contamination is not to exceed in aggregate another sum to be set out in the Memorandum. This aggregate amount (or the balance thereof) is further limited to the lesser of (i) the direct costs reasonably incurred by the Client in cleaning up the site; or (ii) the amount, if any, recoverable by the Consulting Engineer under professional indemnity insurance. The second option excludes the liability of the Consulting Engineer for any claims arising out of, or in connection with, pollution and contamination and fixes the total liability of the Consulting Engineer for each claim to an amount to be set out in the Memorandum.

The wording of ACE (Second Edition 1998) provides:

Option 1

A10 *The liability of the Consulting Engineer for any claim or series of claims arising out of the same occurrence or series of occurrences shall not exceed the sum of £_____ provided that and without prejudice to the generality of the foregoing:*

(a) *the total liability of the Consulting Engineer in respect of all such claims under or in connection with this Agreement arising out of or in connection with pollution and contamination shall not exceed in aggregate the sum of £_____*

(b) *such pollution or contamination liability as determined by the aggregate or balance thereof under (a) shall be further limited to the lesser of (i) the direct costs reasonably incurred by the Client in cleaning up the site of the Project or the Works as the case may be or any part thereof or (ii) the amount, if any, recoverable by the Consulting Engineer under any professional indemnity insurance policy taken out by the Consulting Engineer.*

Option 2

A10 *The liability of the Consulting Engineer for any claim or claims arising out of or in connection with pollution or contamination is excluded. The liability of the Consulting Engineer for any claim or series of claims arising out of the same occurrence or series of occurrences shall not exceed the sum of £_____.*

The ACE (Second Edition 1998) permits a limit to be stated for the time within which claims can be brought:

B8.3 *No action or proceedings under or in respect of this Agreement whether in contract or in tort or in negligence or for breach of statutory duty or otherwise shall be commenced against the Consulting Engineer after the expiry of the period of liability stated in A11 or such earlier date as may be prescribed by law.*

RIBA (CE/99) contains a net contribution clause (see section 9.8). Under clause 7.3 of CE/99 there is also a monetary limit for any loss or damage and this is to be stated in the Letter of Appointment.

Clause 7.2 provides for a limit to be placed on the time within which claims can be brought. It provides:

> 7.2   *No action or proceedings whatsoever for any breach of this Agreement or arising out of or in connection with this Agreement whether in contract, negligence, tort or howsoever shall be commenced against the Architect after the expiry of the period stated in the Letter of Appointment from the date of the last Services performed under the Agreement or (if earlier) practical completion of the construction of the Project.*

In addition to a net contribution clause in Clause 13.1, Clause 13.2 of the Terms of Appointment of the RICS (1999) provides that liability is limited to the amount of professional indemnity insurance required. It provides:

> 13.2   *The liability of the Quantity Surveyor shall be limited to the amount of the professional indemnity insurance required by virtue of Clause 5.1 above.*

Clause 13.3 permits a limit to be placed on the time within which claims for breach of the Agreement (but not other claims) can be brought. It provides:

> 13.3   *No action or proceedings for any breach of this Agreement shall be commenced by either party after the expiry of the period of limitation (specified in Clause 9 of the Form of Enquiry).*

Clause 9 of the Form of Enquiry to RICS (1999) provides the alternative of 6 years (for appointments under hand) and 12 years (for appointments executed as a deed) from practical completion.

The APM (1998) contains an optional limitation of liability clause, providing:

> 6.4   *Where it is stated in the Schedule of Particulars that this Clause 6.4 applies, notwithstanding anything to the contrary contained elsewhere in this Agreement, the Project Manager's liability to the Client under or pursuant to this Agreement and whether in contract, in tort, for breach of statutory duty, for negligence or otherwise shall not exceed the sum stated in the Schedule of Particulars. The Client hereby indemnifies and agrees to keep indemnified the Project Manager from and against liability of any nature whatsoever arising under or pursuant to this Agreement or in relation to the Project in excess of this sum.*

A monetary limit then has to be provided in the Schedule of Particulars to APM (1998). The parties must decide whether this limit is *'for any one claim or series of claims arising from the same original source or cause'* or *'in the aggregate for any one policy year'*.

Chapter 14

Indemnities

14.1 Indemnities and guarantees generally

Indemnity clauses are often included in professional services agreements whereby a professional provides an indemnity to a client against certain liabilities set out in that indemnity. Indemnities have particular characteristics of which the professional should be aware.

A contract of indemnity can be defined in several ways; in its widest sense it is any contract under which a party underwrites as a primary liability the loss or liabilities of another party. A contract of indemnity need not be in writing and can arise through statute or the relationship between the parties. For example, a non-standard professional services agreement may contain an indemnity against all loss or liability incurred by the client as a result of the professional's breach of contract.

A contract of indemnity creates its own independent original obligations and the indemnifying party will be primarily liable for the obligations under the contract of indemnity throughout its term.

An '*indemnity*' can also describe certain contracts of insurance or guarantee (usually described as '*bonds*' in construction contracts) as the purpose of those contracts is to provide some compensation to an innocent party, usually due to a failure of a third party to perform its obligations.

A contract of indemnity is not the same as a contract of guarantee (or bond). The latter is often described as being a collateral contract, existing in parallel with a main contract, under which a guarantor (or surety) assumes a secondary liability for the obligations of a party under the main contract. If the party under the main contract performs its contractual obligations completely and perfectly, the guarantor (or surety) is released from its liability and the contract of guarantee ends. A contract of guarantee must be in writing. Guarantees are discussed in chapter 18.

In this chapter, a contract of indemnity is being used in its narrow sense, that is, to cover the specific forms of indemnities which professionals may be required to give to clients under their appointments.

14.2 Problems with indemnities

Unless indemnities are very carefully worded, there is a risk that the amount that the professional will have to pay under the indemnity in respect of some default on the professional's part will be higher than the damages awarded if the claim had been decided in court. This can apply to amounts payable to the client and also to third parties, because of the professional's default.

An indemnity could, for example, allow a client to recover damages which would:

(1) Not normally be recoverable because they are too remote.
(2) Otherwise be reduced by the client's duty to mitigate its loss or by reason of the client's contributory negligence.
(3) Not be recoverable because they may not have been properly or reasonably incurred.

It is also possible that an indemnity would allow legal costs and expenses to be recovered which would otherwise be disallowed by the court.

A professional does not necessarily have to have been negligent before being liable to pay under an indemnity. If a client has suffered a loss for which the professional is providing an indemnity, the professional has to pay, regardless of any cover (which may be limited to negligent acts or may exclude indemnity clauses) from professional indemnity insurers. The client is therefore under no obligation to prove that the professional failed to exercise reasonable skill and care; it merely has to show that it has suffered an indemnified loss. For example, there might be an indemnity in a contract by a professional to its client against any damage to property owned by the client, even though damage to that property was inevitable when performing the services. Because of the indemnity the client could claim for the damage to its property, even though the professional had not been negligent.

Indemnities are not only asked for by clients to cover their own losses, but can extend to claims brought by third parties against the client in respect of some default of the professional. For example, a contractor could sue the client because of some error in design which is alleged to have caused additional work and delay. It is possible in this situation that a design professional will not know anything about the claim between the contractor and the client nor be involved in any court or arbitration hearing about it, and will only be informed once the amount has been determined by the court or arbitrator when the client seeks to collect that amount from the professional under its indemnity. The problem is likely to become more prevalent as faster alternative dispute resolution procedures, such as adjudication, become more common.

Settlements of claims can also give rise to particular difficulties. For example, a client may decide for commercial reasons to settle a claim with a third party for £500 000 when the damages properly payable by the professional if decided by the court would be £350 000. There may be no opportunity, if the indemnity is drafted in appropriate terms, to argue that the amount the professional should pay should be limited to £350 000. The full amount paid may not be recoverable under the professional's professional indemnity insurance — this will depend on the policy's terms. Even if it is recoverable, the professional's future insurance premiums may be increased because of the size of the payment which had been swollen by the *ex gratia* element.

The length of time within which a client can collect the amount due under an indemnity can also be a problem. Although in practice the client will probably not wait to claim under the indemnity once a claimable event occurs, the client has in fact between 6 and 12 years to do so, depending on whether the indemnity is contained in a contract under hand or signed as a deed.

The limitation period for claims under a contract of indemnity only begins when the person with the indemnity suffers a loss, whereas the limitation period for claims for breach of contract begins when the contract is breached. It is therefore possible that a claim can be made under an indemnity contract after the limitation period in respect of claims under the principal contract has expired.

If indemnities are given to specified third parties as well as the client, those third parties may be entitled to claim under the indemnity directly as a result of the Contracts (Rights of Third Parties) Act 1999 (and see section 2.3). The same could apply to indemnities in respect of claims by specified third parties. Unless the Act is excluded, indemnity clauses will need to be checked for such provisions.

Indemnities are not needed and should therefore be resisted. If a professional is in breach of the terms of a professional services agreement, a client will be entitled to the damages prescribed by law and it may also be able to sue the professional in negligence. If third parties sue the client because of something the professional has done, the professional can be joined in or damages can be claimed from the professional in contribution proceedings. An indemnity therefore only makes it easier for a client to collect money from a professional and increases the damages it can recover. There are no advantages to the professional.

As a general rule, indemnities should only be given where it is absolutely necessary, such as for commercial reasons, for example where a project is particularly wanted. It is important to consider the extent and nature of the indemnity which is being proposed and what types of losses are to be covered, for example personal injury or death, property damage or even all losses arising out of the contract. A widely drafted indemnity clause can create onerous obligations and it may be called upon in situations which the professional had not envisaged. Obvious unacceptably wide indemnities should not be accepted. The terms of any proposed indemnity should also be checked against any insurance policy of the professional.

None of the standard conditions of engagement referred to in this text contain indemnities.

14.3 Some specific indemnities

It is impossible to include every indemnity wording that might appear in non-standard professional services agreements and to comment on them. The following examples illustrate some of the foregoing general principles:

The Consultant shall indemnify the Client against any damages, costs, losses, expenses, actions, claims or proceedings arising out of or caused by any breach of the terms hereof or any negligent act or omission by the Consultant in carrying out or failing to carry out its obligations hereunder, whether express or implied.

This illustrates some of the problems outlined in section 14.2 as follows:

(1) It does not necessarily follow that because a professional has been in breach of its obligations it is liable for all the costs and expenses suffered by a client. Even when this is the case, the courts will provide a system of assessment to establish what costs and expenses are properly recoverable. In this clause, *'any costs or expenses'* would not necessarily be restricted to those the court would order to be paid and thus a professional could pay more than those for which it might otherwise be legally liable.

(2) A breach of the terms of the appointment may not result in any particular loss or damage to the client, but the client could incur costs and expenses in finding this out. These costs and expenses could be recoverable under the quoted indemnity.

(3) The indemnity refers not only to a *'negligent act or omission'* but also to the *'carrying out or failing to carry out its obligations hereunder whether express or implied.'* It may be acceptable to include *'express'* obligations because those will be specifically set out in the appointment − subject to the point that failure to carry out an express obligation may not necessarily result in any damages. However, to extend the indemnity to *'implied obligations'* could be extending the liability of the professional beyond what is reasonable. Who can say what those implied terms or obligations will be − this is an issue the court would have to decide. A professional should therefore resist such a specific inclusion.

The Consultant shall be responsible for any discrepancies, inadequacies, errors or omissions in the documents and information provided by it under this Agreement and the consequences thereof whether or not the Client shall have approved the same. The Consultant shall at its sole expense rectify promptly any such deficiency by amending, replacing or supplementing the deficient document or information as appropriate and shall bear the cost of any consequences thereof and/or shall indemnify the Client against all costs, losses, expenses, damages, claims, actions or proceedings brought or claimed by or on behalf of third parties in respect of any such consequences thereof.

(1) The problems with this clause are as follows: The obligation is to *'rectify promptly any such deficiency ...'*. If the deficiency is such that for example it affects the professional's designs, the professional will have such an obligation in any event. What if the deficiency is a mathematical or detailing error which in fact has no effect on any of the professional's designs or information? In the latter circumstances the professional has no obligation to amend and no liability for *'the cost of any consequences thereof.'* The same would be true if the deficiency did not amount to a breach of contract or negligence. The wording seeks to pre-empt what the consequences of any error might be, instead of leaving it to be sorted out under the common law, which requires that there must be a breach of contract or negligence and that a client has suffered loss or damage which is properly recoverable.

The *'costs of any consequences'* could be outside the scope of the professional's indemnity insurance cover.

(2) The indemnity part of the clause also suffers from the same problem: even if a professional is not liable under the common law for *'any such consequences'*, it could still become liable under the terms of the indemnity for the reasons previously stated.

(3) There is also the same difficulty about *'costs and expenses'* as has been outlined above in relation to the first example.

Some indemnity clauses are not so onerous, for example they may expressly limit the amounts recoverable to those properly recoverable in law and exclude the *ex gratia* element of any settlement. Some, although this is rare, will provide for notice to be given to the professional of any third party claim received which the client considers is covered by the indemnity and/or will allow the professional to take over the conduct of any negotiations and any litigation or arbitration.

It is stressed again that indemnities by a professional should be resisted as the law already provides adequate remedies to a client, both in respect of its own claims and any claims coming from third parties.

There are, possibly, three exceptions to this.

(1) *An indemnity to a client in respect of copyright infringement by a professional.* If it is correctly worded most professionals will accept such an indemnity because copyright is a matter over which the professional has control — that is, the professional will usually be aware whether or not it is infringing someone's copyright when producing a design, report, information, etc.

(2) *Joint ventures.* Because one of the joint venturers can become liable for acts or omissions of a co-joint venturer it is usual for cross-indemnities to be given to enable an innocent joint venturer to collect any amount that it has paid from the co-joint venturer(s).

(3) *Where a limitation or exclusion of liability has been agreed between a client and a professional,* this will protect the professional against third party claims brought against the client, but it will not protect the professional against third party claims made directly against it. If a limitation of liability is agreed, a professional should not have any liability to third parties claiming directly where those claims would exceed the amount of the liability agreed with the client. The professional needs an indemnity from the client against such claims, if the professional is to be protected. However, of the standard conditions referred to in this text, only the APM (1998) contains such an indemnity, even though all the standard conditions have provisions to limit or exclude liability (see section 13.8).

Chapter 15

Set-off, liens, retentions and liquidated damages

15.1 Set-off and abatement

Set-offs have been discussed earlier in section 6.13.

The Construction Act 1996 has recognised set-off but requires the payer to deal with it by way of notice of intention to withhold payment (see section 6.14).

Abatement is technically distinct from set-off. It is usually raised as a defence where an innocent party to a breach of contract is entitled to deduct from the cost of the contract the reduction in value of the relevant goods or services caused by the breach. Abatement is a common law right whereas set-off originated from statute law. Abatement has been available as a defence at common law since the beginning of the last century and is restricted to claims arising out of contracts for the sale of goods or work and materials. Unlike set-off, it is therefore not available under all contracts.

15.2 Liens

In the absence of express contractual provisions to the contrary, a professional has a legal right to retain documents, such as the designs and drawings the professional has prepared or significantly improved, until it is paid for them (at which point they must be handed over). This is known as a *'particular lien'*.

There are various rules covering this right of retention. The lien only covers the costs of preparing the documents concerned, so that any other amounts of money that might be part of the total owed to the professional do not have to be paid in order to secure the release of the documents. Payment for the professional's work must be due. The professional cannot use a lien to obtain an early payment.

The lien only comes into existence when the professional has completed the documents or drawings, although a lien can be claimed for work actually done if the contract is terminated before the work is completed.

The lien only exists while the professional still possesses the work, so that the lien is lost once the work is passed on to a third party. In this respect, a lien is a personal right of the professional.

A lien will often arise in connection with work which will also attract copyright. Copyright, licences and the effect of payment on any licence are discussed in chapter 8.

In practice, there may be a risk of being sued if the exercise of a lien causes delay to the project. For example, the client may seek to recover the costs of a contractor's claims for delay under the contract due to the delayed delivery of drawings. A lien, therefore, may only be valuable as a means of obtaining payment when withholding *'as-built'* drawings or documents that a client might need, say, to complete its health and safety file under the CDM regulations.

15.3 Retentions

Some non-standard professional services agreements allow for retention of a specified amount of the fee until certain events or circumstances have occurred.

Professionals are sometimes engaged on the basis that no fees will be payable until planning permission for the project is obtained. Problems can result if the client abandons the scheme, withdraws the scheme from consideration by the planning committee or if planning permission is available but not *'collected'* by the client (see also text referring to conditional payment in section 6.4).

The risks for the professional will depend on how precisely the amount can be calculated and the definition of the circumstances in which it can be released. The professional will need to consider whether the provisions concerning the retention in the agreement set out clearly when the retained monies will be released. If the test is subjective, for example *'when the client is satisfied that all the services have been completely and correctly carried out'*, it might be difficult to determine when the amount is due. If it is fixed to a certain date, such as *'practical completion'* or *'the Certificate of Making Good'*, this may be more certain provided, of course, these events actually occur. The former occurs in a project that proceeds (although problems could occur if the first contractor becomes insolvent) but the latter frequently does not occur — the client can ensure it does not occur by not allowing the contractor access or agreeing to take a discount in the price in lieu.

15.4 Liquidated damages

The parties to a contract can agree that if the contract is breached by either party, a fixed amount of damages will automatically be recoverable by the innocent party. The purpose of such an agreement is to allow the innocent party to be compensated without the need to show that it has suffered loss and to avoid the costly and often difficult procedures involved in doing so. Sometimes the parties will fix a sum as liquidated damages if a specific breach occurs. Should any other breach occur, the innocent party still needs to sue for unliquidated damages. If the parties have used a liquidated damages clause, and the innocent party's losses exceed the stipulated sum, it cannot disregard the clause and sue for more compensation; in a similar manner the party in default cannot prove that the innocent party has suffered less damage.

In general, the courts will not interfere in any agreement freely entered into by the parties, and they will not prevent a party from making a bad bargain. However, in the area of liquidated damages clauses, the courts have been reluctant to uphold clauses which are expressed to be liquidated damages clauses, but which in practice operate as a penalty to encourage the parties to perform the contract.

A liquidated damages provision must be a genuine pre-estimate of the losses that would be suffered by the innocent party if the obligation under consideration is breached. The courts will treat the clause as a penalty if the damages payable exceed these estimated losses or if the same amount is payable in circumstances that have different financial consequences.

It used to be thought that penalty clauses were unenforceable, but the courts [Court of Appeal in *Jobson* v *Johnson* 1989 1 WLR 1026] have now held that an innocent party can sue on a penalty clause, although it will only recover its actual losses. In some circumstances, although an action can be brought on a penalty clause, or for unliquidated damages where the contract contains a penalty clause, the claimant's damages will be capped at the amount of liquidated damages stated in the contract, even though the clause is unenforceable as a penalty and the actual damages suffered are greater.

Liquidated damages may be included in a non-standard professional services agreement where a professional does not complete services within a pre-agreed timescale or where certain drawings or documents are not provided by a certain time. They are usually expressed in terms of so much money per day of delay.

Proposals to include liquidated damages are inappropriate for professional services agreements and are not needed. The reason is the same as that given for indemnities in chapter 14. If a professional is in breach of contract the client will be entitled to the damages prescribed by law. The client may also have a remedy in negligence. A client does not need a liquidated damages clause in order to recover damages. Generally, too, unlike contractors' liabilities, a professional's liability will be underwritten by professional indemnity insurance.

The problems for a professional in assessing a liquidated damages clause tied to the programme for completion of the services are:

(1) Whether compliance with the programme is something that is entirely within the professional's control and, if not, whether any extensions of time can be given for changes by the client, delay by others, etc., and whether these extensions can be challenged if not correctly given.

(2) Whether the proposed rate of liquidated damages is a genuine pre-estimate of the client's loss.

If liquidated damages are a genuine pre-estimate and there is a total aggregate limit in place, exposure can be limited. If it is not, the professional may have a good chance of arguing that it is a penalty and only the actual damage or loss would be recoverable.

In the case of late delivery of documents, it is difficult to see how the same rate of liquidated damages could apply to all documentation supplied late. Late delivery of documents may have no effect, very little effect or have severe consequences for the whole project.

In one non-standard professional services agreement, liquidated damages for late delivery of documents were combined with liquidated damages for erroneous or incomplete documents. However, as stated, damages that flow from some errors could be very little or none, whereas others could result in very grave consequences. A fixed level of damages would not distinguish between the two. There was also a problem in the interaction in the two provisions — how are the liquidated damages calculated if at the same date the professional is late with some documents and those that are delivered contain errors. Are the liquidated damages paid until all late documents are delivered, and then only a proportion paid until errors have been put right, or do both sets of liquidated damages run until everything is put right?

The professional's professional indemnity insurance needs to be considered. Liquidated damages are often expressly excluded and the cover provided by the policy could be limited to acts of negligence only and the damages which result from any breach of the duty of care. Thus, if the liquidated damages agreed are more than the damages that would have been payable if the claim had been made on the basis of negligence or breach of the duty of care, there would not be a full indemnity to the professional from the insurer.

Chapter 16

Assignments and novations

16.1 Assignments generally

In chapters 2 and 17, it will be seen that the rule of privity of contract which prevents a third party from taking a benefit under a contract can be avoided in several ways, for example through agency principles, the '*Panatown*' principle, the use of collateral contracts or applying the Contracts (Rights of Third Parties) Act 1999 in certain circumstances. The privity rule can also be overcome through the assignment of contractual rights by one party to the contract ('the assignor') to a third party (the 'assignee').

16.2 Legal assignments

The Law of Property Act 1925 provides that a legal right (or '*benefit*') may be assigned provided the assignment is made in writing by the assignor and the other party to the contract is notified of the assignment in writing. The assignment must also transfer the entire benefit under the contract, so that the assignor cannot retain some interest in the contract. The assignment is therefore described as '*absolute*', in the sense that the assignee becomes the new owner of all the rights. The assignment cannot be stated to be by way of charge. If the assignment is valid, it passes the legal rights under the contract to the assignee, as well as the legal and other remedies relating to those rights. These are transferred, however, '*subject to equities*', that is, subject to any rights of set-off or other defences which would have been available to the other party to the contract against the assignor. Once contractual rights have been assigned, therefore, the assignee has the right to bring legal proceedings to enforce those rights in its own name, without the need to join the assignor as a party to the action.

The consent of the other party to the contract to the assignment of the benefits under that contract is not required.

It must be noted, however, that the obligations (or *'burdens'*) under a contract (for example the client's obligation to pay a professional or the professional's obligation to perform the services) cannot be assigned without the consent of the other party. If consent is given, this could constitute a novation of the original contract (see section 16.7).

It should also be noted that although the 1925 Act sets out a mechanism for assigning contractual rights, it has not destroyed the common law and equitable principles, so that an assignment which is void under the 1925 Act, because the formalities have not been complied with, may still take effect as an equitable assignment.

An oral assignment of legal rights could therefore still take effect in equity (see section 16.3).

It has been established by the courts [*St Martins Corporation Limited* v *Sir Robert McAlpine & Sons Limited* (1994)] that an assignment cannot be used to change the nature of the contractual obligations. It is considered that currently the assignee is not allowed to claim more damages than the assignor could have recovered if there had been no assignment, and the assignee cannot use the assignment to raise new heads of claims. The assignment therefore only operates as a mere substitution of the contracting parties.

Many contracts expressly prohibit the assignment of any rights of action in respect of accrued breaches without consent. The House of Lords [*St Martins Corporation Limited* v *Sir Robert McAlpine & Sons Limited* (1994)] held that an assignment which was made in breach of a prohibition on assignment clause in the contract did not give the assignee the rights to sue the original contractor. The House of Lords held that the rights to sue do not vest in the assignee independently of the invalid assignment. They did, however, hold that in such a situation the original contracting parties could still sue each other, even where the owners of a defective building had sold the property and no longer had an interest in it. This conclusion was on the basis that it could be foreseen that any damages caused by a breach of contract would cause loss to a future owner of the property and that the parties made the contract on the footing that they would be able to enforce the contract on behalf of any party suffering the loss.

(See also section 2.3, dealing with the implications of a client acting on behalf of, or for the benefit of, third parties.)

16.3 Equitable assignments

In equity, an assignment is valid even if the formalities have not been complied with, provided the assignee paid for the transfer under the contract of the rights to the assignee. The effect of a valid equitable assignment is the same as for a legal assignment.

In contrast to the provisions of the Law of Property Act 1925, no formalities are required to make an equitable assignment of rights. No specific form of assignment is necessary, and the assignment need not be in writing. The assignor must, however, indicate that the rights have been transferred to another person, whether by request or permission. The equitable assignee cannot, however, sue the other party in its own name – it must join the assignor as a party to action.

As for legal assignment, no equitable assignment of the obligations or burdens of any contract is permitted without the consent of the other party. If consent is given, this could constitute a novation of the original contract (see section 16.7).

16.4 Extracts from standard conditions of engagement

The current standard conditions expressly prohibit assignment without the consent of the other party.

ACE (Second Edition 1998) provides:

> B2.4 *The Consulting Engineer shall not, without the written consent of the Client which consent shall not unreasonably be delayed or withheld, assign or transfer any benefit or obligation under this Agreement.*

And:

> B3.4 *The Client shall not, without the written consent of the Consulting Engineer which consent shall not unreasonably be delayed or withheld, assign or transfer any benefit or obligation under this Agreement.*

RIBA (CE/99) provides:

> 4.1 *Neither the Architect nor the Client shall assign the whole or any part of the Agreement without the consent of the other in writing.*

RICS (1999) provides:

> 3.1 *Neither the Client nor the Quantity Surveyor shall assign the whole or any part of this Agreement without the consent of the other in writing. Such consent shall not be unreasonably withheld.*

APM (1998) provides:

> 11.2 *Neither the Client nor the Project Manager may without the prior approval of the other assign or otherwise transfer this Agreement or all or any of their rights or obligations arising under or out of this Agreement.*

16.5 Assignments in collateral warranties

The assignment clauses in collateral warranties require special consideration. Briefly (this is discussed more fully in chapter 17) a collateral
warranty entered into by a professional with a third party gives that
third party a right to sue the professional when it might not otherwise
have been able to do so. Generally, the terms of the collateral warranty
will set out the damages recoverable by the third party (or set some
limit on these) and stipulate the time within which claims can be
brought. Sometimes, however, collateral warranties are unlimited as to
damages and silent as to the time within which claims can be brought.
If assignment of the collateral warranty by the third party is prohibited,
the risk to the professional of being sued upon the collateral warranty
would come to an end once the third party had ceased to have any interest
in the building or project which is the subject of the collateral warranty. If,
however, the benefit of the collateral warranty can be assigned (as will be
the case if nothing is said), the professional is at risk of being sued by the
assignees until the time limit for bringing claims under the collateral
warranty has expired. This could mean that many subsequent assignees
may have the right to bring claims against the professional, although
any restrictions in the original collateral warranty as to the amount that
can be recovered will also apply to those claims. Professionals will
therefore usually seek either expressly to exclude any right to assign
the benefit of a collateral warranty or restrict the number of such
assignments. It also needs to be remembered that even if a claim by an
assignee is unsuccessful, the professional will incur time and expense
in dealing with that claim which may not be recoverable.

16.6 Effect of the Contracts (Rights of Third Parties) Act 1999 on assignment

The ability of a professional to protect itself against future claims by
limiting or excluding the right to assign the benefit of a contract with
clients or of collateral warranties entered into with third parties has
been affected by the Contracts (Rights of Third Parties) Act 1999. Under
the Act a third party may be entitled to enforce a term of a contract in
certain circumstances (see section 2.3). The Act provides that the third
party must be expressly identified by name or as a member of a class or
as answering a particular description. Thus, a generic description of
third parties can be used in the contract between the client and the
professional, such as 'occupiers', 'funders', 'tenants' or 'purchasers'. Third
parties coming within these descriptions have the right to enforce a
term of the contract against the professional, such as the right expressed

to be for the benefit of all tenants to have an air-conditioning system designed with reasonable skill and care. There would be no limit on the number of tenants who can sue the professional if the air-conditioning system has been negligently designed, provided they come within the description and subject to the statutory time limits for bringing their claim. In the example given, any *'tenant'* of a building described as such in the appointment, be it the first or any subsequent tenant, would be able to sue the professional, even though the same tenant would not have been able to do so under a collateral warranty to a tenant if it was outside the permitted number of assignments (see section 16.5).

16.7 Novations generally

As has been said, the only way in which contractual obligations or burdens can be assigned, either in law or in equity, is with the consent of the other contracting party. This is achieved by the parties to the original contract and the third party to whom the obligations are being assigned entering into a new appointment — a novation agreement — whereby it is agreed that the obligations will now be undertaken by the third party.

Strictly, a novation agreement is one which substitutes one party for another or substitutes the original contract for one on the same terms. It should not change the terms of the original contract.

As a novation agreement replaces the original contract, the usual requirements for the validity of contracts will apply on the making of the agreement.

16.8 Novation by a client

A professional does not have to agree to a third party taking over its client's obligations under the professional's appointment. This would include the obligation to pay the professional's fees. There could be real objections to this. For example, the professional may not wish to work for that particular client, the client might be close to insolvency or there may be a conflict of interest. Some appointments may provide for the assignment of the burdens and benefits of the contract without consent, or may oblige the professional to agree in advance to a novation in a certain form to a third party. This is often the case, where there is to be a design and build contractor and the client wishes to novate its professionals to that contractor (see section 16.11).

The novation agreement should be drafted on the basis that the retiring party is discharged from any further liability and thus steps out of the contract completely, and the new party assumes responsibility for all the contractual obligations, including past obligations.

However, most people use '*novation*' somewhat loosely to cover, for example, an arrangement where the whole benefit and only part of the burden is assigned with consent. For example, when a new client takes over an appointment, the client usually agrees to pay future fees but often does not wish to take on the burden of paying fees accrued but not paid, or responsibility for certain past decisions of the first client.

This is not satisfactory. The new client is going to want to sue the professional for any breaches that may have occurred before the new client took over and it should work both ways. The professional will not want to sue the old client for some things (and particularly not for non-payment of fees if the reason the appointment is being novated is that the client is in financial difficulties) and the new client for others.

There should also be no variation to the time within which claims can be brought. The time limits to apply should be those which would have applied if the original client had remained the professional's client throughout. Some novation agreements try to give new clients extra time for bringing claims in respect of pre-existing breaches. This should not be accepted by a professional. Also, if the original appointment was under hand, a novation agreement should not be signed as a deed.

Any novation agreement should therefore be checked for any unusual or onerous terms in the same way that any other contract would be checked.

16.9 Novation by a professional

Most appointments state that a professional must not assign its obligations, for example the performance of the services, without the client's consent. The client then has the opportunity to check and approve the new proposed professional's abilities to carry out those obligations. There is therefore a prohibition on the assignment of obligations without consent in the ACE (Second Edition 1998), RIBA (CE/99), RICS (1999) and APM (1998) (see section 16.4). This would apply also to any proposed transfer of burdens or obligations from one legally separate part of the professional's organisation to another.

16.10 Interaction with sub-contracting

Although a party to a contract may not, without the consent of the other party, transfer its obligations to a third party, it is generally entitled to arrange for those obligations to be performed on its behalf, say by a sub-consultant, while remaining liable for any defect in such performance (see section 9.3). Where a professional is employed for the professional's special skill and knowledge, there may be an implied prohibition against sub-contracting. It is best, therefore, to obtain consent to any sub-contracting, in advance, in the original appointment document.

16.11 Novation to a design and build contractor

A professional may be engaged by a client for initial outline designs and costing and then novated to a design and build contractor in order to finalise the details. Such a novation can only take place with the professional's consent.

However, some appointments provide that the professional has to agree in advance to this without identifying the new employer and without the form of novation being agreed. The professional must reserve the right to refuse to accept a new employer for the reasons given in section 16.8 and the form of novation should be agreed before the appointment is signed.

Some clients try to ensure that some of the obligations of the professional continue to be owed to the client so that, for example, they can ask the professional to continue to supervise the works on behalf of the client or report to it on various matters during construction. This should be resisted, not only because of the likely conflict of interest but also because the contractor is now the professional's client and it is the contractor who should be notified of these matters, not the client.

The same thing can be achieved by clients if there is a collateral warranty back to the client in respect of the services now to be carried out by the professional for the design and build contractor. Again, these warranties should be in the usual form, that is, to use reasonable skill and care in the performance of the professional's services under the appointment with the design and build contractor and no additional duties direct to the client should be included, such as the duty to report to or carry out an inspection for the client. The duty reserved to the original client (or to a provider of finance) may be to issue one or more certificates as to the value of work carried out, for example for the purpose of funds drawn down from the provider of finance. In order properly to issue such certificates, periodic inspection of the works will be necessary, whether or not the contractor required it or is prepared to pay for it (see also section 2.6).

Chapter 17

Collateral warranties

17.1 What are collateral warranties?

To understand collateral warranties, it is necessary to go back briefly to the law of negligence and the question of to whom it is that the duty of care is owed. The common law duty of a professional is to take reasonable skill and care in the performance of professional services. A professional owes a client a concurrent duty in contract and in tort. However, the courts [*Murphy* v *Brentwood District Council* (1991)] decided that a professional owes a non-client a duty in tort only in respect of personal injury and damage to third party property.

In the mid 1980s the courts were reluctant to impose a duty of care in negligence by a professional to anyone other than to the client with whom the professional had a contract. This gave the client problems with prospective, and usually (but not exclusively) building, occupiers (such as users, purchasers and tenants) who could be taking over a potentially defective building without the possibility of suing the contractor or designer who might have been at fault. This was because the construction team had no direct contract with the occupiers who would probably not be able to show they were owed a duty of care by the construction team in negligence. They could not claim against the client because the client had not designed or constructed the building. The client would probably not be able to bring a claim on the occupier's behalf (even if the client could be persuaded to do so) because, having sold the building or let it on full repairing leases, the client had suffered no loss and thus had no basis for a claim. Funders were also concerned because, if the client had financial difficulties and the funder exercised a right to take over and complete the building (or sold it in a half constructed state), the funder might have no legal cause of action against the construction team.

The concept of a warranty was evolved to try to create a direct contract, a *'collateral warranty'*, between the funder, purchasers/tenants, future occupiers, etc., on the one hand and the contractor and the rest of the construction team on the other. If there was poor construction, defective design or even inspection, those third parties could then sue the contractor and/or the rest of the construction team, including professionals directly in contract.

The position in law has now evolved so that it is becoming easier for such claims to be brought by third parties against the construction team, and decisions by the courts [for example *Alfred McAlpine* v *Panatown* (2000) and *St Martins Corporation Limited* v *Sir Robert McAlpine & Sons Limited* (1994)] together with the Contracts (Rights of Third Parties) Act 1999, have also affected the position (see section 2.3). For the time being, however, it is anticipated that collateral warranties will still be demanded.

A collateral warranty is described as such because it is a contract which is collateral to the construction contract or the professional appointment. It is also a statement or representation about what a contractor or professional did, since it is often signed after the works are completed.

A collateral warranty gives third parties the right to sue the giver of the warranty when they might not otherwise have that right in law. The question of what matters the third party can sue in respect of and the extent of the damages recoverable will depend on the wording of the collateral warranty itself. A professional should question signing a collateral warranty, especially if not being paid extra to do so. If there are no overriding commercial reasons, why should the professional extend its risks for nothing? A professional will be under no obligation to sign, for example if the client has forgotten to include in the professional services agreement an undertaking that the professional would sign a warranty or has failed to agree an acceptable form of wording with the professional. The client then approaches the professional at the end of the provision of services or the end of the project, asking for the warranties to give to future owners/occupiers. The professional could then refuse or if, for commercial reasons, the professional wishes to give one, it can at least dictate the terms and obtain a fee which adequately reflects the additional risks and additional administrative costs incurred. One of the terms that might be refused is that of accepting any adjudication procedures. The collateral warranty will probably not be a construction contract, the option to use the Scheme for Construction Contracts would not be available, and there is no advantage to a professional in accepting adjudication (see section 21.8).

17.2 Limitations on collateral warranties

If collateral warranties cannot be avoided they should be limited in at least three ways to reduce the risks to the professional.

(1) *They should be limited in number.* Many proposed appointments try to oblige the professional to give collateral warranties to any

funders, future owners, occupiers or users. This may not be limited to the first of such people and all would potentially have a right to sue the professional for an unlimited amount.

(2) *There should be limitations on the time within which the collateral warranty has to be entered into or on when claims can be brought.* Many appointments simply say that the collateral warranties must be given '*at any time*'. This could mean that years after a project is completed, a client finds a tenant/purchaser and can ask for a warranty. If the warranty is to be signed as a deed, the tenant/purchaser will then have 12 years from the date of the warranty to sue, and this could be 18 or more years after the original duties have been completed. If such a clause is agreed to, the professional should ensure that the collateral warranty itself has a finite time limit, fixed to a date such as practical completion, within which claims can be brought under the collateral warranty, preferably limited to, say, 6 years. (It should be noted, however, that such a limitation may be subject to the reasonableness test under the Unfair Contract Terms Act 1977 (see chapter 13).) Alternatively, the appointment should state that there is a limited time after the services have been completed within which the professional can be asked to sign them. The professional also needs to consider the implications of signing the collateral warranty under hand or signed as a deed (see section 3.14). The collateral warranty limitation period should mirror at most the period in the original appointment, that is, if the latter was signed under hand, the collateral warranty should not be signed as a deed.

(3) *The liability of the professional under the collateral warranty should be limited.* (It would otherwise be unlimited.) The professional should consider the obligations contained in a collateral warranty and assess the risk of any breach of those obligations to determine the appropriate limit of liability in exactly the same way as for the appointment itself. Generally, all warranties (except possibly to a funder) include some limitation of liability. Because a funder's warranty often permits the funder to step in and become the employer on certain terms, many professionals take the view that the funder should be treated as the client and thus will agree to become liable to a funder for matters they would not accept for a purchaser or tenant. Net contribution clauses are often accepted in purchaser and tenant warranties (see sections 9.8 and 13.3). Ideally, limitation of liability and net contribution clauses should be included in all the warranties or an aggregate limit of liability agreed which covers all the warranties given and the original appointment. Thus, if the client and all the tenants of a building brought claims totalling £10 million, an agreed aggregate limitation

of liability of £5 million which covered the appointment and the warranties would restrict the amount recoverable to £5 million (subject to the '*reasonableness*' test — see chapter 13). Also, particularly for purchaser and tenant warranties, some limitation on the damages recoverable should be included, such as the maximum liability being no more than the cost of repairs. This is particularly important where the professional is dealing with environmental matters and the possibility of pollution and contamination claims, where insurance cover may be more limited than for other sorts of claims.

17.3 Extracts from standard conditions of engagement

ACE (Second Edition 1998) provides:

> *B8.7 When the Client and the Consulting Engineer have so agreed before the commencement of the appointment, the Consulting Engineer shall enter into and provide collateral warranties for the benefit of other parties. It shall be a condition of the provision of such warranties that they shall give no greater benefit to those to whom they are issued in quantum, duration or otherwise than is given to the Client under the terms of this Agreement. Should the Client request alterations to the previously agreed terms or the execution of warranties in addition to those previously agreed, and the Consulting Engineer consents to such request, these may be entered into and provided by the Consulting Engineer for such additional fee or other consideration as the parties may agree.*

The Guidance on Completion explains that B8.7 is drafted on the basis that the client and the consulting engineer agree before the commencement of the appointment whether or not collateral warranties are to be given and their terms. Only the British Property Federation (BFP) forms (CoWa/F third edition (1992) for a funder and CoWa/P&T second edition (1993) for purchasers and tenants) are currently recommended (see section 17.4).

RIBA (CE/99) provides:

> *7.5 Where the Client has notified, prior to the signing of this Agreement, that he will require the Architect to enter into an agreement with a third party or third parties, and the terms of which and the names or categories of other parties who will sign similar agreements are set out in an annex to this Agreement, then the Architect shall enter such agreement or agreements within a reasonable period of being requested to do so by the Client.*

RICS (1999) provides:

> *7.1 As and when requested by the Client the Quantity Surveyor shall provide the collateral warranties required under Clause 10 of the Form*

> *of Enquiry, provided insurance cover is available in accordance with Clause 5 above.*

Clause 10 in the Form of Enquiry refers to the same BPF forms as are referred to in the ACE Guidance on Completion. In addition, there is space to indicate how many funders, purchasers and tenants will be entitled to a collateral warranty; how many times the collateral warranties can be assigned; whether the collateral warranties are to be executed under hand or as a deed and for any other amendments to be specified.

The APM (1998) contains no obligation concerning the provision of collateral warranties.

17.4 The British Property Federation forms of collateral warranty generally

Several standard forms of collateral warranty exist. Those produced by the BPF are collateral warranties for funders, and for purchasers and tenants. Copies of both are included as Appendices A1 and A2, respectively. The BPF forms do not, of course, cover all of the matters that can be included in collateral warranties and advice should be taken on them. However, the following sections concerning the BPF forms illustrate some of the issues that collateral warranties give rise to (see also section 21.8). The BPF forms, for example, do not have an express provision that the professional shall have no greater obligation to the purchaser/tenant than to the employer under the original professional services agreement. Because of other limitations in the BPF forms, this is not essential. However, other warranties should, if possible, have such a limitation so that a professional is able to use any limitation of liability in the original appointment to limit liability to the purchaser/ tenant under the proposed collateral warranty.

17.5 The British Property Federation purchaser/tenant warranties

Clause 1: The duty of care clause. This states the common law duty of reasonable skill and care. Anything higher needs to be considered carefully. Just because the original appointment may contain a higher duty of care, there is no reason why a warranty should.

If a warranty is being signed after the services or obligations have been completed, the professional should not state that it *'will continue to use reasonable skill and care.'* This could be construed as a continuing obligation to monitor its design or to check materials. This should not be agreed, unless the professional is being paid specifically to do it.

Clause 1(a)–1(c): Limitation of liability. Part 1(a) of the clause limits the damages recoverable from a professional by the purchaser or tenant to the cost of repairs and to the amount of the professional's net contribution if this is applicable (see chapter 13 on this topic generally). Clause 1(c) allows the professional to take advantage of any limitation in the original appointment (see above) or raise equivalent rights in defence of liability as it would have against the client under the original appointment. (This presupposes there are such limitations in the appointment. If there are not, further consideration may be needed as to whether any further limitations should be expressly stated in the collateral warranty.)

Clause 2: Deleterious/prohibited materials. This clause is typical but ought to be deleted or amended to reflect the obligations in the original appointment, if any, unless, of course, the latter is more onerous (see section 4.7).

Clause 3: Fees and expenses up to date. This clause should be deleted unless all fees and expenses have been paid. It will affect the licence given under Clause 5.

Clause 4: Authority of purchaser/tenant to issue directions. This is a useful reminder of the status of a purchaser/tenant in the construction process. The purchaser/tenant is not the client and is therefore not empowered to give instructions. If any are needed, they should be given by the client and any question of the extent of the instruction and/or additional payment agreed with the client. Without this, if the professional acted on the instructions of the purchaser/tenant, it could find that this is outside the professional's original appointment or even in breach of obligations under that appointment and that there is no entitlement to payment.

Clause 5: Licence to use documents, etc. The licence is widely drawn and it may be necessary to consider some restrictions on it (see section 8.3). The point to note, however, is that it is *'subject to the Firm having received payment of any fees due.'* This is a valuable condition enabling the professional to refuse to give a licence until it has been paid all the fees that are due to it (see comments on the funder's warranty form in section 17.6). However, if the professional has not been paid and clause 3 of the BPF form is not amended when the collateral warranty is signed, the professional may not be able to exercise its right to withhold the licence.

Clause 6: Maintenance of insurance. This needs to be checked to see that it correctly reflects the basis of the professional's insurance cover, for example if there is a limitation on some sorts of cover this should be stated. As to the amount, there is no reason for this to be the amount of the professional's insurance or the amount that the professional undertakes to maintain under the original appointment. It should be appropriate for the risks undertaken under the warranty and no more, bearing in mind any limitations in Clause 1.

The period for which insurance will be maintained will depend on the period of liability agreed under Clause 9 (see also sections 12.10 and 12.11).

Clause 7: Number of assignments. The number of assignments should be as limited as possible (see section 16.5).

Clause 8: Time within which claims can be brought. The wording of the clause should be expanded because of recent case law to read:

> *No action or proceedings under or in connection with this Agreement, whether in contract or in tort, in negligence or for breach of statutory duty or otherwise shall be commenced against the Firm after the expiry of _____ years from the date of practical completion of the Premises under the Building Contract or such earlier date as may be prescribed by law.*

If practical completion is not applicable to the professional's original appointment, another certain date should be used.

Limitation periods and other time-related issues have been discussed earlier in the text (see section 13.6).

17.6 The British Property Federation funder's warranty

The BPF funder's warranty is similar to the purchaser/tenant warranty but includes '*step in*' provisions. The following deals only with the differences in the funder's warranty and the '*step in*' provisions.

Clauses 1(a) and 1(b): Limitation of liability. Liability is limited to the professional's net contribution only, if this is applicable (see section 9.8).

Clauses 5–7: Rights to step in. These clauses allow the funder to '*step in*' and take over the original appointment in circumstances where there is a termination of the finance agreement by the funder and the professional would otherwise be able to exercise its right to terminate the appointment. The act of '*stepping in*' is, in fact, a novation of the original appointment (see section 16.7).

Clause 7: Liability for payment. This expressly provides that the funder has to accept liability for payment of all fees payable to the professional and for the performance of all the client's obligations.

Clause 8: Licence to use documents. The licence to the funder is subject to the payment of fees. This is important where a funder has a right to take over the development and decides not to take over the appointment of the professional but to appoint another professional. If the collateral warranty gave the funder a licence which was not subject to this proviso the funder would be able to use the professional's drawings and other documents to complete the development, even if the original professional had not been paid all outstanding fees. The same principles apply to any other party with '*step in*' rights, such as a purchaser.

17.7 Non-standard collateral warranties

All clauses in non-standard collateral warranties should be considered as carefully as the clauses in non-standard professional services agreements.

Of particular concern are clauses which extend the duty of care, impose further direct obligations, seek to impose warranties for fitness for purpose or absolute obligations, clauses regarding *'reliance'* on the professional, extensions to the obligations to insure, and indemnities. If there is a provision allowing a funder or a purchaser a right to take over the professional's appointment if a right to terminate has arisen under the original appointment, it is necessary to make sure that notice periods are not too long. The professional is likely to want to terminate in the event of non-payment but there may be a long notice period under the original appointment before it is allowed to do so. To that has to be added any notice period in the warranty. It could therefore be many weeks or months before the professional will know whether or not the funder is going to take over the professional's appointment. If the funder decides not to, the professional is at risk of never recovering payment of the outstanding fees. The professional has to continue working until the notice periods have expired — putting further fees at risk.

17.8 Adjudication in collateral warranties

It is quite possible to incorporate adjudication procedures within collateral warranties. As with any other express contract clauses agreed by both parties, once signed, these must be adhered to, except, possibly, if a collateral warranty is a *'construction contract'* as defined by the Construction Act 1996 (see section 7.5). In that case a referring party has a right (that is, an option) to refer a dispute to an adjudication procedure complying with at least the minimum requirements of the Act. If the existing express adjudication procedures already comply with those requirements, they must be followed by the parties. If one express procedure is not Act-compliant, the whole of the Scheme for Construction Contracts (England and Wales) Regulations 1998 (the Scheme) procedures apply, if that option is chosen by the referring party.

It may be difficult to determine whether collateral warranties are *'construction contracts'*. It is considered that they will be *'construction contracts'* only where:

(1) They are in favour of funders who have exercised their rights under the collateral warranty to step in and take over the professional's original appointment, thus becoming the professional's client.

(2) There is a specific provision in the collateral warranty under which the professional provides services or advice direct to purchasers, tenants or others in relation to '*construction operations*'.

The Act intended to provide a rough and ready way of settling disputes during construction operations and was mainly directed at the contracting side of the industry. Usually, once a tenant, purchaser or others have taken possession, '*construction operations*' will be over. Further, adjudication, which is aimed at providing a quick provisional decision, is not suitable for resolving the highly technical legal disputes that might arise under collateral warranties. These will in particular concern whether or not the professional has been in breach of its duty of care or of other obligations under the original appointment and the extent of the damages. Adjudication for disputes under collateral warranties which are not '*construction contracts*' should be resisted.

Adjudication is dealt with in more detail in chapter 21, as are the issues to be considered for adjudication with collateral warranties.

Chapter 18

Guarantees and bonds

18.1 General

Historically, bonds were introduced to cover contractors' insolvency and the cost to a client of finding another contractor to complete the works (usually at an increased cost) and the cost of the delay to the project. Some clients such as government bodies or local authorities ask for performance bonds or performance guarantees from their professionals as well as from contractors. They are not appropriate for professionals and should be resisted where possible.

The risk of a professional's failure to perform is best managed through requiring it to maintain adequate professional indemnity insurance. This is usually much higher than the value of a bond.

The cost of bonds and guarantees has to be funded and this puts up the cost of providing the services, particularly of those who do not regularly need to provide bonds.

18.2 Basic characteristics

A bond is an undertaking under seal or signed as a deed to make a payment. There are two categories of bond:

(1) *Single bond.* This is an undertaking to pay a certain sum of money on a fixed date or on the happening of a certain event.
(2) *Conditional bond (also known as a double bond).* This falls into two categories:
    (a) on-demand bonds, under which payment must be made if the demand satisfies the conditions stated in the bond (for example presentation of an engineer's certificate or statement by the employer that the contractor is in default under the construction contract and that specified losses have been suffered);

(b) default bonds, which are in the nature of guarantees, under which payment need only be made when the claimant, usually the employer, establishes first a breach and, second, a loss. Frequently, the loss has to be established by means of court or arbitration proceedings.

A guarantee is a promise by the guarantor (usually) to pay money to a specified party (the beneficiary) if a third party defaults on a promise to pay money or perform obligations under a contract, for example a construction contract. The obligation under that construction contract is described as the primary obligation, and the obligation under the guarantee is described as the secondary obligation. A guarantee does not have to be executed under seal or signed as a deed, provided it is in writing and signed by the guarantor. Guarantees can include indemnities (see chapter 14).

Bonds and guarantees suffer from imprecise and confusing terminology. For example, a document entitled *'performance bond'* or *'default bond'* is, in reality, normally a guarantee. The term *'conditional bond'* (which may be either a conditional on-demand bond or a default bond) is frequently used to describe a document which is, in reality, a default bond (sometimes called an *'on default'* bond). Further, one standard *'bond'* in the industry (which in reality is a guarantee) is described as a *'guarantee bond'*.

For those reasons, it is necessary to distinguish between a guarantee and a bond.

18.3 Guarantees

As explained, under a guarantee a guarantor (usually a bank, surety or insurance company) undertakes to see that a party (usually a contractor) fulfils its contract with another party (the client), or undertakes to perform the first party's obligations if that party fails to. If the contractor fails to fulfil its obligations, the contractor is liable for breach of the contract with the client. A guarantor's primary obligation is to see that the contractor performs the stated obligations (hence, these are often called *'performance guarantees'* or, less accurately, *'performance bonds'*), or the guarantor pays a sum by way of compensation.

Under a guarantee, the guarantor normally has all the defences open to the party whose performance is being guaranteed. This could include rights of set-off and cross-claims.

Further, the beneficiary claiming under the guarantee must prove the loss suffered as a result of the default of the primary obligor (usually the contractor). This means that it is not until the beneficiary has ascertained the extra costs of completing the works, the delay and any other loss or damage suffered, and, if necessary, proved this through court or arbitration proceedings (or in some cases adjudication), that payment has to be made by the guarantor. If, at the time of default, the obligor/contractor has outstanding claims (for example for variations, loss and expense and extensions of time) those claims will have to be ascertained prior to payment under the guarantee in order to determine the beneficiary's net loss.

18.4 On-demand bonds

This type of bond usually requires a simple demand made of the bondsman in good faith by the client, usually in the case of a contractor's bonds accompanied by an architect's or engineer's certificate. The bondsman is then under an obligation to pay the full amount of the bond.

The bondsman who receives a valid demand is not required to enquire into the actual loss suffered by the client — which may turn out to be less than the amount of the bond — although if the loss is demonstrably less than the sum demanded, it may be possible to challenge the amount payable in equity. Nothing is allowed for any cross-claims or set-off to which the professional may be entitled.

The advantages to the client of such a bond are that the client has only to assert the breach/non-performance specified in the bond, make the notice in the prescribed manner and collect the money.

The disadvantage to the professional where it gives an on-demand bond is that the money paid by the bondsman to the client may be immediately recoverable from the professional under a counter-indemnity required by the bondsman as a condition of providing the bond. It is common for the counter-indemnity to be drafted in such a way that the professional has no choice but to pay immediately. If that is not the case, the professional may be able to avoid paying under the counter-indemnity if the professional can prove that the amount claimed by the beneficiary was not due, did not take into account any cross-claims, or had been claimed improperly.

If, for example, the client owed professional fees including additional fees of £20 000 and then as a result of an alleged default collected, say, £50 000 due under the bond, the professional is then £70 000 out of pocket. The professional has to initiate proceedings or arbitration (and incur the costs of doing that) in order to try to recover the money due from the client. There may also be additional interest charges to the bank because of the effect of calling the bond on the professional's overdraft.

If there was no bond, the professional would be able to bring a claim against the client for the outstanding fees. The client would then claim and have to prove both that there had been a breach of contract and that it had suffered damages. If the client's counterclaim was less than the amount of fees due or was totally unjustified, the court could order that something be paid on account by the client to the professional and during the process, or until the matter was settled, both sides would be out of pocket and both sides would have to bear the costs of pursuing their claims. This sort of procedure provides an impetus to settle, a factor which is missing if the client has a bond.

Bonds also have implications for the professional's indemnity insurance. Some insurers may not be prepared to indemnify a professional against amounts payable under bonds unless both of the following apply:

(1)   The amount payable is clearly in respect of some liability covered by the policy.
(2)   The amount payable by the insurers equals or exceeds the amount paid by the surety.

18.5 Matters to be considered by professionals

Bonds for professionals are rarely standard. The following lists some of the points to be considered:

(1)   The form of the bond must be agreed at the time of the appointment. Is the proposed bond attached to the appointment? Some proposed appointments oblige the professional to provide a bond, but no sample form is attached. Sometimes a form of bond is attached but the client is allowed to make *'reasonable revisions'* to it. This is unacceptable as it may be difficult to reconcile what the client may think is reasonable with what a professional may think is reasonable.
(2)   Is the surety required to pay once it has received a demand in a certain form, or are other conditions to be complied with, for example must there be some assertion of non-performance or breach? The latter is, of course, preferable.
(3)   Can the surety question whether the sum is due in whole or in part? Generally this is precluded as the surety does not want to demand proof or require further evidence because of administrative inconvenience. However, it would be helpful if the surety were at least required to give notice to the professional before paying out to give it an opportunity to challenge what is being claimed.
(4)   Do any matters discharge the liability of the surety, other than the completion of the services, for example suspension of services, variations to the contract, termination of the contract, any waiver

by the client, any other bond taken by the client, or any breach by the client? Sometimes it is essential for a professional to have a provision allowing the discharge of the bond in some of these, or similar, circumstances.

(5) How long does the bond last? Some bonds last for the length of the contract plus a further specified period, thus enabling a client to call on the bond after the professional's services are completed without having to formulate a detailed claim. In other forms of bond, once the amount of the bond is paid, or the last completion certificate for the whole project issued, the bond is discharged. Ideally, the bond should not extend beyond the completion of the services.

(6) Is the amount of the bond clear? The amount should not exceed 10% of the contract sum, or a reasonable percentage of the fee and/or be reasonable for that particular project. If there are provisions which allow the sum to be called upon in tranches, the total aggregate sum must also be clear.

(7) What is the bond for? If it is for insolvency, 10% should be acceptable (as for contractors). If it is for liability for negligence, it may be for a much larger sum. In those circumstances, the professional should question whether a bond is appropriate.

When the professional receives the draft bond from the surety, the bond details should be compared by the professional with the client's requirements before submission to the client. Copies of all bonds provided to clients by a professional organisation should be kept in a central register so that the professional can monitor them and ensure that they are discharged.

18.6 Parent company guarantees

Generally, guarantees are provided by parent companies to guarantee the performance of a subsidiary under a contract. Sometimes they require the guarantor to take over and complete the work. They should generally only be required if the subsidiary's assets are disproportionately small when compared to the value of the commission or if it is a shell company and not an established soundly financed company. A professional should not be required to give both a bond and a parent company guarantee as this would be covering the same risks twice.

Parent company guarantees should never extend the parent company's liability beyond that of the subsidiary company. They are sometimes coupled with an indemnity from the parent company to the client in respect of claims against the subsidiary. If so, the terms of the indemnity will need to be considered (see chapter 14).

A form of wording such as the following might assist a professional in negotiating to remove a requirement for a parent company guarantee.

[The Professional] is one of the UK's leading [consultancies, architectural practices, quantity surveying firms] ... with a [xxx] million turnover and around [xxx] staff. It is thus not merely an operating company with negligible assets and there is no anticipation that [the professional] will become insolvent. We therefore see no reason why an undertaking from our holding company [xxx Holdings Ltd] to complete our services will assist you, not least because [xxx Holdings Ltd] does not itself provide [consultancy] services.

Chapter 19

The Construction (Design and Management) Regulations 1994 (the CDM Regulations)

19.1 Relevance to professionals

A professional may be affected by the Construction (Design and Management) Regulations 1994 ('the CDM Regulations') if one of the following.

(1) A designer.
(2) A Client's agent.
(3) A planning supervisor.

This chapter considers the obligations that may be imposed on professionals by the CDM Regulations. Being statutory requirements, it is unnecessary in conditions of appointment to set out the duties of the designer or Planning Supervisor under the CDM Regulations.

However, many non-standard professional services agreements do contain specific CDM obligations and often paraphrase them or include duties not imposed by the CDM Regulations at all. Before provisions in non-standard professional services agreements can be considered it is necessary to understand the background to the CDM Regulations, the criminal and civil liabilities imposed by the CDM Regulations and the duties imposed on Clients, designers and planning supervisors.

19.2 The statutory framework

The CDM Regulations were issued under the Health and Safety at Work etc Act 1974 to implement the 1992 Temporary or Mobile Construction Sites EC Directive. This imposed requirements and prohibitions on the health and safety aspects of *'construction work'* which is very widely defined and in any particular case the definition itself should be referred to. In summary, *'construction work'* is the carrying out of any building, civil engineering or engineering construction works. It includes the construction, alteration, conversion, fitting out, commissioning, renovation, repair, upkeep or maintenance and decommissioning, demolition or dismantling of '*a structure*'. It also covers the preparation for an intended structure, including site clearance or investigation; laying and installing foundations and de-assembly of prefabricated elements to form a structure; commissioning, maintenance and repair, and the installation of services which are normally found within a structure.

'*Structure*' is also defined very widely in the CDM Regulations and includes not only all traditional forms of structure but almost all other forms of construction, such as railway lines, docks, harbours, tunnels, bridges, reservoirs, pipes, cables, roads, airfield cables, sewers, sea defence works, earthworks, dams, underground tanks, as well as formwork and falsework and other temporary works and any fixed plant, the installation, commissioning, decommissioning or dismantling of which involves a risk of a person falling more than 2 metres.

The CDM Regulations will apply to all construction work except that carried out for domestic clients or small-scale projects as defined in the CDM Regulations.

There are two significant exceptions.

(1) Regulation 13, which applies to designers, is applicable to all projects.
(2) All the CDM Regulations apply to the demolition or dismantling of a structure, unless it is for a domestic client.

The CDM Regulations do not apply to construction work where the local authority is the enforcing authority.

The Health and Safety Commission has also issued an Approved Code of Practice (ACOP) which gives practical guidance on the implementation of the CDM Regulations. Failure to comply with ACOP is not a criminal offence, but it can be used as proof that a person has contravened the CDM Regulations or a section of the Health and Safety at Work etc Act 1974.

19.3 Criminal and civil liability

Breach of the CDM Regulations (as of the other health and safety legislation) is a criminal offence and can lead to a prosecution and, if convicted, a fine. Such a fine is not recoverable under professional indemnity insurance, as this is against public policy, but in some cases insurance may cover or contribute to defence costs.

The CDM Regulations impose no civil liability except in two cases: (i) where the Client allows work to start before a compliant health and safety plan is in place; and (ii) where the principal contractor fails to take reasonable steps to ensure that only authorised persons are allowed on to the site.

However, a criminal conviction will be powerful evidence in any claims for negligence and there is no doubt that the contractual arrangements between the Client and planning supervisors, designers and principal contractors impose contractual duties in relation to the CDM Regulations which could give rise to liabilities.

19.4 The client and client's agents

It is essential to be able to identify '*the Client*' for the purposes of the CDM Regulations. This is not necessarily the professional's client. Clients have extensive obligations under the CDM Regulations. Professionals can find themselves acting as Client's agents and therefore responsible for some or all of the Client's obligations under the CDM Regulations and be liable to prosecution if they are in breach of those obligations.

The Client is defined in Regulation 2(1) as '*any person for whom a project is carried out, whether carried out by another person or in-house.*' A project is any project '*which includes or is intended to include construction work.*' A domestic client as defined in the CDM Regulations is not '*a Client*'.

If the Client wishes to appoint an agent it is necessary first to check the competence of the agent to perform the Client's duties. Where an agent is appointed, the agent has to make a declaration to the HSE in the appropriate form that the agent will act as '*Client*' for the purposes of the CDM Regulations. If the declaration is not made, any requirement imposed on '*the Client*' by the CDM Regulations will also be imposed on any agent of the Client in so far as it relates to any matters within its authority. This could be potentially dangerous for a professional who advises a Client, because the professional could be '*an agent*' for the purposes of the CDM Regulations. The agent could be in breach of the CDM Regulations unless the Client provides the agent with all it needs in order to comply with the Client's obligations under the CDM Regulations. A professional or planning supervisor who is asked to help the Client with its obligations can be an '*agent*' and could become vulnerable to prosecution.

19.5 The client's obligations

There are eight CDM Regulations imposing obligations on '*the Client*' and these are summarised as follows:

(1) To appoint a planning supervisor and a principal contractor as soon as is practicable.

(2)   To check the competence and resources of:
      (a) the planning supervisor;
      (b) all contractors including the principal contractors and nominated sub-contractors;
      (c) all designers;
      (d) the Client's agent (although this is only in relation to competence).

      It should be noted, however, that anybody employing any designer and any contractor (not only the principal contractor) also has to check their competence and resources before they arrange for a designer to prepare a design or for a contractor to carry out or manage construction work.

      The CDM Regulations and ACOP give detailed guidance as to these checks and when they should be carried out.
(3)   To obtain information concerning the premises and to make available and update information in the health and safety file.
(4)   To ensure that construction work does not start until there is a compliant health and safety plan.

19.6 Designers

The CDM Regulations apply to any person who prepares a design in connection with a project. This will include a professional. A *'design'* is defined to include drawings, design details, specifications and bills of quantities.

If a designer arranges for another designer to be appointed (for example where a sub-contractor or another designer are to carry out some of the design) the designer has a duty to check the competence and resources of that sub-contractor or sub-consultant in respect of its function as a designer.

19.7 The designer's obligations

The designer's obligations are set out in Regulation 13. They are summarised as follows:

(1)   To advise the Client of the Client's obligations.

      A designer, before preparing a design, must advise the Client of the Client's duties under the CDM Regulations. These, of course, include the duty to be satisfied with the competence and resources of that same designer.

      (*'The Client'* for the project may not necessarily be the designer's employer.)

The designer also has a duty to advise the Client of practical guidance issued from time to time by the HSE, such as ACOP.

(2) To ensure that the design includes, among the design considerations, adequate regard to various matters.

Regulation 13(2) sets out those matters to which designers must have adequate regard. They are the need to:

(a) avoid foreseeable risks to the health and safety of any person at work carrying out construction work or cleaning work in or on the structure at any time, or of any person who may be affected by the work of such a person at work;

(b) combat at source risks to the health and safety of any such person;

(c) give priority to measures which will protect all such persons over measures which only protect each person carrying out such work.

(3) To ensure that the design includes adequate information.

This is described as being information about any aspect of the project of structure or materials (including articles or substances) which affect the health or safety of any person at work carrying out construction work or cleaning work, etc.

This information must be given to the planning supervisor for inclusion in the health and safety file and/or plan.

(4) To co-operate with the planning supervisor and with other designers.

This is to enable each of them to comply with the statutory provisions concerning health and safety.

19.8 The planning supervisor's obligations

There are eight main planning supervisor obligations set out in CDM Regulations 7, 14 and 15, which are summarised as follows:

(1) To notify the HSE of the project.

(2) To ensure the design contains certain matters.

The planning supervisor must ensure that any design includes, among the design considerations provided by designers, adequate regard to the matters in Regulation 13 and that the requisite information is provided by designers identified in accordance with Regulation 13 and put the necessary information in the health and safety file and/or plan.

This obligation also applies to designs prepared during the construction phase or designs altered during the construction phase.

(3) To ensure co-operation between designers.

(4) To advise on competence and resources.

The planning supervisor must be in a position to give adequate advice to the Client and contractors on the competence and resources of designers and/or of any contractor.

(5) To advise the Client whether the principal contractor's part of the health and safety plan complies with the CDM Regulations.

(6) To ensure the health and safety file is prepared and contains certain information.

(7) To review, amend or revise the health and safety file and ensure it is handed to the Client on completion.

(8) To ensure that a health and safety plan is prepared with the requisite information.

19.9 Appointment as a designer/planning supervisor

The obligations of a designer or planning supervisor are imposed by statute and last only while acting as designer or planning supervisor and while construction work lasts. An appointment therefore should make it clear that a professional acting in either capacity will have no further responsibility to the Client for any of the duties undertaken if the appointment is terminated before construction works are completed.

For each appointment it may also be necessary to consider whether there needs to be included any specific obligations on the Client regarding information a professional may need as designer or planning supervisor, either from the Client or third parties from whom the Client can obtain it. This will include information about the site and the project for the health and safety plan and file. If a planning supervisor is to advise on the competence and resources of other designers and/or of contractors, the planning supervisor will need information from them which only the Client may be able to obtain. The appointment may need to include an obligation on the Client to achieve the necessary co-operation between designers and the planning supervisor. Provisions about a timetable may also be necessary. A planning supervisor should also consider whether a right to terminate its appointment in certain circumstances should be included, for example if it is not possible to get the information or co-operation needed to do the job, or if the Client will not comply with its obligations.

No duties to supervise the principal contractor or other contractors' obligations under the CDM Regulations should be undertaken by designers or the planning supervisor. ACOP paragraph 68 provides:

The Regulations do not require architects or engineers ... (where they act as designers or are appointed as Planning Supervisors) to dictate construction methods or to exercise a health and safety management function over contractors as they carry out construction work. Neither do the Regulations place a duty on architects and engineers visiting site . . . to review and report on all aspects of health and safety. Where unsafe practices are noticed these need to be drawn to the attention of the responsible person, the principal contractor and contractor as appropriate.

There is no need for an appointment to list the designer's services as the obligation is imposed by statute. Wording which simply refers to Regulation 13, such as *'The Designer shall comply with all its obligations under Regulation 13 of the Construction (Design and Management) Regulations 1994'*, should be acceptable.

If the obligations are set out in full, the wording should be identical to that in Regulation 13.

The same principles apply to the planning supervisor, save that any reference to specific CDM Regulations in the acceptable form of words should be to:

Regulations 7, 14 and 15(1), (2) and (3) of the Construction (Design and Management) Regulations 1994.

Regulation 14 contains some duties that the Client may not require the planning supervisor to undertake or there may be alternative ways of complying with those duties. It is best, therefore, to clarify at an early stage what the planning supervisor will and will not be doing and put this into the appointment, using the words of the CDM Regulations.

Paraphrases or extensions of the duties under the CDM Regulations included in appointments for designers or planning supervisors are dangerous because they can be misleading and/or they can increase the professional's risk — by extending the duties beyond those in the CDM Regulations. The professional will have to comply with any additional or different obligations set out in its appointment as well as the designer's or planning supervisor's obligations in the CDM Regulations.

ACE (Second Edition 1998) does not contain any specific CDM services, but does include a reminder to the lead consultant to discuss with the Client the role of the consulting engineer and the relationship of the latter with, and need for, *inter alia*, any planning supervisor.

Under RIBA (CE/99) the architect has a duty to advise the Client of the duties of the Client under the CDM Regulations, to receive information about the site from the Client and, where applicable, to co-operate with, and pass information to, the planning supervisor, in particular for the pre-tender health and safety plan, and provide drawings showing the building and main lines of drainage and other information for the health and safety file.

The Client has a specific CDM obligation:

3.7   The Client shall, where required by CDM Regulations:

> .1 *comply with his obligations under the CDM Regulations and in any conflict between the obligations under the Regulations and this Agreement, the former shall take precedence;*
> .2 *appoint a competent Planning Supervisor;*
> .3 *appoint a competent Principal Contractor.*

RICS (1999) does not mention the CDM Regulations but risk assessment and management services can be additional services, and the quantity surveyor can be appointed as planning supervisor.

APM (1998) does not include any reference to the CDM Regulations but there is a duty to ascertain the statutory duties applicable to the project and to develop a brief which includes these. The monitoring duties could include the monitoring of others' CDM obligations.

Neither a designer nor a planning supervisor should warrant or undertake to the Client that it has the requisite competence to act as designer or planning supervisor, or that it has, or will, allocate adequate resources. It is for the Client to check competence and resources. If such a warranty is given and if, for example, a planning supervisor's appointment is terminated because the planning supervisor has not sufficient resources, the Client may be able to recover from the planning supervisor all the costs of delay while a new planning supervisor is appointed, and any difference in the fee.

19.10 Collateral warranties for a designer/planning supervisor

The CDM Regulations are concerned with obligations before and during the construction of the works only. The designer's obligations are confined to the design period, whereas the planning supervisor's duties are carried out during the design and construction phases and both relate to the health and safety implications of design. Planning supervisors are also concerned with the preparation of a health and safety plan during construction work and preparation of a health and safety file. Planning supervisors are not, however, responsible for information in the file — that is the responsibility of the designer, contractor or sub-contractor who provided it. The planning supervisor has no duties after the file has been handed to the Client at the end of the construction work.

It is therefore not appropriate that collateral warranties in respect of CDM obligations should be given to funders, tenants or purchasers, as the performance of these duties has no implications for purchasers and tenants who do not take an interest until after construction is completed (except perhaps where funders might step in and take over the project and thus become *'the Client'* for that project). Further, the CDM

Regulations have already imposed the penalty of a criminal prosecution and the possibility of a fine if there is a breach of the CDM Regulations by a designer or planning supervisor, and specifically excluded civil liability (see section 19.3).

It was therefore not the intention of the legislators that the CDM Regulations should create new civil liabilities or extend to the civil liabilities that are created by warranties. If collateral warranties are given, therefore, care should be taken to preserve the right to argue that no additional civil liability can be created.

Chapter 20

Law and jurisdiction, and dispute resolution

20.1 Law and jurisdiction

The law and jurisdiction that governs a professional services agreement may be dealt with expressly or be left to be decided when a dispute arises. Clearly, the former is sensible where there is any overseas element in, or related to, an appointment. In the absence of an express or implied choice of law, it will, when the occasion arises, be for the court to decide which law governs the contract and which court should hear any dispute. Factors taken into account include an assessment of the *'connections'* of a contract with any law or jurisdiction, for example the place where the contract was negotiated, the place where the contract was entered into, the place of performance of the contract, the location of the subject matter of the contract and the domicile, residence, nationality, place of incorporation and place of business of the parties.

The choice of law and jurisdiction can be important because the damages that may be awarded overseas (for example the USA) may be greater than those that would be awarded in England under English law. Thus, if a professional has an English law clause in an agreement with a sub-consultant, but a foreign law clause in the principal consultancy agreement, there is a risk that the same sort of damages will not be payable under both. It is therefore essential that the sub-consultancy agreement is drafted *'back to back'* with the principal agreement on this issue.

Dealing with the proceedings and attending court will be more time consuming and expensive in some countries. Further, it may be necessary to check if there are any restrictions or exclusions in the professional indemnity insurance that limit the insurance cover available in different regions.

In contracts with an overseas element, it is fairly common to find a clause which includes a provision such as *'the parties hereby submit to the exclusive jurisdiction of the English courts'* or *'the parties submit to the non-exclusive jurisdiction of the English courts.'*

Where there is an *'exclusive jurisdiction'* clause, the contract requirement takes effect to the exclusion of the jurisdiction that would otherwise be imposed by, for example, the Brussels Convention or by the *'connection'* test mentioned in the first paragraph above. A *'non-exclusive jurisdiction'* clause is a way of conferring jurisdiction on the court stated in the clause, in addition to the jurisdictions that would have existed under the Brussels Convention or under the *'connection'* test. It is a very persuasive factor in the choice of the appropriate court for proceedings, but not always decisive.

To avoid doubts as to which country's laws apply and questions of jurisdiction, the following can be used, as in ACE (Second Edition 1998):

A18 *This Agreement shall be governed and construed in all respects in accordance with the laws of England/Scotland and each party hereby submits to the non-exclusive jurisdiction of the English/ Scottish courts.*

The RIBA (CE/99) provides:

1.3 *The law applicable to this Agreement shall be that stated in the Letter of Appointment and, if not so stated, shall be the law of England and Wales.*

The RICS (1999) does not mention law or jurisdiction.
The APM (1998) provides:

15.1.1 *This Agreement shall be governed by and construed in accordance with the Laws of England and Wales.*

20.2 Dispute resolution processes

There are various ways, apart from negotiation, in which a dispute can be resolved. This text deals briefly with litigation, arbitration, mediation, conciliation, expert determination and adjudication.

Litigation and arbitration are considered to be the traditional methods of resolving disputes. They are methods where, to a greater or lesser extent, control of the management of the dispute is taken away from the parties. A final and binding decision is reached, subject only to rights of appeal where these exist.

The other processes are those normally referred to as alternative dispute resolution (ADR). There is no definition of the term ADR, but it is a useful way of referring to various dispute resolution processes. With one exception, they are consensual processes. They do not, unless the parties agree otherwise, result in final and binding decisions that exclude the *'traditional'* processes of litigation or arbitration should the dispute need to be taken further. The exception is expert determination. This process would normally be commenced as a result of an express contractual clause, although it could be arranged *ad hoc* as circumstances require.

20.3 Litigation

Litigation is available in relation to any dispute unless the parties have agreed to resolve the dispute by a different process. This may be by way of an express term in the appointment or a separate *ad hoc* agreement after a dispute has arisen. Even where parties agree to resolve their dispute by means other than litigation, the court may retain residual powers that cannot be excluded.

The advantages of litigation are that the court possesses greater powers than arbitrators, the quality of judges in the High Court and the Technology and Construction Court is very high, and the judges and the rooms for interlocutory hearings and trials are provided free by the state. In appropriate cases, legal aid is available for litigation, but not for arbitration.

Some of the traditional criticisms of litigation are now out of date. The waiting time for trial dates has been reduced dramatically and radical changes to the rules governing civil litigation have streamlined the litigation process and trimmed costs. Changes include the introduction of pre-action protocols that require claimants to provide much more information to a prospective defendant prior to the commencement of proceedings. There is now a greater opportunity to investigate and, if appropriate, negotiate and settle claims prior to proceedings being commenced.

Litigation provides a forum where all parties involved in a particular problem or dispute, for example an employer, architect, consulting engineer, main contractor and sub-contractor, can have all the claims decided by the same judge at the same time.

20.4 Arbitration

The advantages of arbitration are perceived to be that it is a more informal and flexible procedure, the dispute can be dealt with by appropriately technically qualified arbitrators, and it is a private process generating much less publicity than litigation. On the other hand, some argue that: (i) major arbitrations all too often mirror litigation procedures; (ii) it has been too easy to hijack, resulting in delays and disruption to the proceedings; (iii) the quality of arbitrators can be variable, and (iv) the parties have to pay for the time of the arbitrator and for the rooms for all hearings.

Those criticisms have been addressed in part by the Arbitration Act 1996 which gives the parties more autonomy and the arbitrators greater powers. Also, the arbitrator-appointing institutions have been seeking to maintain and improve the quality and training of arbitrators. A dispute before a good-quality, experienced arbitrator, keen to get on with the matter and not afraid to use his powers, can be very effective.

The ACE (Second Edition 1998) does not provide for arbitration and ultimately any dispute must be resolved by litigation.

The RIBA (CE/99) provides that the parties can choose whether arbitration or litigation should apply. If it is arbitration, the arbitrator's decision is final. In England and Wales, however, disputes regarding sums under £5000 can be litigated. The client gives the architect an indemnity against the architect's costs and a reasonable sum in respect of time spent if the architect obtains a judgment or award or the client fails to obtain a judgment or award.

The RICS (1999) provides that disputes may be referred to arbitration under the CIC's Model Arbitration Rules.

The APM (1998) provides that any dispute or difference shall be subject to the exclusive jurisdiction of the English courts.

20.5 Mediation

Mediation is a process in which a neutral third party — the mediator — seeks to assist the parties in reaching a negotiated settlement of the dispute. It is a consensual process, with the result that no party can be forced to participate in a mediation and, if it agrees to take part, can still walk away from the process at any time.

One of the benefits of mediation is that the solutions do not have to be simply the payment of money. Where long-term relationships exist between the parties, it is often the maintenance of those long-term relationships that is more important than determination of the precise amount of money due from one to the other by means of an adversarial dispute. The latter could lead to the relationship between the parties being damaged irreparably with the result that no further business will be conducted between them.

A mediator may be chosen by the parties or be selected by one of the bodies which holds itself out as providing mediation services. Once a mediator is appointed, it is usual for the parties to be asked to prepare a brief summary of their case prior to the date fixed for the mediation. Mediation is normally commenced with an initial session conducted by the mediator with all parties and their representatives present when each party is asked to present its case.

The mediator will usually make it a prerequisite of the mediation that each party will be represented by a senior executive who has the power to make decisions in relation to the dispute and to reach a settlement.

The parties then normally retire to private rooms. The mediator will visit the parties in turn in what are usually termed *'caucus'* sessions. In these sessions, the mediator discusses the issues, seeks to clarify the parties' cases and to ascertain the parties' real interests and what they want or need out of the settlement. The mediator must treat all information given to him with the utmost confidence unless expressly authorised to release it.

Mediation is a relatively short process. The majority of mediations last no more than 1 or 2 days. As a result, the whole mediation process, from the appointment of the mediator to completion, can take place in 3 or 4 weeks.

20.6 Conciliation

The terms *'conciliation'* and *'mediation'* are often used interchangeably where the conciliator performs a role identical to that of a mediator. Generally, the term *'mediation'* has become more popular in recent years. There is no mandatory format for either mediation or conciliation, with the result that the processes are difficult to define with any degree of accuracy. Having said that, it is believed that there are no mediation schemes in common usage in which the mediator forces a solution on the parties or recommends to them a particular solution. Conciliation, on the other hand, can be more proactive and a conciliator is frequently empowered to make recommendations or suggestions to the parties as to how the dispute should be resolved.

20.7 Expert determination

Expert determination is a process which is usually agreed by the parties to be final and conclusive, and in the past, was used most often in relation to valuations of property and shares and for rent reviews by surveyors. Recently, it has become more popular in other fields, such as construction.

The procedure to be adopted will be determined by the expert and will vary depending on the nature of the dispute. In straightforward disputes, the matter can be disposed of on the basis of written statement of cases. In more complex disputes, the expert may ask such questions and make such investigations as he thinks necessary in the circumstances. Usually, the expert is not restricted to the evidence submitted to him by the parties. It is often the case that the parties are relying on the expert's knowledge and expertise in a particular field. This, in itself, can reduce the length of submissions necessary by the parties. Expert determination thus gives the parties and the expert a high degree of flexibility in determining the procedure, with no necessity for pleadings, disclosure, witness evidence and a hearing.

20.8 Adjudication

Adjudication is dealt with in detail in chapter 21.

Chapter 21

Adjudication

21.1 Introduction

Adjudication is a process by which parties refer a dispute to an impartial third party — the adjudicator — to decide the issue in dispute. The parties will normally provide an adjudicator with a range of powers to enable him to reach a decision. An adjudicator's decision can be agreed by the parties to be both final and binding, although usually it is simply binding until such time as one of the parties takes the matter to litigation or arbitration.

21.2 Adjudication and the courts

The Technology and Construction Court gives priority to adjudication matters and invariably enforces adjudicators' decisions, allowing little scope for appeals except on the basis of an adjudicator exceeding his jurisdiction, or if there have been procedural irregularities.

21.3 Insurance considerations

As an adjudicator's decision is enforceable in the courts, a professional will have a legal liability to comply with that decision. Assuming it is a monetary decision, the insured under a civil liability policy will be entitled to an indemnity from insurers, subject to any terms and conditions of the policy.

If an adjudicator decides against a professional in relation to, say, defects in design and/or inspection, there is a presumption that the adjudicator has decided that the professional has been negligent. This is particularly so if the relevant adjudication procedures require the adjudicator to reach a decision in accordance with the applicable law relating to the contract. On that basis the insured, under a negligence policy, will be entitled to an indemnity from insurers, subject to the terms and conditions of the policy.

Where an adjudicator is entitled to reach a decision on the basis of a fair and commercially reasonable view, or at his absolute discretion, and with no reasons in a decision to show otherwise, insurers can argue that there has been no finding of negligence against the professional and that they are not obliged to provide an indemnity under a negligence policy.

Most professional indemnity insurers are providing cover for adjudicators' decisions, although in some cases this has been on the basis of an *'exclusion and buy-back'*, that is, it has to be bought as an extension of cover. Usually additional conditions are required, such as: (i) very early/immediate notice of adjudication is to be provided directly to insurers (compliance being a condition precedent to cover); (ii) cover only to be provided where an adjudicator is under an obligation to reach a decision on the basis of the legal entitlements of the parties, and (iii) the onus is on the insured to show that an adverse adjudicator decision was the direct result of negligence by the insured in the conduct of professional activities.

21.4 Adjudication under the Construction Act 1996 and the statutory Scheme

The Construction Act 1996 gives either party to a *'construction contract'* a right (that is, it is not obligatory) at any time to refer a dispute arising under that contract to adjudication under a procedure that complies with the Act. In other words, a referring party has a right (that is, an option) to refer a dispute to an adjudication procedure complying with at least the minimum requirements of the Act.

The Act applies to a professional services agreement to carry out architectural, design or surveying work, or to provide advice on a building, engineering, interior or exterior decoration or on the laying-out of landscape, in each case in relation to *'construction operations'*. *'Construction operations'* are defined in the Act and have been further clarified by the courts. A detailed consideration is outside the scope of this text, but it is considered that most, but not all, construction professional services agreements will fall within the Act. Further investigation and possibly legal advice may be necessary to clarify this in the circumstances pertaining to any particular agreement.

The Act requires that all *'construction contracts'* contain certain minimum adjudication provisions, otherwise the Scheme for Construction Contracts (England and Wales) Regulations 1998 (the Scheme) will apply. The Scheme describes adjudicator appointment procedures and states how the adjudicator must conduct the adjudication. If no adjudication procedures are incorporated into an agreement or if adjudication procedures already incorporated within an agreement do not comply with the provisions in the Act, a referring party has the option to use the Scheme instead. Thus, if there are existing express adjudication procedures that already comply with those requirements, they must be followed by the parties. If one express procedure is not Act-compliant, the whole of the Scheme procedures apply, if that option is chosen by the referring party.

Where the Scheme has been adopted in this way, neither party can amend it. (However, if the words of the Scheme are used as the basis of new adjudication procedures, the Scheme can be amended, as long as the resulting procedures still comply with the Act.)

21.5 Non-statutory standard adjudication procedures

There are a number of standard adjudication procedures published by construction industry-related organisations, such as the ICE and the CIC. Some large organisations, such as the Highways Agency, also produce their own procedures. While the intention of most is to comply with the minimum adjudication requirements of the Act, often those minimum requirements are enhanced. Where such procedures are to be incorporated into professional services agreements, they need to be considered from both the professional's and insurer's points of view for acceptability and whether the professional is more likely to be the referring or responding party.

Matters to be considered include:

(1) Sometimes an adjudicator may be allowed or obliged to give reasons for a decision, sometimes not, and sometimes the agreement of both parties is needed. It is desirable that the option to give reasons is included, otherwise the opportunity to identify any grounds for appeal is reduced.

(2) Some procedures require an adjudicator's decision to be based on the facts and applicable law, some are silent and/or may permit a decision on, say, commercial or fair and reasonable grounds. For reasons given earlier, the latter may not be acceptable to insurers.

(3) Some procedures permit set-off, others do not. Whether this is acceptable will depend on the nature of the Construction Contract.

(4) The method of enforcement of a decision might be different.

(5) Sometimes referred disputes will be only those '*arising under the contract*', but in others they must arise '*under or in connection with the contract*' or '*in relation to or arising out of*' the contract. The Act wording '*arising under the contract*' should be used.

(6) An adjudicator will usually have to act impartially, and sometimes fairly and impartially (or other variations, including '*in accordance with natural justice*'). The Act wording '*to act impartially*' should be used.

(7) The adjudicator should be someone qualified to deal with disputes arising under the appointment.

(8) Sometimes a decision may be expressly agreed to be final and binding, or the agreement provides that the decision will become final and binding if certain actions do, or do not, take place. This would prevent later arbitration or litigation and can be unacceptable to insurers. It is preferable to use the wording of the Act: '*binding until the dispute is finally determined by legal proceedings, by arbitration (if the contract provides for arbitration or the parties otherwise agree to arbitration) or by agreement.*'

(9) The adjudicator's powers may differ regarding the allocation of fees and costs between the parties. Each party should bear its own costs.

(10) The scope of an adjudicator's indemnity can vary.

(11) The parties may or may not be entitled to be legally represented at any meetings an adjudicator may wish to have.

21.6 Non-standard *ad hoc* adjudication procedures

Sometimes individual organisations, such as contractors, will produce their own, even ad hoc project-specific, adjudication procedures. These are often biased towards the position the drafter believes his own organisation is most likely to be in, for example a contractor as the responding party and a sub-contractor (or sub-professional) as the referring party. Sometimes the bias is obvious, such as the referring party having to bear both parties' costs (in order to deter disputes being referred), or the use of payment of any adjudication amounts awarded into joint signature shareholder accounts until a further decision has been made by arbitration or the courts (thus delaying actual payment). The adjudication procedure must comply with the express requirements of the Act or the referring party will be able to use the Scheme instead. Where the agreement is not a '*construction contract*', the parties are free to agree any adjudication procedure and will be obliged to comply with what is signed. These adjudication procedures therefore need reviewing, negotiating (and possibly not accepting), like any other conditions of engagement.

21.7 Adjudication as referring party

Where professional services agreement disputes arise during the performance of those professional services, they are most likely to be claims for late or non-payment of fees by a client, with the professional as the referring party. The professional can only gain, and not be any worse off, from the adjudication process and may have the use of any money awarded, unless and until the other party goes to arbitration or the courts. As with any other claim for fees, the professional needs to consider whether referring a dispute concerning fees to adjudication will result in the client referring a dispute alleging negligence on the part of the professional to adjudication. Adjudication will usually be supported by professionals when they see themselves as the referring party. They should review adjudication procedures to check whether they might increase the professional's costs or delay payment.

21.8 Adjudication as responding party

In some instances, a professional is more likely to be the responding party in an adjudication. For example, disputes arising under collateral warranties are more likely to concern an alleged breach of contract by the professional, with the professional as the responding party. A professional will generally be in the position of no gain. If the adjudicator makes a decision against the professional, that decision has to be complied with straight away and might involve large amounts of money, even if the dispute is later referred to arbitration or the courts. The availability of insurance cover for amounts higher than any excess is important, and insurers usually require that they are advised and involved as soon as possible.

Before accepting any collateral warranties containing adjudication procedures, it is therefore essential first to check that adjudication in collateral warranties is not excluded from the professional's professional indemnity insurance. If there is no such exclusion, it is necessary to check that the proposed adjudication procedures do not contain any clauses that would not be acceptable to insurers or must be negotiated out for insurance or other reasons. Negotiation is not possible if the Scheme applies (and probably not in practice for other standard procedures), although it might be feasible for non-standard and non-'*construction contract*' procedures. If satisfactory negotiation is not possible, a decision on whether to sign a collateral warranty would have to be taken commercially, including an assessment of the perceived risk and, where relevant, the availability of non-insurance funds.

21.9 Adjudication provisions in standard conditions of engagement

ACE (Second Edition 1998) provides:

   9.1   The parties shall attempt in good faith to settle any dispute by mediation.

> 9.2 *Where this Agreement is a construction contract within the meaning of the Housing Grants, Construction and Regeneration Act 1996 either party may refer any dispute arising under this Agreement to adjudication in accordance with the Construction Industry Council Model Adjudication Procedure.*

If the appointment is not a *'construction contract'* there will be no referral of any dispute to adjudication under ACE (Second Edition 1998).

RIBA (CE/99) provides that the parties may attempt to settle any dispute by negotiation or in accordance with the RIBA Conciliation Procedure, and where the applicable law is that of England and Wales any dispute referred to adjudication is to be in accordance with CIC Model Adjudication Procedure. (Different provisions apply where Scottish law applies.)

RICS (1999) have also adopted the CIC Model Adjudication Procedure with an agreement that prior to referring a dispute to adjudication the parties will attempt to agree a settlement in good faith. Neither party is entitled to raise any right of set-off, counterclaim and/or abatement in respect of enforcement proceedings.

The APM (1998) provides:

> 14.1 *Any dispute or difference which cannot be resolved amicably between the parties shall in the first instance be referred to the Adjudication Procedure. For the purposes of the Housing Grants, Construction and Regeneration Act 1996, the Adjudication Procedure is deemed to be incorporated into this Agreement.*

The adjudication procedure is to be the CDR Rules for Adjudication unless the parties indicate otherwise. Neither party is entitled to raise any rights of set-off, counterclaim or abatement and in any proceedings to enforce an adjudicator's decision the court is not entitled to open up the adjudicator's decision for inspection or review other than to determine whether the decision has been reached in accordance with the adjudication procedure.

As the adjudication procedures in the RIBA (CE/99), RICS (1999) and APM (1998) are not restricted to *'construction contracts'*, all disputes under those conditions can be referred to adjudication.

Chapter 22

Management of risks

22.1 Risk management generally

Having identified and discussed ways of handling the risks inherent in professional services agreements, we discuss in this final chapter procedures to manage those risks. Each organisation will have different concerns and management structures and the following is therefore a broad outline only.

In order to minimise risks, a professional organisation should:

(1) Assess clauses in each potential agreement singly, and then in conjunction with the rest of the agreement, to determine the risks.
(2) Negotiate to delete or reduce the impact of the risks that are of concern.
(3) Consider its own financial capacity to meet the potential liability including the availability of insurance cover and its own assets.
(4) Make a commercial decision as to whether or not to sign the final agreement.

It will be realised that some forms of activities carry inordinately high risks, often in terms of consequential costs, for the amount of fee income involved, for example site investigations of potentially contaminated land. Even an agreement to limit liability in such a case may not be effective.

22.2 Internal procedures

Because professional services can carry high potential risks, formal internal procedures are necessary to deal with appointments.

An initial step must be to establish the effective lines of communication between those in the organisation responsible for deciding what professional services agreements can be accepted and those knowledgeable about insurance cover, total company exposures, the possible consequences of claims, etc. Small practices may handle all such matters at partner/director level. Alternatively, it may be necessary for specialist members of staff to be available to provide advice to project managers on agreements and to assist in negotiations with clients.

There should also be standard procedures for dealing with the risks arising under agreements. For example, risks could be categorised in order of importance. At one end of the scale could be those requirements that are unacceptable (for example, unqualified, wide-ranging indemnities or *'fitness for purpose'* clauses) or outside company policy, for example, parent company guarantees. At the other end could be those requirements that could be accepted in certain circumstances (for example, those increasing the standard of care above *'reasonable skill and care'*) for a particular client or a particular project.

It should then be decided which risks need to be considered and/or which need advice from the organisation's legal advisers, and which risks need sanctioning at which level within the professional's organisation. These decisions will take into account commercial aspects, such as the size and type of job, how much the work is wanted, maintenance of relationships with the proposers of the agreement, etc.

Acceptable alternative forms of words can be prepared for the more common problem clauses to aid negotiations if those are handled in-house. Legal advisers and insurers or brokers will need to be involved in this.

However, for each agreement, the final commercial decision as to whether or not to accept risk must be taken by a knowledgeable professional at the appropriate level in the organisation who has taken account of any necessary independent advice. Appropriate training may be necessary.

22.3 Conclusions

It is only by establishing, implementing and auditing the organisation's risk management procedures that a professional can expect to control this important, but potentially high-risk, area of activity. When sufficient records become available, the results of these procedures should, in the long term, show that more effective control leads to reduced loss and fewer claims. The professional can also use this record to negotiate better insurance terms through brokers. A direct comparison should become possible between the additional management salary costs of implementing the strategy and the resulting savings in average annual uninsured losses and premium, thus providing an ongoing assessment of the cost-effectiveness of the risk management process.

Appendices

Standard collateral warranties

A1 British Property Federation, CoWa/F Third Edition (1992)

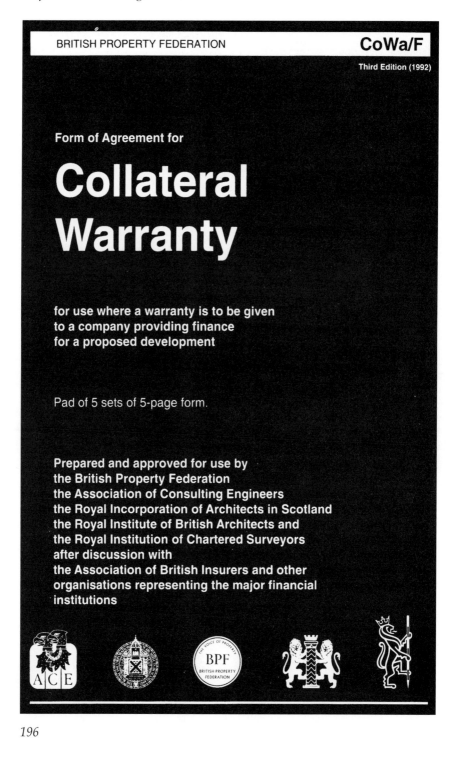

BRITISH PROPERTY FEDERATION

CoWa/F

Third Edition (1992)

Form of Agreement for

Collateral Warranty

for use where a warranty is to be given
to a company providing finance
for a proposed development

Pad of 5 sets of 5-page form.

Prepared and approved for use by
the British Property Federation
the Association of Consulting Engineers
the Royal Incorporation of Architects in Scotland
the Royal Institute of British Architects and
the Royal Institution of Chartered Surveyors
after discussion with
the Association of British Insurers and other
organisations representing the major financial
institutions

Form of Agreement for

Collateral Warranty
for funding institutions

CoWa/F

The forms in this pad are for use where a warranty is to be given to a company providing finance for a proposed development. They must not in any circumstances be provided in favour of prospective purchasers or tenants.

General advice

1. The term "collateral agreement", "duty of care letter" or "collateral warranty" is often used without due regard to the strict legal meaning of the phrase. It is used here for agreements with a funding institution putting up money for construction and development.

2. The purpose of the Agreement is to bind the party giving the warranty in contract where no contract would otherwise exist. This can have implications in terms of professional liability and could cause exposure to claims which might otherwise not have existed under Common Law.

3. The information and guidance contained in this note is designed to assist consultants faced with a request that collateral agreements be entered into.

4. The use of the word "collateral" is not accidental. It is intended to refer to an agreement that is an adjunct to another or principal agreement, namely the conditions of appointment of the consultant. It is imperative therefore that before collateral warranties are executed the consultant's terms and conditions of appointment have been agreed between the client and the consultant and set down in writing.

5. Under English Law the terms and conditions of the consultant's appointment may be "under hand" or executed as a Deed. In the latter case the length of time that claims may be brought under the Agreement is extended from six years to twelve years.

6. Under English Law this Form of Agreement for Collateral Warranty is designed for use under hand or to be executed as a Deed. It should not be signed as a Deed when it is collateral to an appointment which is under hand.

7. The acceptance of a claim under the consultant's professional indemnity policy, brought under the terms of a collateral warranty, will depend upon the terms and conditions of the policy in force at the time when a claim is made.

8. Consultants with a current indemnity insurance policy taken out under the RIBA, RICSIS, ACE or RIASIS schemes will not have a claim refused simply on the basis that it is brought under the terms of a collateral warranty provided that warranty is in this form. In other respects the claim will be treated in accordance with policy terms and conditions in the normal way. **Consultants insured under different policies** must seek the advice of their brokers or insurers.

9. **Amendment to the clauses should be resisted.** Insurers' approval as mentioned above is in respect of the unamended clauses only.

Commentary on Clauses

Recitals A, B and C are self-explanatory and need completion. The Consultant is described in the form as "The Firm". The following notes are to assist in understanding the use of the document:

Clause 1
This confirms the duty of care that will be owed to the Company. The words in square brackets enable the clause to reflect exactly the provisions contained within the terms and conditions of the Appointment.

Paragraphs (a) and (b) qualify and limit in two ways the Firm's liability in the event of a breach of the duty of care.

1 (a) By this provision the Firm's potential liability is limited. The intention is that the effect of "several" liability at Common Law is negated. When the Firm agrees - probably at the time of appointment - to sign a warranty at a future date, the list should include the names, if known, or otherwise the description or profession, of those responsible for the design of the relevant parts of the Development and the general contractor. When the warranty is signed, the list should be completed with the names of those previously referred to by description or profession.

1 (b) By this clause, the Company is bound by any limitations on liability that may exist in the conditions of the Appointment. Furthermore, the consultant has the same rights of defence that would have been available had the relevant claim been made by the Client under the Appointment.

Clause 2
As a consultant it is not possible to give assurances beyond those to the effect that materials as listed have not been nor will be specified. Concealed use of such materials by a contractor could possibly occur, hence the very careful restriction in terms of this particular warranty. Further materials may be added.

Clause 4
This obliges the consultant to ensure that all fees due and owing including VAT at the time the warranty is entered into have been paid.

Clause 5
This entitles the funding organisation to take over the consultant's appointment from the client on terms that all fees outstanding will be discharged by the funding authority (see Clause 7).

Clause 6
This affects the consultant's right to determine the appointment with the client in the sense that the funding authority will be given the opportunity of taking over the appointment, again subject to the payment of all fees which is the purpose of **Clause 7**.

Clause 8
Reasonable use by the Company of drawings and associated documents is necessary in most cases. By this clause, the Company is given the rights that might be reasonably expected but it does not allow the reproduction of the designs for any purpose outside the scope of the Development.

Clause 9
This confirms that professional indemnity insurance will be maintained in so far as it is reasonably possible to do so. Professional indemnity insurance is on the basis of annual contracts and the terms and conditions of a policy may change from renewal to renewal.

Clause 11
This clause indicates the right of assignment by the funding institution.

Clause 11S
This is applicable in Scotland in relation to assignations.

Clause 12
This identifies the method of giving Notice under Clauses 5, 6, 11 &11S

Clause 13
This needs completion. The clause makes clear that any liability that the Firm has by virtue of this Warranty ceases on the expiry of the stated period of years after practical completion of the Premises. (Note: the practical completion of the Development may be later).

Under English law the period should not exceed 6 years for agreements under hand, nor 12 years for those executed as a Deed.

In Scotland, the Prescription and Limitations (Scotland) Act 1973 prescribes a 5 year period.

Clause 14 and Attestation below
The appropriate method of execution by the Firm, the Client and the Company should be checked carefully.

Clause 14S and Testing Clause below
This assumes the Firm is a partnership and the Client and the Company are Limited Companies. Otherwise legal advice should be taken.

Published by
The British Property Federation Limited
35 Catherine Place, London SW1E 6DY Telephone: 0171-828 0111

© The British Property Federation, The Association of Consulting Engineers, The Royal Incorporation of Architects in Scotland, The Royal Institute of British Architects and The Royal Institution of Chartered Surveyors. 1992.

ISBN 0 900101 08 6

N.B. The above advice and commentary is not intended to affect the interpretation of this Collateral Warranty. It is based on the terms of insurance current at the date of publication. All parties to the Agreement should ensure the terms of insurance have not changed.

Warranty Agreement   CoWa/F

Note

This form is to be used where the warranty is to be given to a company providing finance for the proposed development. Where that company is acting as an agent for a syndicate of banks, a recital should be added to refer to this as appropriate.

THIS AGREEMENT

(In Scotland, leave blank. For applicable date see Testing Clause on page 5)

is made the .... day of .... 19 ....

BETWEEN:-

(insert name of the Consultant)

(1) ....

of/whose registered office is situated at ....

.... ("the Firm");

(insert name of the Firm's Client)

(2) ....

whose registered office is situated at ....

.... ("the Client"); and

(insert name of the financier)

(3) ....

whose registered office is situated at ....

("the Company" which term shall include all permitted assignees under this agreement).

WHEREAS:-

A. The Company has entered into an agreement ("the Finance Agreement") with the Client for the provision of certain finance in connection with the carrying out of

(insert description of the works)

....

....

(insert address of the development)

at ....

....

....("the Development").

(insert date of appointment)
(delete/complete as appropriate)

B. By a contract ("the Appointment") dated ....
the Client has appointed the Firm as [architects/consulting structural engineers/consulting building services engineers/   surveyors] in connection with the Development.

(insert name of building contractor or "a building contractor to be selected by the Client")

C. The Client has entered or may enter into a building contract ("the Building Contract") with

....

....

....

for the construction of the Development.

NOW IN CONSIDERATION OF THE PAYMENT OF ONE POUND (£1) BY THE COMPANY TO THE FIRM (RECEIPT OF WHICH THE FIRM ACKNOWLEDGES) IT IS HEREBY AGREED as follows:-

(delete "and care" or "care and diligence" to reflect terms of the Appointment)

1. The Firm warrants that it has exercised and will continue to exercise reasonable skill [and care] [care and diligence] in the performance of its duties to the Client under the Appointment. In the event of any breach of this warranty:

    (a) the Firm's liability for costs under this Agreement shall be limited to that proportion of the Company's losses which it would be just and equitable to require the Firm to pay having regard to the extent of the Firm's responsibility for the same and on the basis that ......

(insert the names of other intended warrantors)

    ....

    ....

    ....

    ....

    .... shall be deemed to have provided contractual undertakings on terms no less onerous than this Clause 1 to the Company in respect of the performance of their services in connection with the Development and shall be deemed to have paid to the Company such proportion which it would be just and equitable for them to pay having regard to the extent of their responsibility;

    (b) the Firm shall be entitled in any action or proceedings by the Company to rely on any limitation in the Appointment and to raise the equivalent rights in defence of liability as it would have against the Client under the Appointment;

(delete where the Firm is the quantity surveyor)

2. [Without prejudice to the generality of Clause 1, the Firm further warrants that it has exercised and will continue to exercise reasonable skill and care to see that, unless authorised by the Client in writing or, where such authorisation is given orally, confirmed by the Firm to the Client in writing, none of the following has been or will be specified by the Firm for use in the construction of those parts of the Development to which the Appointment relates:-

    (a) high alumina cement in structural elements;

    (b) wood wool slabs in permanent formwork to concrete;

    (c) calcium chloride in admixtures for use in reinforced concrete;

    (d) asbestos products;

    (e) naturally occurring aggregates for use in reinforced concrete which do not comply with British Standard 882: 1983 and/or naturally occurring aggregates for use in concrete which do not comply with British Standard 8110: 1985.

(further specific materials may be added by agreement)

    (f)

    ]

3. The Company has no authority to issue any direction or instruction to the Firm in relation to performance of the Firm's services under the Appointment unless and until the Company has given notice under Clauses 5 or 6.

4. The Firm acknowledges that the Client has paid all fees and expenses properly due and owing to the Firm under the Appointment up to the date of this Agreement. The Company has no liability to the Firm in respect of fees and expenses under the Appointment unless and until the Company has given notice under Clauses 5 or 6.

5. The Firm agrees that, in the event of the termination of the Finance Agreement by the Company, the Firm will, if so required by notice in writing given by the Company and subject to Clause 7, accept the instructions of the Company or its appointee to the exclusion of the Client in respect of the Appointment upon the terms and conditions of the Appointment. The Client acknowledges that the Firm shall be entitled to rely on a notice given to the Firm by the Company under this Clause 5 as conclusive evidence for the purposes of this Agreement of the termination of the Finance Agreement by the Company.

6. The Firm further agrees that it will not without first giving the Company not less than twenty one days' notice in writing exercise any right it may have to terminate the Appointment or to treat the same as having been repudiated by the Client or to discontinue the performance of any services to be performed by the Firm pursuant thereto. Such right to terminate the Appointment with the Client or treat the same as having been repudiated or discontinue performance shall cease if, within such period of notice and subject to Clause 7, the Company shall give notice in writing to the Firm requiring the Firm to accept the instructions of the Company or its appointee to the exclusion of the Client in respect of the Development upon the terms and conditions of the Appointment.

7. It shall be a condition of any notice given by the Company under Clauses 5 or 6 that the Company or its appointee accepts liability for payment of the fees and expenses payable to the Firm under the Appointment and for performance of the Client's obligations including payment of any fees and expenses outstanding at the date of such notice. Upon the issue of any notice by the Company under Clauses 5 or 6, the Appointment shall continue in full force and effect as if no right of termination on the part of the Firm had arisen and the Firm shall be liable to the Company and its appointee under the Appointment in lieu of its liability to the Client. If any notice given by the Company under Clauses 5 or 6 requires the Firm to accept the instructions of the Company's appointee, the Company shall be liable to the Firm as guarantor for the payment of all sums from time to time due to the Firm from the Company's appointee.

8. The copyright in all drawings, reports, models, specifications, bills of quantities, calculations and other similar documents provided by the Firm in connection with the Development (together referred to in this Clause 8 as "the Documents") shall remain vested in the Firm but, subject to the Firm having received payment of any fees agreed as properly due under the Appointment, the Company and its appointee shall have a licence to copy and use the Documents and to reproduce the designs and content of them for any purpose related to the Premises including, but without limitation, the construction, completion, maintenance, letting, promotion, advertisement, reinstatement, refurbishment and repair of the Development. Such licence shall enable the Company and its appointee to copy and use the Documents for the extension of the Development but such use shall not include a licence to reproduce the designs contained in them for any extension of the Development. The Firm shall not be liable for any such use by the Company or its appointee of any of the Documents for any purpose other than that for which the same were prepared by or on behalf of the Firm.

9. The Firm shall maintain professional indemnity insurance in an amount of not less than

(insert amount)

pounds (£   )

for any one occurrence or series of occurrences arising out of any one event for a period

(insert period)

of   years from the date of practical completion of the Development for the purposes of the Building Contract, provided always that such insurance is available at commercially reasonable rates. The Firm shall immediately inform the Company if such insurance ceases to be available at commercially reasonable rates in order that the Firm and the Company can discuss means of best protecting the respective positions of the Company and the Firm in respect of the Development in the absence of such insurance. As and when it is reasonably requested to do so by the Company or its appointee under the Clauses 5 or 6, the Firm shall produce for inspection documentary evidence that its professional indemnity insurance is being maintained.

200

10. The Client has agreed to be a party to this Agreement for the purposes of acknowledging that the Firm shall not be in breach of the Appointment by complying with the obligations imposed on it by Clauses 5 and 6.

(delete if under Scots law)

[11. This Agreement may be assigned by the Company by way of absolute legal assignment to another company providing finance or re-finance in connection with the carrying out of the Development without the consent of the Client or the Firm being required and such assignment shall be effective upon written notice thereof being given to the Client and to the Firm.]

(delete if under English law)

[11S. *The Company shall be entitled to assign or transfer its rights under this Agreement to any other company providing finance or re-finance in connection with the carrying out of the Development without the consent of the Client or the Firm being required subject to written notice of such assignation being given to the Firm in accordance with Clause 12 hereof.*]

12. Any notice to be given by the Firm hereunder shall be deemed to be duly given if it is delivered by hand at or sent by registered post or recorded delivery to the Company at its registered office and any notice given by the Company hereunder shall be deemed to be duly given if it is addressed to "The Senior Partner"/"The Managing Director" and delivered by hand at or sent by registered post or recorded delivery to the above-mentioned address of the Firm or to the principal business address of the Firm for the time being and, in the case of any such notices, the same shall if sent by registered post or recorded delivery be deemed to have been received forty eight hours after being posted.

(complete as appropriate)

13. No action or proceedings for any breach of this Agreement shall be commenced against the Firm after the expiry of .... years from the date of practical completion of the Premises under the Building Contract.

(delete if under Scots law)

[14. The construction validity and performance of this agreement shall be governed by English Law and the parties agree to submit to the non-exclusive jurisdiction of the English Courts.

(alternatives: delete as appropriate)

[**AS WITNESS** the hands of the parties the day and year first before written.

(for Agreement executed under hand and NOT as a Deed)

Signed by or on behalf of the Firm ....

in the presence of: ....

Signed by or on behalf of the Client ....

in the presence of: ....

Signed by or on behalf of the Company ....

in the presence of: ....]

(this must only apply if the Appointment is executed as a Deed)

[**IN WITNESS WHEREOF** this Agreement was executed as a Deed and delivered the day and year first before written.

by the Firm

....

....

....

by the Client

....

....

....

by the Company

....

....

....]]

Professional services agreement

[14S. *This Agreement shall be construed and the rights of the parties and all matters arising hereunder shall be determined in all respects according to the Law of Scotland.*

IN WITNESS WHEREOF *these presents are executed as follows:-*

SIGNED by the above named Firm at ....

on the ....day of.............................Nineteen hundred and..............................

as follows:-

...(Firm's signature)

Signature...Full Name ....

Address ....

...Occupation ....

Signature...Full Name ....

Address ....

...Occupation ....

SIGNED by the above named Client at ....

on the ....day of.........................Nineteen hundred and..............................

as follows:-

For and on behalf of the Client

...Director/Authorised Signatory

...Director/Authorised Signatory

SIGNED by the above named Company at ....

on the ....day of.........................Nineteen hundred and..............................

as follows:-

For and on behalf of the Company

...Director/Authorised Signatory

...Director/Authorised Signatory]

A2 British Property Federation, CoWa/P&T Second Edition (1993)

BRITISH PROPERTY FEDERATION	CoWa/P&T
	Second Edition (1993)

Form of Agreement for

Collateral Warranty

**for use where a warranty is to be given to a
purchaser or tenant of premises
in a commercial and/or industrial development**

Pad of 5 sets of 4-page form.

**Prepared and approved for use by
the British Property Federation
the Association of Consulting Engineers
the Royal Incorporation of Architects in Scotland
the Royal Institute of British Architects and
the Royal Institution of Chartered Surveyors**

Form of Agreement for

Collateral Warranty
for purchasers & tenants | CoWa/P&T

The forms in this pad are for use where a warranty is to be given to a purchaser or tenant of a whole building in a commercial and/or industrial development, or a part of such a building. It is essential that the number of warranties to be given to tenants in one building should sensibly be limited.

General advice

1. The term "collateral agreement", "duty of care letter" or "collateral warranty" is often used without due regard to the strict legal meaning of the phrase. It is used here for agreements with tenants or purchasers of the whole or part of a commercial and/or industrial development.

2. The purpose of the Agreement is to bind the party giving the warranty in contract where no contract would otherwise exist. This can have implications in terms of professional liability and could cause exposure to claims which might otherwise not have existed under Common Law.

3. The information and guidance contained in this note is designed to assist consultants faced with a request that collateral agreements be entered into.

4. The use of the word 'collateral' is not accidental. It is intended to refer to an agreement that is an adjunct to another or principal agreement, namely the conditions of appointment of the consultant. It is imperative therefore that before collateral warranties are executed the consultant's terms and conditions of appointment have been agreed between the client and the consultant and set down in writing.

5. Under English Law the terms and conditions of the consultant's appointment may be 'under hand' or executed as a Deed. In the latter case the length of time that claims may be brought under the Agreement is extended from six years to twelve years.

6. Under English Law this Form of Agreement for Collateral Warranty is designed for use under hand or to be executed as a Deed. It should not be signed as a Deed when it is collateral to an appointment which is under hand.

7. The acceptance of a claim under the consultant's professional indemnity policy, brought under the terms of a collateral warranty, will depend upon the terms and conditions of the policy in force at the time when a claim is made.

8. Consultants with a current indemnity insurance policy taken out under the RIBA, RICSIS, ACE or RIASIS schemes will not have a claim refused simply on the basis that it is brought under the terms of a collateral warranty provided that warranty is in this form. In other respects the claim will be treated in accordance with policy terms and conditions in the normal way. **Consultants insured under different policies** must seek the advice of their brokers or insurers.

9. **Amendment to the clauses should be resisted.** Insurers' approval as mentioned above is in respect of the unamended clauses only.

Commentary on Clauses

Recital A.

This needs completion.

When this warranty is to be given in favour of a purchaser or tenant of part of the Development, the following words in square brackets must be deleted.

["The Premises" are also referred to as "the Development" in this Agreement".]

Care must be taken in describing "the Premises" accurately.

When this warranty is to be given in favour of a purchaser or tenant of the entire development, the terms "the Premises" and "the Development" are synonymous.

The following words in square brackets must be deleted

[forming part of. ....

at. .... ("the Development").]

Recitals B & C

These are self explanatory but need completion.

Clause 1

This confirms the duty of care that will be owed to the Purchaser/the Tenant. The words in square brackets enable the clause to reflect exactly the provisions contained within the terms and conditions of the Appointment.

Paragraphs (a),(b) and (c) qualify and limit in three ways the Firm's liability in the event of a breach of the duty of care.

1 (a)   By this provision, the Firm is liable for the reasonable costs of repair renewal and or reinstatement of the Development insofar as the Purchaser/the Tenant has a financial obligation to pay or contribute to the cost of that repair. Other losses are expressly excluded.

1 (b)   By this provision the Firm's potential liability is limited. The intention is that the effect of "several" liability at Common Law is negated. When the Firm agrees - probably at the time of appointment - to sign a warranty at a future date, the list should include the names, if known, or otherwise the description or profession, of those responsible for the design of the relevant parts of the Development and the general contractor. When the warranty is signed, the list should be completed with the names of those previously referred to by description or profession.

1 (c)   By this clause, the Purchaser/ the Tenant is bound by any limitations on liability that may exist in the conditions of the Appointment. Furthermore, the consultant has the same rights of defence that would have been available had the relevant claim been made by the Client under the Appointment.

1 (d)   This states the relationship between the Firm and any consultant employed by the Purchaser/the Tenant to survey the premises.

Clause 2

As a consultant it is not possible to give assurances beyond those to the effect that materials as listed have not been nor will be specified. Concealed use of such materials by a contractor could possibly occur, hence the very careful restriction in terms of this particular warranty. Further materials may be added.

N.B.   The above advice and commentary is not intended to affect the interpretation of this Collateral Warranty. It is based on the terms of insurance current at the date of publication. All parties to the Agreement should ensure the terms of insurance have not changed.

Clause 3

This obliges the consultant to ensure that all fees due and owing including VAT at the time the warranty is entered into have been paid.

Clause 4

This is included to make it clear that the Purchaser/the Tenant has no power or authority to direct or instruct the Firm in its duties to the Client.

Clause 5

Reasonable use by the Purchaser/the Tenant of drawings and associated documents is necessary in most cases. By this clause, the Purchaser/the Tenant is given the rights that might be reasonably expected but it does not allow the reproduction of the designs for any purpose outside the scope of the Development.

Clause 6

This confirms that professional indemnity insurance will be maintained in so far as it is reasonably possible to do so. Professional indemnity insurance is on the basis of annual contracts and the terms and conditions of a policy may change from renewal to renewal.

Clause 7

This allows the Purchaser/the Tenant to assign the benefit of this Warranty provided it is done by formal legal assignment and relates to the entire interest of the original Purchaser/Tenant. By this clause any right of assignment may be limited or extinguished. If it is to be extinguished the word "not" shall be inserted after "may" and all words after "the Purchaser/the Tenant" deleted. If it is agreed that there should be a limited number of assignments, the precise number should be inserted in the space between "assigned" and "by the Purchaser/the Tenant".

Clause 7S

This is applicable in Scotland in relation to assignations. Completion is as for Clause 7.

Clause 8

This identifies the method of giving Notice under Clause 7 & 7S.

Clause 9

This needs completion. The clause makes clear that any liability that the Firm has by virtue of this Warranty ceases on the expiry of the stated period of years after practical completion of the Premises. (Note: the practical completion of the Development may be later).

Under English law the period should not exceed 6 years for agreements under hand, nor 12 years for those executed as a Deed.

In Scotland, the Prescription and Limitations (Scotland) Act 1973 prescribes a 5 year period.

Clause 10 and Attestation below

The appropriate method of execution by the Firm and the Purchaser/the Tenant should be checked carefully.

Clause 10S and Testing Clause below

This assumes the Firm is a partnership and the Purchaser/the Tenant is a Limited Company. Otherwise legal advice should be taken.

Published by
The British Property Federation Limited
35 Catherine Place, London SW1E 6DY Telephone: 0171-828 0111

© The British Property Federation, The Association of Consulting Engineers, The Royal incorporation of Architects in Scotland, The Royal Institute of British Architects and The Royal Institution of Chartered Surveyors. 1992.

ISBN 0 900101 08 7

Warranty Agreement   CoWa/P&T

(In Scotland, leave blank. For applicable date see Testing Clause on page 4)

THIS AGREEMENT

is made the .... day of 199

BETWEEN:-

(insert name of the Consultant)

(1) ....

of/whose registered office is situated at ....

.... ("the Firm"), and

(insert name of the Purchaser/the Tenant)

(2) ....

whose registered office is situated at ....

....

(delete as appropriate)

("the Purchaser"/"the Tenant" which term shall include all permitted assignees under this Agreement).

WHEREAS:-

(delete as appropriate)

A. The Purchaser/the Tenant has entered into an agreement to purchase/an agreement to lease/a lease with

....

.... ("the Client") relating to

(insert description of the premises)

....

....

....

....("the Premises")

(delete as appropriate)

[forming part of ....

....

....

(insert description of the development)

(insert address of the development)

at ....

.... ("the Development").]

(delete as appropriate)

["The Premises" are also referred to as "the Development" in this Agreement.]

(insert date of appointment)
(delete/complete as appropriate)

B. By a contract ("the Appointment") dated ....
the Client has appointed the Firm as [architects/consulting structural engineers/consulting building services engineers/   surveyors] in connection with the Development.

C. The Client has entered or may enter into a contract ("the Building Contract") with

(insert name of building contractor or "a building contractor to be selected by the Client")

....

....

....

for the construction of the Development.

NOW IN CONSIDERATION OF THE PAYMENT OF ONE POUND (£1) BY THE PURCHASER/ THE TENANT TO THE FIRM (RECEIPT OF WHICH THE FIRM ACKNOWLEDGES) IT IS HEREBY AGREED as follows:-

(delete as appropriate to reflect terms of the Appointment)

1. The Firm warrants that it has exercised and will continue to exercise reasonable skill [and care] [care and diligence] in the performance of its services to the Client under the Appointment. In the event of any breach of this warranty:

   (a) subject to paragraphs (b) and (c) of this clause, the Firm shall be liable for the reasonable costs of repair renewal and/or reinstatement of any part or parts of the Development to the extent that

   – the Purchaser/the Tenant incurs such costs and/or
   – the Purchaser/the Tenant is or becomes liable either directly or by way of financial contribution for such costs.

   The Firm shall not be liable for other losses incurred by the Purchaser/the Tenant.

   (b) the Firm's liability for costs under this Agreement shall be limited to that proportion of such costs which it would be just and equitable to require the Firm to pay having regard to the extent of the Firm's responsibility for the same and on the basis that ....

(insert the names of other intended warrantors)

   ....
   ....
   ....
   ....
   ....shall
   be deemed to have provided contractual undertakings on terms no less onerous than this Clause 1 to the Purchaser/the Tenant in respect of the performance of their services in connection with the Development and shall be deemed to have paid to the Purchaser/the Tenant such proportion which it would be just and equitable for them to pay having regard to the extent of their responsibility;

   (c) the Firm shall be entitled in any action or proceedings by the Purchaser/the Tenant to rely on any limitation in the Appointment and to raise the equivalent rights in defence of liability as it would have against the Client under the Appointment;

   (d) the obligations of the Firm under or pursuant to this Clause 1 shall not be released or diminished by the appointment of any person by the Purchaser/the Tenant to carry out any independent enquiry into any relevant matter.

(delete where the Firm is the quantity surveyor)

2. [Without prejudice to the generality of Clause 1, the Firm further warrants that it has exercised and will continue to exercise reasonable skill and care to see that, unless authorised by the Client in writing or, where such authorisation is given orally, confirmed by the Firm to the Client in writing, none of the following has been or will be specified by the Firm for use in the construction of those parts of the Development to which the Appointment relates:-

   (a) high alumina cement in structural elements;

   (b) wood wool slabs in permanent formwork to concrete;

   (c) calcium chloride in admixtures for use in reinforced concrete;

   (d) asbestos products;

   (e) naturally occurring aggregates for use in reinforced concrete which do not comply with British Standard 882: 1983 and/or naturally occurring aggregates for use in concrete which do not comply with British Standard 8110: 1985.

(further specific materials may be added by agreement)

   (f)

   In the event of any breach of this warranty the provisions of Clauses 1a, b, c]
   and d shall apply.

CoWa/P&T   2nd Edition   Page 2
© BPF, ACE, RIAS, RICS, RIBA 1993

Professional services agreement

3. The Firm acknowledges that the Client has paid all fees and expenses properly due and owing to the Firm under the Appointment up to the date of this Agreement.

4. The Purchaser/the Tenant has no authority to issue any direction or instruction to the Firm in relation to the Appointment.

5. The copyright in all drawings, reports, models, specifications, bills of quantities, calculations and other documents and information prepared by or on behalf of the Firm in connection with the Development (together referred to in this Clause 5 as "the Documents") shall remain vested in the Firm but, subject to the Firm having received payment of any fees agreed as properly due under the Appointment, the Purchaser/the Tenant and its appointee shall have a licence to copy and use the Documents and to reproduce the designs and content of them for any purpose related to the Premises including, but without limitation, the construction, completion, maintenance, letting, promotion, advertisement, reinstatement, refurbishment and repair of the Premises. Such licence shall enable the Purchaser/the Tenant and its appointee to copy and use the Documents for the extension of the Premises but such use shall not include a licence to reproduce the designs contained in them for any extension of the Premises. The Firm shall not be liable for any use by the Purchaser/the Tenant or its appointee of any of the Documents for any purpose other than that for which the same were prepared by or on behalf of the Firm.

(insert amount)

(insert period)

6. The Firm shall maintain professional indemnity insurance in an amount of not less than pounds (£   ) for any one occurrence or series of occurrences arising out of any one event for a period of   years from the date of practical completion of the Premises under the Building Contract, provided always that such insurance is available at commercially reasonable rates. The Firm shall immediately inform the Purchaser/the Tenant if such insurance ceases to be available at commercially reasonable rates in order that the Firm and the Purchaser/the Tenant can discuss means of best protecting the respective positions of the Purchaser/the Tenant and the Firm in the absence of such insurance. As and when it is reasonably requested to do so by the Purchaser/the Tenant or its appointee the Firm shall produce for inspection documentary evidence that its professional indemnity insurance is being maintained.

(insert number of times)

(delete if under Scots law)

[7. This Agreement may   be assigned   by the Purchaser/the Tenant by way of absolute legal assignment to another person taking an assignment of the Purchaser's/the Tenant's interest in the Premises without the consent of the Client or the Firm being required and such assignment shall be effective upon written notice thereof being given to the Firm. No further assignment shall be permitted.]

(insert number of times)

(delete if under English law)

[7S. *The Purchaser/the Tenant shall   be entitled to assign or transfer his/their rights under this Agreement   to any other person acquiring the Purchaser's/the Tenant's interest in the whole of the Premises without the consent of the Firm subject to written notice of such assignation being given to the Firm in accordance with Clause 8 hereof. Nothing in this clause shall permit any party acquiring such right as assignee or transferee to enter into any further assignation or transfer to anyone acquiring subsequently an interest in the Premises from him.*]

8. Any notice to be given by the Firm hereunder shall be deemed to be duly given if it is delivered by hand at or sent by registered post or recorded delivery to the Purchaser/the Tenant at its registered office and any notice given by the Purchaser/the Tenant hereunder shall be deemed to be duly given if it is addressed to "The Senior Partner"/"The Managing Director" and delivered by hand at or sent by registered post or recorded delivery to the above-mentioned address of the Firm or to the principal business address of the Firm for the time being and, in the case of any such notices, the same shall if sent by registered post or recorded delivery be deemed to have been received forty eight hours after being posted.

(complete as appropriate)

9. No action or proceedings for any breach of this Agreement shall be commenced against the Firm after the expiry of   years from the date of practical completion of the Premises under the Building Contract.

(delete if under
Scots law)

[10. The construction validity and performance of this Agreement shall be governed by English law and the parties agree to submit to the non-exclusive jurisdiction of the English Courts.

(alternatives:
delete as
appropriate)

[AS WITNESS the hands of the parties the day and year first before written.

Signed by or on behalf of the Firm ....

(for Agreement
executed under hand and
NOT as a Deed)

in the presence of: ....

Signed by or on behalf of the Purchaser/the Tenant ....

in the presence of: ....]

(this must only
apply if the
Appointment
is executed
as a Deed)

[IN WITNESS WHEREOF this Agreement was executed as a Deed and delivered the day and year first before written.

by the Firm

....

....

....

....

by the Purchaser/the Tenant

....

....

....

....]]

(delete if under
English law)

10S. *This Agreement shall be construed and the rights of the parties and all matters arising hereunder shall be determined in all respects according to the Law of Scotland.*

IN WITNESS WHEREOF these presents are executed as follows:-

SIGNED by the above named Firm at ....

on the ....*day of* ....*Nineteen hundred and* ....

as follows:-

....*(Firm's signature)*

Signature ....*Full Name* ....

Address ....

....*Occupation* ....

Signature ....*Full Name* ....

Address ....

....*Occupation* ....

SIGNED by the above named Purchaser/Tenant at ....

on the ....*day of* ....*Nineteen hundred and* ....

as follows:-

For and on behalf of the Purchaser/the Tenant

....*Director/Authorised Signatory*

....*Director/Authorised Signatory*]